Jack the Ripper

TREVOR MARRIOTT

Jack the Ripper

THE 21st CENTURY INVESTIGATION

JOHN BLAKE

Published by John Blake Publishing Ltd,
3 Bramber Court, 2 Bramber Road,
London W14 9PB, England

www.blake.co.uk

First published in paperback in 2007

ISBN: 978 1 84454 370 0

British Library Cataloguing-in-Publication Data:

A catalogue record for this book is available from the British Library.

Design by www.envydesign.co.uk

Printed in the UK by CPI Bookmarque, Croydon, CR0 4TD

1 3 5 7 9 10 8 6 4 2

Papers used by John Blake Publishing are natural, recyclable products made
from wood grown in sustainable forests. The manufacturing processes conform
to the environmental regulations of the country of origin.

Every attempt has been made to contact the relevant copyright-holders,
but some were unobtainable. We would be grateful if the appropriate
people could contact us.

CONTENTS

PART TWO:
ON THE TRAIL OF THE RIPPER

INTRODUCTION

Jack the Ripper: man or myth, fact or fiction? Whoever he was, his identity remains a mystery. The horrendous murders attributed to the unknown killer spread terror among the residents of London's East End and soon his nickname was known the world over.

'Jack' was the most common alias for a man, real or fictitious, in Victorian times, a few examples being Jack Tar, Jack O'Lantern and Jack Frost. And the name Jack the Ripper set a trend in evocative nicknames for murderers, and since then there have been the Yorkshire Ripper, the Boston Strangler, the Axeman of New Orleans and many more.

Between April 1888 and July 1889 an area of east London witnessed a series of horrific murders, initially known as the 'Whitechapel murders'. All of them remain unsolved to this day. The unidentified killer, who soon came to be known as 'Jack the Ripper', stalked the dimly lit, fog-blanketed streets of the East End with a single, brutal ambition — murder. With malice a forethought, and under the cover of darkness, he lurked in the shadows, awaiting his prey, before slaughtering and butchering the helpless street women of the area.

Once the terrifying string of murders had begun, where would it end? Would the killer be caught? Who would turn out to be the most notorious serial criminal of all time? It was the officers of Scotland Yard and the City of London Police who were entrusted with the task of apprehending the brutal killer. They failed to do so, but did they fail honourably? Some researchers have suggested the police, in fact, knew who the killer was but, for reasons known only to the higher echelons of the police and the government, they chose not to bring the culprit to court or ever to reveal his identity and therefore were complicit in one of the biggest criminal cover-ups of all time.

In 1888, the police did not have the benefit of modern forensic methods, such as DNA testing and fingerprinting, which are readily available to police officers today. They had to rely on old-fashioned methods of detecting crime: catching the criminal committing the crime; finding witnesses who saw the crime being committed; or arresting a person on suspicion of having committed the crime, in the hope that he or she would confess.

More than a century has passed since the Ripper's crimes were committed, yet the search for his identity still goes on. In fact, the mystery has deepened so much that the truth about the murders is thoroughly obscured. Innumerable press stories, books, plays, films and even musicals have dramatised and distorted the facts, with the unfortunate result that the public accepts the fiction more readily than the reality.

So, how did I, a modern-day criminal investigator, come to be interested in these horrific murders? It all goes back to the early 1960s, when I went to a concert and saw, for the first time, a pop singer by the name of Screaming Lord Sutch, who, as Lord Sutch, later became the leader of a British political party known as the Monster Raving Loony Party. Sutch had just released a record called 'Jack the Ripper', which became a minor hit, and when performing the number on stage he portrayed the killer and acted out the murders. He went on to perform this grisly routine in dance halls around Britain and Europe. I saw Sutch many times but I guess that on hearing his song for the first time is when my interest in Jack the Ripper was born.

After joining the Bedfordshire Police in 1970, I was in uniform only a short while before being promoted to the Criminal Investigation Department (CID), where I worked on many murders. As well as serving in various specialist police departments, including those dealing with burglary and robbery, I spent a short time in Special Branch. All the while, my fascination with the Whitechapel murders grew, to the extent that I knew that some day I would have to satisfy my curiosity. Later, with a great deal of free time on my hands, I made the decision to reinvestigate these unsolved murders. I felt that all the experience, knowledge and insight into the criminal mind I had gained by interviewing and talking to murderers, rapists and robbers would be invaluable in my attempt to view the murders through the eyes of the killer or killers, as the case might be.

I would look closely at the murders themselves, the victims and the suspects at the time, and at both the evidence available at that time and the new evidence and new suspects that have emerged in the intervening years. I would also need to analyse the new evidence recently put forward, with a view to either proving or disproving some of the accepted theories about the murders which have been with us for many years. In doing so, I hoped I might find something new that would unlock the mystery of Jack the Ripper's identity.

What I discovered during my investigation was startling. The result is that I feel I can now introduce a major doubt into the number of Whitechapel murders, the suspects and, in fact, the whole mystery of Jack the Ripper.

Before analysing the murders, I decided to get an idea of what life was like in the East End in 1888. All the murders were committed in squalid, poor areas and all the victims were prostitutes. In those days, many prostitutes were forced to work the streets by gangs who inflicted violence on these poor women if they did not obey them and hand over money they earned through prostitution. It is documented that, at the time of the murders, there were some 1,600 prostitutes in the East End.

The population of the whole area is believed to have been about 900,000, 80,000 of whom resided in Whitechapel. The 'poor' made up about 8 per cent of the population of the East End and consisted of men, women and children who worked as builders, market porters, dock workers or in other trades, earning a meagre but regular income of between 18 and 21 shillings a week. (Before decimalisation, 20 shillings equalled £1.) The 'very poor' totalled about 11 per cent of the population and their income fell below this level. If the first group struggled to make ends meet, the second lived in utter poverty. Two per cent of the population was designated as being of the lowest class: down-and-outs and the homeless. In one district alone, it was documented that there were 146 registered lodging-houses, with more than 6,000 beds, for such people. Some of these premises contained as few as four beds, while others had as many as 350. For those who could not afford lodgings there was no other option but to sleep in the streets and alleys.

PART ONE
VICTIMS

It is widely accepted that Jack the Ripper killed five women. However, my investigation revealed that nine women were murdered. All were killed in similar circumstances and all the murders occurred in or near Whitechapel, east London, between 2 April 1888 and 13 February 1891. So, has everyone been wrong all these years? Were the police of the day blinkered in the way they investigated the murders? Did the Ripper kill the canonical five women? Or was it more? Or was he responsible for fewer murders than he has been given credit for? Could another person or persons have murdered some of the victims? All are interesting questions that I hoped to be able to answer as a result of my investigation.

Who were the women murdered during this reign of terror? In Part One, I discuss each victim in chronological order and in doing so draw on the inquests conducted by Her Majesty's Coroner. These reports not only helped me to build up a better picture of each victim but also gave me the opportunity to assess the police investigation and any other evidence which may have come out during the course of the inquests but which may have been overlooked. The inquest reports from which I quote are as reported in *The Times* and the *Daily Telegraph* at the time.

But first let us be clear what a coroner's court is and what jurisdiction a coroner has. A coroner's court is convened to investigate the death of a person or persons and to establish how death occurred. The jury is made up of members of the public and presided over by the coroner, who is appointed by the reigning monarch. He (or she) is either a doctor or other medical person, in either case with great experience. He acts exactly as a judge does in a crown court. The only difference is that, unlike in a crown court, the normal rules of evidence do not apply and instead hearsay evidence and evidence of opinion are admissible.

The jury and the witnesses are sworn in and the witnesses give their evidence on oath. This evidence will have been obtained in advance by police officers by means of witness statements. At the end of the inquest, the coroner directs the jury to reach a verdict. This verdict is either death by murder by a specific named person or by person or persons unknown, manslaughter, suicide, accident or misadventure. If none of these verdicts applies, an open verdict is recorded.

CHAPTER ONE

EMMA SMITH

Emma Elizabeth Smith, 45-year-old mother of two and a prostitute, was attacked in Osborn Street, off Whitechapel Road, on 2 April 1888, four months before the main series of murders started. A blunt instrument was savagely thrust into her vagina and she died in hospital the next day. The only other wounds she had were cuts and abrasions to her head and one ear.

Was Emma Smith the first Ripper victim? Or could she have been attacked by one of the many gangs who frequented the Whitechapel area, extorting money from prostitutes and other downtrodden women in return for their protection? It wasn't until September 1888 that Smith was first looked on as a possible Ripper victim, and then only by the press, and only because other, later victims had their sexual organs attacked and mutilated and because the attack occurred in the same locality as those on later victims. The inquest was presided over by Mr Wynne E Baxter, the Coroner for East Middlesex:

Saturday, 7 April 1888
... **Mrs Mary Russell**, deputy keeper of a common lodging-house, stated that she had known the deceased

for about two years. On the evening of Bank Holiday 2nd April she left home at 7 o'clock, and returned about 4 or 5 the next morning in a dreadful state. Her face and head were much injured, one of her ears being nearly torn off. She told the witness that she had been set upon and robbed of all her money. She also complained of pains in the lower part of the body. Witness took her to the hospital, and when passing along Osborn Street the deceased pointed out the spot where she was assaulted. She said there were three men, but she could not describe them.

Mr George Haslip, house surgeon, stated that when the deceased was admitted to the hospital she had been drinking but was not intoxicated. She was bleeding from the head and ear, and had other injuries of a revolting nature. Witness found that she was suffering from rupture of the peritoneum, which had been perforated by some blunt instrument used with great force. The deceased told him that at 1.30 am that morning she was passing near Whitechapel Church when she noticed some men coming towards her. She crossed the road to avoid them, but they followed, assaulted her, took all the money she had, and then committed the outrage. She was unable to say what kind of instrument was used, nor could she describe her assailants, except that she said that one was a youth of 19. Death ensued on Wednesday morning 4th April through peritonitis set up by the injuries.

Margaret Hayes, living at the same address as the deceased, deposed to seeing Mrs Smith in company with a man at the corner of Farrant Street and Burdett Road. The man was dressed in a dark suit and wore a white silk handkerchief round his neck. He was of medium height, but witness did not think she could identify him. ...

> The jury returned a verdict of 'Wilful murder against some person or persons unknown.'

I conclude from this report that Emma Smith's death was in no way connected to the later murders. As the report confirms, Whitechapel was a crime-ridden area where violent assault and murder were common occurrences. Smith was probably attacked and punished for disobeying one of the many gangs responsible for running prostitutes at that time, and her attack illustrates the degree of violence to which these gangs would resort.

The report states that she told two separate people that she had been attacked by a group or gang of men. She may or may not have known their identities. In any event, she did not name anyone. I believe that, if she did know the names of some or all of her attackers, she chose not to give them for fear of reprisal.

CHAPTER TWO

MARTHA TABRAM

A plump, middle-aged prostitute, Martha Tabram was stabbed to death in George Yard on 7 August 1888.

On the previous evening Tabram was seen with another prostitute in various public houses in Whitechapel. At around 11.45pm she was seen going into George Yard with a soldier, presumably to have sex. There were no more sightings of her before her body was found at 4.45am on the stairs in George Yard Buildings, a tenement block. A resident of the building used the stairs at 1.30am and saw nothing suspicious. Another, on returning home at 3.30am, saw what he thought was someone sleeping on the stairs and paid no attention.

At 4.45am, a third resident was on his way to work. By this time, daylight was breaking and he found Tabram lying in a pool of blood on the stairs. Her lower garments were in a state of disarray, suggesting intercourse had taken place. (There is some evidence of this having occurred with later Ripper victims.)

A police surgeon visited the scene at 5.30am and estimated the time of death at around 2.30–2.45am. There were 39 stab wounds.

In the report of the inquest, presided over by Mr G Collier, Deputy Coroner for South East Middlesex, the doctor stated that the focus of the wounds was the breasts, belly and groin. In his opinion, he said, a right-handed attacker inflicted all but one of the wounds, and all but one seemed to have been the result of an 'ordinary pen-knife'. There was, however, one wound on the sternum which appeared to have been inflicted by a dagger or bayonet.

Day One: Thursday, 9 August 1888
... **Dr T.R. Killeen**, of 68, Brick-lane, said that he was called to the deceased, and found her dead. She had 39 stabs on the body. She had been dead some three hours. Her age was about 36, and the body was very well nourished. Witness had since made a post-mortem examination of the body. The left lung was penetrated in five places, and the right lung was penetrated in two places. The heart, which was rather fatty, was penetrated in one place, and that would be sufficient to cause death. The liver was healthy, but was penetrated in five places, the spleen was penetrated in two places, and the stomach, which was perfectly healthy, was penetrated in six places. The witness did not think all the wounds were inflicted with the same instrument. The wounds generally might have been inflicted by a knife, but such an instrument could not have inflicted one of the wounds, which went through the chest-bone. His opinion was that one of the wounds was inflicted by some kind of dagger, and that all of them were caused during life.

The Coroner said he was in hope that the body would be identified, but three women had identified it under three different names. He therefore proposed to leave that question open until the next occasion. [The inquest was adjourned for a fortnight.]

Day Two: Thursday, 23 August 1888

... The body has been identified as that of Martha Tabram, aged 39 or 40 years, the wife of a foreman packer at a furniture warehouse.

Henry Samuel Tabram, 6, River Terrace, East Greenwich, husband of the deceased woman, said he last saw her alive about 18 months ago, in the Whitechapel Road. They had been separated for 13 years, owing to her drinking habits. ...

Henry Turner, a carpenter, staying at the Working Men's Home, Commercial Street, Spitalfields, stated that he had been living with the woman Tabram as his wife for about nine years. Two or three weeks previously to this occurrence he ceased to do so. He had left her on two or three occasions in consequence of her drinking habits, but they had come together again. He last saw her alive on Saturday, the 4th inst., in Leadenhall Street. He then gave her 1 shilling and sixpence to get some stock. When she had money she spent it in drink. While living with witness deceased's usual time for coming home was about 11 o'clock. As far as he knew she had no regular companion and he did not know that she walked the streets. ...

Mary Ann Connolly ('Pearly Poll'), who at the suggestion of [Detective] Inspector [Edmund] Reid [H Division, Metropolitan Police] was cautioned in the usual manner before being sworn, stated she had been for the last two nights living at a lodging-house in Dorset Street, Spitalfields. Witness was a single woman. She had known the woman Tabram for about four or five months. She knew her by the name of Emma. She last saw her alive on Bank Holiday night, when witness was with her about three-quarters of an hour, and they separated at 11.45pm. Witness was with Tabram and two soldiers, one a private and one a corporal. She did not know what regiment they belonged to, but they had white bands round their caps. After they separated, Tabram went away with the private, and witness accompanied the corporal up Angel Alley. There was no quarrelling between any of them. Witness had been to the barracks to identify the soldiers, and the two men she picked out were, to the best of her belief, the men she and Tabram were with. The men at the Wellington Barracks were paraded before witness. One of the men picked out by witness turned out not to be a corporal, but he had stripes on his arm.

Detective Inspector Reid made a statement of the efforts made by the police to discover the perpetrator of the murder. Several persons had stated that they saw the deceased woman on the previous Sunday with a corporal, but when all the corporals and privates at the Tower and Wellington Barracks were paraded before them they failed to identify the man. The military authorities afforded every facility to the police. 'Pearly Poll' picked out two men belonging to the Coldstream Guards at the Wellington Barracks. One of those men had three good conduct stripes, and he was proved beyond doubt to have been with his wife from 8 o'clock on the Monday night until 6 o'clock the following morning. The other man was also proved to have been in barracks at 10.05 p.m. on Bank Holiday night. ...

The Coroner having summed up, the jury returned a verdict to the effect that person or persons unknown had murdered the deceased.

After closely examining all the facts of this murder, I decided there are many which suggest Martha Tabram's murder was not connected to Emma Smith's but may be connected to later murders attributed to Jack the Ripper.

The wounds inflicted on Tabram, while savage in their execution, were just stab wounds, as described. The later victims' bodies were subjected to even more savage attack and mutilation. In Tabram's case, by contrast with these others, her sexual organs were not attacked or mutilated.

It should also be noted that she may have been killed either during sexual intimacy or shortly afterwards. The reason for her attack could have been that she was caught trying to rob her client – a practice common in those days among prostitutes while engaging in sexual acts.

Among all the later victims there was only one instance of a clear sign of intimacy having taken place at the time of death, and that was in the case of Alice McKenzie, whose clothes were found up around her chest. Some of these victims, however, were found with their clothes in disarray, and there is evidence to suggest that some of them were throttled to the point of unconsciousness or strangled. In Tabram's case, there was no evidence of this.

As to the doctor's suggestion that the attacker may have been right-handed, I suggest, having studied sketches of the pattern and location of the wounds, that the attacker could equally have been right-handed or left-handed.

Most experts do not believe that Martha Tabram was murdered by the Ripper, but, having looked closely at this murder, I cannot rule out the possibility that she was an early victim of his. Her body was subjected to dozens of stab wounds. Her killer at this time had with him only a small knife, and not being able to savagely mutilate the bodies, as was perhaps his intention, later changed his weapon to a longer-bladed knife.

The specific wound which the doctor says may have been caused by a dagger, I suggest he may be wrong. This area of the body is a very fleshy area and a stab in that area would split the skin, making a wound which would give the appearance that a larger knife had been used. This could also have been one of the first wounds inflicted on her and could have been inflicted with such force as to penetrate deeper than the stab wounds which followed.

CHAPTER THREE

MARY ANN NICHOLS

Mary Ann Nichols, known as Polly, was 43 when she was murdered in a narrow, cobbled street called Buck's Row (now Durward Street) on Friday, 31 August 1888. The prostitute was last seen alive around 2.30am and was found in the street at 3.45am. Witnesses who found her suggest she may have been clinging to life. If that was so, the killer was very lucky not to have been seen either committing the killing or making his escape.

The inquest into the death of 'a woman supposed to be Mary Ann Nichols' was presided over by Mr Wynne E Baxter, the Coroner for South East Middlesex. Material from the inquest report follows.

Day One: Saturday, 1 September 1888
… **Edward Walker**: I live at 15, Maidwell Street, Albany Road, Camberwell, and have no occupation. I was a smith when I was at work, but I am not now. I have seen the body in the mortuary, and to the best of my belief it is my daughter; but I have not seen her for three years. I recognise her by her general appearance and by a little mark she has had on her forehead since she was a child. She also had either one or two teeth out, the same as the

woman I have just seen. My daughter's name was Mary Ann Nichols, and she had been married twenty-two years. Her husband's name is William Nichols, and he is alive. He is a machinist. They have been living apart about seven or eight years. I last heard of her before Easter. She was forty-two years of age. ...

Coroner: Have you any reasonable doubt that this is your daughter?

Walker: No, I have not. ...

Constable John Neil (J Division): Yesterday morning I was proceeding down Buck's Row, Whitechapel, going towards Brady Street. There was not a soul about. I had been round there half an hour previously, and I saw no one then. I was on the right-hand side of the street, when I noticed a figure lying in the street. ... Deceased was lying lengthways along the street, her left hand touching the gate. I examined the body by the aid of my lamp, and noticed blood oozing from a wound in the throat. She was lying on her back, with her clothes disarranged. I felt her arm, which was quite warm from the joints upwards. Her eyes were wide open. Her bonnet was off and lying at her side, close to the left hand. ... [Dr Henry Llewellyn] arrived in a very short time. ... The doctor looked at the woman and then said, 'Move her to the mortuary [at Whitechapel Workhouse Infirmary]. She is dead, and I will make a further examination of her.' We placed her on the ambulance, and moved her there. Inspector Spratling came to the mortuary, and while taking a description of the deceased turned up her clothes, and found that she was disembowelled. This had not been noticed by any of them before. On the body was found a piece of comb and a bit of looking glass. No money was found, but an unmarked white handkerchief was found in her pocket.

Coroner: Did you notice any blood where she was found?

Constable Neil: There was a pool of blood just where her neck was lying. It was running from the wound in her neck.

Coroner: Did you hear any noise that night?

Constable Neil: No; I heard nothing. The farthest I had been that night was just through the Whitechapel Road and up Baker's Row. I was never far away from the spot.

Coroner: Whitechapel Road is busy in the early morning, I believe. Could anybody have escaped that way?

Constable Neil: Oh yes, sir. I saw a number of women in the main road going home. At that time anyone could have got away. …

Dr Henry Llewellyn: On Friday morning I was called to Buck's Row about 4am. The constable told me what I was wanted for. On reaching Buck's Row I found the deceased woman laying flat on her back in the pathway, her legs extended. I found she was dead, and that she had severe injuries to her throat. Her hands and wrists were cold, but the body and lower extremities were warm. I examined her chest and felt the heart. It was dark at the time. I believe she had not been dead more than half-an-hour. I am quite certain that the injuries to her neck were not self-inflicted. There was very little blood round the neck. There were no marks of any struggle or of blood, as if the body had been dragged. …
[In the mortuary I] saw that the abdomen was cut very extensively. I have this morning made a post-mortem examination of the body. I found it to be that of a female about forty or forty-five years. Five of the teeth are missing, and there is a slight laceration of the tongue. On the right side of the face there is a bruise running

along the lower part of the jaw. It might have been caused by a blow with the fist, or pressure by the thumb. On the left side of the face there was a circular bruise, which also might have been done by the pressure of the fingers. On the left side of the neck, about an inch below the jaw, there was an incision about four inches long and running from a point immediately below the ear. An inch below on the same side, and commencing about an inch in front of it, was a circular incision terminating at a point about three inches below the right jaw. This incision completely severs all the tissues down to the vertebrae. The large vessels of the neck on both sides were severed. The incision is about eight inches long. These cuts must have been caused with a long-bladed knife, moderately sharp, and used with great violence. No blood at all was found on the breast [area] either of the body or clothes. There were no injuries about the body till just about the lower part of the abdomen. Two or three inches from the left side was a wound running in a jagged manner. It was a very deep wound, and the tissues were cut through. There were several incisions running across the abdomen. On the right side there were also three or four similar cuts running downwards. All these had been caused by a knife, which had been used violently and been used downwards. The wounds were from left to right, and might have been done by a left-handed person. The same instrument had done all the injuries. ...

Day Two: Monday, 3 September 1888
[Detective Sergeant Enright of Scotland Yard, after telling the coroner that two workhouse officials had stripped the body] said the clothes, which were lying in a heap in the

[mortuary] yard, consisted of a reddish-brown ulster, with seven large brass buttons, and a brown dress, which looked new. There were also a woollen and a flannel petticoat, belonging to the workhouse. Inspector Helson had cut out pieces marked 'P. R., Princes-road,' with a view to tracing the body. There was also a pair of stays, in fairly good condition, but witness did not notice how they were adjusted. ...

The Foreman of the jury asked whether the stays were fastened on the body.

Inspector [John] Spratling [J Division, Metropolitan Police] replied that he could not say for certain. There was blood on the upper part of the dress body, and also on the ulster, but he only saw a little on the under linen, and that might have happened after the removal of the body from Buck's Row. The clothes were fastened when he first saw the body. The stays did not fit very tightly, for he was able to see the wounds without unfastening them. About six o'clock that day he made an examination at Buck's Row and Brady Street, which ran across Baker's Row, but he failed to trace any marks of blood. ...

Witness also visited half a dozen persons living in the same neighbourhood, none of whom had noticed anything at all suspicious. ...

Inspector Jos. Helson deposed that he first received information about the murder at 6.45am on Friday morning. He afterwards went to the mortuary, where he saw the body with the clothes still on it. The dress was fastened in front, with the exception of a few buttons, the stays, which were attached with clasps, were also fastened. He noticed blood on the hair, and on the collars of the dress and ulster, but not on the back of the skirts. There were no cuts in the clothes, and no indications of any struggle having taken place. The only suspicious mark discovered in the neighbourhood of Buck's Row was in Broad Street, where there was a stain which might have been blood.

Witness was of opinion that the body had not been carried to Buck's Row, but that the murder was committed on the spot. ...

Emily Holland, a married woman, living at 18, Thrawl Street, said deceased had stayed at her lodgings for about six weeks, but had not been there during the last ten days or so. About half-past two on Friday morning witness saw deceased walking down Osborn Street, Whitechapel Road. ...

Day Three: 17 September 1888

Dr Llewellyn, recalled, said he had re-examined the body and there was no part of the viscera missing. ...

Robert Mann, the keeper of the mortuary, said the police came to the workhouse, of which he was an inmate. He went, in consequence, to the mortuary at 5 am He saw the body placed there, and then locked the place up and kept the keys. After breakfast witness and Hatfield, another inmate of the workhouse, undressed the woman.

Day Four: Saturday, 22 September 1888

... The Coroner then summed up. Having reviewed the career of the deceased from the time she left her husband, and reminded the jury of the irregular life she had led for the last two years, Mr Baxter proceeded to point out that the unfortunate woman was last seen alive at half-past two o'clock on Saturday morning, Sept 1, by Mrs Holland, who knew her well. Deceased was at that time much the worse for drink, and was endeavouring to walk eastward down Whitechapel. What her exact movements were after this it was impossible to say; but in less than an hour and a quarter her dead body was discovered at a spot rather under three-quarters of a mile distant. The time at which the body was found cannot have been far from 3.45 am, as it is fixed by so many independent data. The condition of the body appeared to prove conclusively that the deceased was killed on the exact spot in which she was found. There was not a trace of blood anywhere, except at the spot where her neck was lying, this circumstance being sufficient to justify the assumption that the injuries to the throat were committed when the woman was on the ground, whilst the state of her clothing and the absence of any blood about her legs suggested that the abdominal injuries were inflicted whilst she was still in the same position.

Coroner: It seems astonishing at first thought that the culprit should have escaped detection, for there must surely have been marks of blood about his person. If, however, blood was principally on his hands, the presence of so many slaughter houses in the neighbourhood would make the frequenters of this spot familiar with blood stained clothes and hands, and his appearance might in that way have failed to attract attention while he passed from Buck's Row in the twilight into Whitechapel Road, and was lost sight of in the morning's market traffic. We cannot altogether leave unnoticed the fact that the death that you have been investigating is one of four presenting many points of similarity, all of which have occurred within the space of about five months, and all within a very short distance of the place where we are sitting. All four victims were women of middle age, all were married, and had lived apart from their husbands in consequence of intemperate habits, and were at the time of their death leading an irregular life, and eking out a miserable and precarious existence in common lodging-houses. In each case there were abdominal as well as other injuries. In each case the injuries were inflicted after midnight, and in places of public resort, where it would appear impossible but that almost immediate detection should follow the crime, and in each case the inhuman and dastardly criminals are at large in society. Emma Elizabeth Smith, who received her injuries in Osborn Street on the early morning of Easter Tuesday, April 3rd, survived in the London Hospital for upwards of twenty-four hours, and was able to state that she had been followed by some men, robbed and mutilated, and even to describe imperfectly one of them. Martha Tabram was found at 3 am on Tuesday, August 7th, on the first floor landing of George Yard buildings, Wentworth Street, with thirty-nine puncture wounds on her body. In addition to these, and the case under your consideration, there is the case of Annie Chapman, still in the hands of another jury. The instruments used in the two earlier cases are dissimilar. In the first it was a blunt instrument, such as a walking stick; in the second, some of the wounds, were thought to have been made by a dagger, but in the two recent cases the instruments suggested by the medical witnesses are not so different. Dr Llewellyn says the injuries on Nichols could have been produced by a strong bladed instrument, moderately sharp. Dr Phillips is of opinion that those on Chapman were by a very sharp knife, probably with a thin, narrow blade, at least six to eight inches in length, probably longer. The similarity of the injuries in the two cases is considerable. There are bruises about the face in both cases; the head is nearly severed from the body in both cases; there are other dreadful injuries in both cases; and those injuries, again, have in each case been performed with anatomical knowledge. Dr Llewellyn seems to incline to the opinion that the abdominal injuries were first, and caused instantaneous death; but, if so, it seems difficult to understand the object of such desperate injuries to the throat, or how it comes about that there was so little bleeding from the several arteries, that the clothing on the upper surface was not stained, and, indeed, very much less bleeding from the abdomen than from the neck. Surely it may well be that, as in the case of Chapman, the dreadful wounds to the throat were inflicted first and the others afterwards. This is a matter of some importance when we come to consider what possible motive there can be for all this ferocity. Robbery is out of the question; and there is nothing to suggest jealousy; there could not have been any quarrel, or it would have been heard. I suggest to you as a possibility that these two women may have been murdered by the same man with the same object, and that in the case of Nichols the wretch was disturbed before he had accomplished his object, and having failed in the open street he tries again, within a week of his failure, in a more secluded place. ...

The jury, after a short consultation, returned a verdict of wilful murder against some person or persons unknown. ...

The murder of Mary Ann Nichols was certainly the first in a series of savage and brutal murders, which it is suggested were the work of the same killer. It is obvious that a long-bladed knife was used to inflict the wounds, making the murder different from that of Martha Tabram.

Nichols's throat had been slashed so deeply that the head was nearly severed. She appeared to have been either knocked or throttled unconscious. This would account for the lack of blood on her clothes and, perhaps, a distinct lack of blood on her attacker. If she was already dead before her throat was cut and her body mutilated, this would explain the lack of blood, as the heart would have already stopped, causing minimal blood loss. In addition, it was a cold night and blood loss is reduced when the heart slows down because of the body being cold.

Like Dr Killeen in the case of Martha Tabram, Dr Llewellyn went out on a limb in suggesting that Nichols's attacker was left-handed since some of the wounds ran from left to right. I disagree. I am right-handed and it is much easier for a right-handed man to strike from left to right than it is for a left-handed man to do so.

There is no doubting that Nichols was subjected to a violent attack, but was her throat cut before the other wounds were inflicted? One of the police officers at the inquest, Inspector Helson, gave evidence that there were no cuts to her clothing. To me this suggests that the murderer lifted the victim's clothes in order to mutilate the body – a sign of a very organised killer. Another indication of a calculated approach is that, even though engaged in a frenzied attack, the murderer clearly remained alert to sight and sound of passers-by, so that he would have time to escape if necessary.

There were no witnesses and no descriptions of anyone seen with Nichols before her death or at the spot where she was murdered. Her killer vanished unseen into the darkness and the mist.

CHAPTER FOUR

ANNIE CHAPMAN

Forty-seven year-old prostitute Annie Chapman was found dead in the back yard at 29 Hanbury Street on 8 September 1888. Her throat, like Mary Ann Nichols's, was dissevered deeply. She had been disembowelled and her uterus was missing at the time of the post-mortem. Her intestines had been placed over her right shoulder and other parts of her digestive system were on her left side.

She was last seen alive at around 5.30am, talking to a man near to where her body was found. This man was described as shabbily dressed, over 40 years of age, with a dark complexion, possibly of foreign appearance. He was wearing a brown deerstalker hat and what is believed to have been a dark overcoat.

Assuming the time was reported accurately, it would have been nearly daylight when this man was seen with Annie Chapman. This was the first piece of 'direct' evidence to be relied upon. A few moments after Chapman was seen with the man, Albert Cadoch, a young carpenter living at 27 Hanbury Street, walked into his back yard, probably to use the outhouse, and, passing the five-foot-tall wooden fence that separated his yard from that of number 29, he heard voices close by. All he could make out was a woman saying, 'No!' Then he heard something falling against the fence. Had he looked over the fence he may well have seen Chapman's killer.

Dr George Bagster Phillips examined the body of Annie Chapman at 6.30am in the back yard of 29 Hanbury Street. The following is from the report of his inquest testimony.

> The left arm was placed across the left breast. The legs were drawn up, the feet resting on the ground, and the knees turned outwards. The face was swollen and turned on the right side. The tongue protruded between the front teeth, but not beyond the lips. The tongue was evidently much swollen. The front teeth were perfect as far as the first molar, top and bottom, and very fine teeth they were. The body was terribly mutilated ... the stiffness of the limbs was not marked, but was evidently commencing. He noticed that the throat was disseered deeply; that the incision through the skin was jagged and reached right round the neck ... On the wooden paling between the yard in question and the next, smears of blood, corresponding to where the head of the deceased lay, were to be seen. These were about 14 inches from the ground, and immediately above the part where the blood from the neck lay. He should say that the instrument used at the throat and abdomen was the same. It must have been a very sharp knife with a thin narrow blade, and must have been at least 6 in. to 8 in. in length, probably longer. He should say that the injuries could not have been inflicted by a bayonet or a sword. They could have been done by such an instrument as a medical man used for post-mortem purposes, but the ordinary surgical cases might not contain such an instrument. Those used by the slaughtermen, well

ground down, might have caused them. He thought the knives used by those in the leather trade would not be long enough in the blade. There were indications of anatomical knowledge ... he should say that the deceased had been dead at least two hours, and probably more, when he first saw her; but it was right to mention that it was a fairly cool morning, and that the body would be more apt to cool rapidly from its having lost a great quantity of blood. There was no evidence ... of a struggle having taken place. He was positive the deceased entered the yard alive ...

From Dr Phillips's second report, prepared after the post-mortem examination, we learn:

He noticed the same protrusion of the tongue. There was a bruise over the right temple. On the upper eyelid there was a bruise, and there were two distinct bruises, each the size of a man's thumb, on the forepart of the top of the chest. The stiffness of the limbs was now well marked. There was a bruise over the middle part of the bone of the right hand. There was an old scar on the left of the frontal bone. The stiffness was more noticeable on the left side, especially in the fingers, which were partly closed. There was an abrasion over the ring finger, with distinct markings of a ring or rings. The throat had been severed as before described. The incisions into the skin indicated that they had been made from the left side of the neck. There were two distinct clean cuts on the left side of the spine. They were parallel with each other and separated by about half an inch. The muscular structures appeared as though an attempt had been made to separate the bones of the neck. There were various other mutilations to the body, but he was of the opinion that they occurred subsequent to the death of the woman, and to the large escape of blood from the division of the neck.

The deceased was far advanced in disease of the lungs and membranes of the brain, but they had nothing to do with the cause of death. The stomach contained little food, but there was not any sign of fluid. There was no appearance of the deceased having taken alcohol, but there were signs of great deprivation and he should say she had been badly fed. He was convinced she had not taken any strong alcohol for some hours before her death. The injuries were certainly not self-inflicted. The bruises on the face were evidently recent, especially about the chin and side of the jaw, but the bruises in front of the chest and temple were of longer standing – probably of days. He was of the opinion that the person who cut the deceased's throat took hold of her by the chin, and then commenced the incision from left to right. He thought it was highly probable that a person could call out, but with regards to an idea that she might have been gagged he could only point to the swollen face and the protruding tongue, both of which were signs of suffocation.

The abdomen had been entirely laid open: the intestines, severed from their mesenteric attachments, had been lifted out of the body and placed on the shoulder of the corpse; whilst from the pelvis, the uterus and its appendages with the upper portion of the vagina and the posterior two thirds of the bladder, had been entirely removed. No trace of these parts could be found and the incisions were cleanly cut, avoiding the rectum, and dividing the vagina low enough to avoid injury to the cervix uteri. Obviously the work was that of an expert – of one, at least, who had such knowledge of anatomical or pathological examinations as to be enabled to secure the pelvic organs with one sweep of the knife, which must therefore have at least 5 or 6 inches in length, probably more. The appearance of the cuts confirmed him in the opinion that the instrument, like the one which divided the neck, had been of a very sharp character. The mode in which the knife had been used seemed to indicate great anatomical knowledge.

The doctor stated, 'He himself could not have performed all the injuries he described, even without a struggle, in under a quarter of an hour. If he had done it in a deliberate way such as would fall to the duties of a surgeon it probably would have taken him the best part of an hour.'

Day One: Monday, 10 September 1888
... The jury viewed the corpse at the mortuary in Montague Street, but all evidences of the outrage to which the deceased had been subjected were concealed. The clothing was also inspected, and subsequently the following evidence was taken.

John Davies: I am a carman employed at Leadenhall Market. I have lodged at 29, Hanbury Street for a fortnight, and I occupied the top front room on the third floor with my wife and three sons, who live with me. On Friday night I went to bed at 8pm and my wife followed about half an hour later. ... I was awake from 3am to 5am on Saturday, and then fell asleep until 5.45am when the clock at Spitalfields Church struck. I had a cup of tea and went downstairs to the back yard. ...

There are three stone steps, unprotected, leading from the door to the yard, which is at a lower level than that of the passage. Directly I opened the door I saw a woman lying down in the left hand recess, between the stone steps and the fence. She was on her back, with her head towards the house and her legs towards the woodshed. The clothes were up to her groins. I did not go into the yard, but left the house by the front door, and called the attention of two men to the circumstances. ...

Coroner: Have you ever seen the deceased before?

Davies: No.

Coroner: Were you the first down in the house that morning?

Davies: No; there was a lodger named Thompson, who was called at half-past three. ...

Amelia Palmer: I live at 35, Dorset Street, Spitalfields, a common lodging-house. Off and on I have stayed there three years. I am married to Henry Palmer, a dock labourer. He was foreman, but met with an accident at the beginning of the year. I go out charring. My husband gets a pension, having been in the Army Reserve. I knew the deceased very well, for quite five years. I saw the body on Saturday at the mortuary, and am quite sure that it is that of Annie Chapman. She was a widow, and her husband, Frederick Chapman, was a veterinary surgeon in Windsor. ...

Coroner: Has she lived at 30, Dorset Street?

Palmer: Yes, about two years ago, with a man who made wire sieves, and at that time she was receiving 10 shillings a week from her husband by post office order, payable to her at the Commercial Road. This payment stopped about eighteen months ago, and she then found, on inquiry of some relative, that her husband was dead. ...

Coroner: Do you know of any one that would be likely to have injured her?

Palmer: No. ...

Timothy Donovan (of 35 Dorset Street, Spitalfields): I am the deputy of a common lodging-house. I have seen the body of the deceased, and have identified it as that of a woman who stayed at my house for the last four months. She was not there last week until Friday afternoon, between two and three o'clock. I was coming out of the office after getting up, and she asked me if she could go down in the kitchen, and I said, 'Yes,' and asked her where she had been all the week. She replied that she had been in the infirmary, but did not say which.

A police officer stated that the deceased had been in the casual ward. ...

Coroner: Was she the worse for drink when you saw her last?

Donovan: She had had enough; of that I am certain. She walked straight. Generally on Saturdays she was the worse for drink. She was very sociable in the kitchen. I said to her, 'You can find money for your beer, and you can't find money for your bed.' She said she had been only to the top of the street – where there is a public-house.

Coroner: Did you see her with any man that night?

Donovan: No, sir.

Coroner: Where did you think she was going to get the money from?

Donovan: I did not know. She used to come and stay at the lodging-house on Saturdays with a man – a pensioner – of soldierly appearance, whose name I do not know.

Coroner: Have you seen her with other men?

Donovan: At other times she has come with other men, and I have refused her.

Coroner: You only allow the women at your place one husband?

Donovan: The pensioner told me not to let her a bed if she came with any other man. She did not come with a man that night. I never saw her with any man that week. ...

Coroner: When was the pensioner last with deceased at the lodging-house?

Donovan: On Sunday, Sept. 2nd. I cannot say whether they left together. I have heard the deceased say, 'Tim, wait a minute. I am just going up the street to see if I can see him.' She added that he was going to draw his pension. This occurred on Saturday, Aug. 25th, at 3am.

In reply to the Coroner, the police said nothing was known of the pensioner.

Donovan: I never heard deceased call the man by any name. He was between forty and forty-five years of age, about 5 ft. 6 in. or 5 ft. 8 in. in height. Sometimes he would come dressed as a dock labourer; at other times he had a gentlemanly appearance. His hair was rather dark. I believe she always used to find him at the top of the street. Deceased was on good terms with the lodgers. About Tuesday, Aug. 28th, she and another woman had a row in the kitchen. I saw them both outside. As far as I know she was not injured at that time. I heard from the watchman that she had had a clout. I noticed a day or two afterwards, on the Thursday, that she had a slight touch of a black eye. She said, 'Tim, this is lovely,' but did not explain how she got it. The bruise was to be seen on Friday last. I know the other woman, but not her name. Her husband hawks laces and other things.

John Evans: I am night watchman at 35, Dorset Street, and have identified the deceased as having lived at the lodging-house. I last saw her there on Saturday morning, and she left at about 1.45am. I was sent down in the kitchen to see her, and she said she had not sufficient money. When she went upstairs I followed her, and as she left the house, I watched her go through a court called Paternoster Street, into Brushfield Street, and then turn towards Spitalfields Church. Deceased was the worse for drink, but not badly so. She came in soon after twelve (midnight), when she said she had been over to her sister's in Vauxhall. She sent one of the lodgers for a pint of beer, and then went out again, returning shortly before a quarter to two. I knew she had been living a rough nightlife. She associated with a man, a pensioner, every Saturday, and this individual called on Saturday at 2.30 p.m. and inquired for the deceased. He had heard something about her death, and came to see if it was true. I do not know his name or address. When I told him what had occurred he went straight out, without saying a word, towards Spitalfields Church. I did not see deceased and this man leave the house last Sunday week. ...

Day Two: Wednesday, 12 September 1888
Fontain Smith (printer's warehouseman): I have seen the body in the mortuary, and recognise it as that of my eldest sister, Annie, the widow of John Chapman. ... I last saw her alive a fortnight ago, in Commercial Street, where I met her promiscuously. Her husband died at Christmas, 1886. ...

James Kent (packing-case maker, of 20 Drew's Blocks, Shadwell): I work for Mr Bayley, 23A, Hanbury Street, and go there at 6am. On Saturday I arrived about ten minutes past that hour. Our employer's gate was open, and there I waited for some other men. Davis, who lives two or three doors away, ran from his house into the road and cried, 'Men, come here.' James Green and I went together to 29, Hanbury Street and on going through the passage, standing on the top of the back door steps, I saw a woman lying in the yard between the steps and the partition between the yard and the next. Her head was near the house, but no part of the body was against the wall. The feet were lying towards the back of Bayley's premises. (Witness indicated the precise position upon a plan produced by the police officers.) Deceased's clothes were disarranged, and her apron was thrown over them. I did not go down the steps, but went outside and returned after Inspector Chandler had arrived. I could see that the woman was dead. She had some kind of handkerchief around her throat, which seemed soaked in blood. The face and hands were besmeared with blood, as if she had struggled. She appeared to have been on her back and fought with her hands to free herself. The hands were turned toward her throat. The legs were wide apart, and there were marks of blood upon them. The entrails were protruding, and were lying across her left side. ...

Amelia Richardson (of 29 Hanbury Street): I am a widow, and occupy half of the house – i.e., the first floor, ground floor, and workshops in the cellar. I carry on the business of a packing-case maker there. My son John, aged thirty-seven, and a man Francis Tyler, who have worked for me eighteen years, use the shops. The latter ought to have come at 6am, but he did not arrive until eight o'clock, when I sent for him. He is often late when we are slack. My son lives in John Street, Spitalfields, and he works also in the market on market mornings. At 6am my grandson, Thomas Richardson, aged fourteen, who lives with me, got up. I sent him down to see what was the matter, as there was so much noise in the passage. He came back and said, 'Oh, grandmother, there is a woman murdered.' I went down immediately, and saw the body of the deceased lying in the yard. There was no one there at the time, but there were people in the passage. Soon afterwards a constable came and took possession of the place. As far as I know the officer was the first to enter the yard.

Coroner: Which room do you occupy?

Mrs Richardson: The first floor front, and my grandson slept in the same room on Friday night. I went to bed about half-past nine, and was very wakeful half the night. I was awake at three am, and only dozed after that.

Coroner: Did you hear any noise during the night?

Mrs Richardson: No. ...

Coroner: Were the front and back doors always left open?

Mrs Richardson: Yes, you can open the front and back doors of any of the houses about there. They are all let out in rooms. People are coming in or going out all the night.

Coroner: Did you ever see anyone in the passage?

Mrs Richardson: Yes, about a month ago I heard a man on the stairs. I called [the lodger] Thompson, and the man said he was waiting for market.

Coroner: At what time was this?

Mrs Richardson: Between half past three and four o'clock. I could hear anyone going through the passage. I did not hear any one going through on Saturday morning.

Coroner: You heard no cries?

Mrs Richardson: None.

Coroner: Supposing a person had gone through at half past three, would that have attracted your attention?

Mrs Richardson: Yes.

Coroner: You always hear people going to the back yard?

Mrs Richardson: Yes; people frequently do go through.

Coroner: People go there who have no business to do so?

Mrs Richardson: Yes; I daresay they do.

Coroner: On Saturday morning you feel confident no one did go through?

Mrs Richardson: Yes; I should have heard the sound.

Coroner: They must have walked purposely quietly?

Mrs Richardson: Yes; or I should have heard them. …

Harriett Hardiman (of 29 Hanbury Street, cats' meat saleswoman, the occupier of the ground-floor front room): I went to bed on Friday night at half-past ten. My son sleeps in the same room. I did not wake during the night. The trampling through the passage at about six o'clock awakened me. My son was asleep, and I told him to go to the back as I thought there was a fire. He returned and said that a woman had been killed in the yard. I did not go out of my room. I have often heard people going through the passage into the yard, but never got up to look who they were.

John Richardson (of John Street, Spitalfields, market porter): I assist my mother in her business. I went to 29, Hanbury Street, between 4.45am and 4.50am on Saturday last. I went to see if the cellar was all-secure, as some while ago there was a robbery there of some tools.

I have been accustomed to go on market mornings since the time when the cellar was broken in.

Coroner: Was the front door open?

Richardson: No, it was closed. I lifted the latch and went through the passage to the yard door.

Coroner: Did you go into the yard?

Richardson: No, the yard door was shut. I opened it and sat on the doorstep, and cut a piece of leather off my boot with an old table-knife, about five inches long. I kept the knife upstairs at John Street. I had been feeding a rabbit with a carrot that I had cut up, and I put the knife in my pocket. I do not usually carry it there. After cutting the leather off my boot I tied my boot up, and went out of the house into the market. I did not close the back door. It closed itself. I shut the front door.

Coroner: How long were you there?

Richardson: About two minutes at most.

Coroner: Was it light?

Richardson: It was getting light, but I could see all over the place.

Coroner: Did you notice whether there was any object outside?

Richardson: I could not have failed to notice the deceased had she been lying there then. I saw the body two or three minutes before the doctor came. I was then in the adjoining yard. Thomas Pierman had told me about the murder in the market. When I was on the doorstep I saw that the padlock on the cellar door was in its proper place.

Coroner: Did you sit on the top step?

Richardson: No, on the middle step; my feet were on the flags of the yard.

Coroner: You must have been quite close to where the deceased was found?

Richardson: Yes, I must have seen her.

Coroner: You have been there at all hours of the night?

Richardson: Yes.

Coroner: Have you ever seen any strangers there?

Richardson: Yes, plenty, at all hours – both men and women. I have often turned them out. We have had them on our first floor as well, on the landing.

Coroner: Do you mean to say that they go there for an immoral purpose? **Richardson**: Yes, they do. ...

Mrs Richardson, recalled, said she had never missed anything, and had such confidence in her neighbours that she had left the doors of some rooms unlocked.

Coroner: Had you an idea at any time that a part of the house or yard was used for an immoral purpose?

Mrs Richardson (emphatically): No, sir.

Coroner: Did you say anything about a leather apron?

Mrs Richardson: Yes, my son wears one when he works in the cellar.

Coroner: It is rather a dangerous thing to wear, is it not?

Mrs Richardson: Yes. On Thursday, Sept. 6, I found my son's leather apron in the cellar mildewed. He had not used it for a month. I took it and put it under the tap in the yard, and left it there. The police, who took charge of it, found it there on Saturday morning. The apron had remained there from Thursday to Saturday.

Coroner: Was this tap used?

Mrs Richardson: Yes, by all of us in the house. The apron was on the stones. The police took away an empty box, used for nails, and the steel out of a boy's gaiter. There was a pan of clean water near to the tap when I went in the yard at six o'clock on Saturday. It was there on Friday night at eight o'clock, and it looked as if it had not been disturbed.

Coroner: Did you ever know of strange women being found on the first-floor landing?

Mrs Richardson: No.

Coroner: Your son had never spoken to you about it?

Mrs Richardson: No.

John Pizer was then called.

Pizer: I live at 22, Mulberry Street, Commercial-road East. I am a shoemaker.

Coroner: Are you known by the nickname of 'Leather Apron'?

Pizer: Yes, sir.

Coroner: Where were you on Friday night last?

Pizer: I was at 22, Mulberry Street. On Thursday, the 6th inst. I arrived there.

Coroner: From where?

Pizer: From the west end of town.

Coroner: I am afraid we shall have to have a better address than that presently. What time did you reach 22, Mulberry Street?

Pizer: Shortly before 11pm.

Coroner: Who lives at 22, Mulberry Street?

Pizer: My brother and sister-in-law and my stepmother. I remained indoors there.

Coroner: Until when?

Pizer: Until Sergeant Thicke arrested me, on Monday last at 9am.

Coroner: You say you never left the house during that time?

Pizer: I never left the house.

Coroner: Why were you remaining indoors?

Pizer: Because my brother advised me.

Coroner: You were the subject of suspicion?

Pizer: I was the object of a false suspicion.

Coroner: You remained on the advice of your friends?

Pizer: Yes; I am telling you what I did.

Coroner: It was not the best advice that you could have had. You have been released, and are not now in custody?

Pizer: I am not. I wish to vindicate my character to the world at large.

Coroner: I have called you in your own interests, partly with the object of giving you an opportunity of doing so. Can you tell us where you were on Thursday, August 30th?

Pizer (after considering): In the Holloway Road.

Coroner: You had better say exactly where you were. It is important to account for your time from that Thursday to the Friday morning.

Pizer: What time, may I ask?

Coroner: It was the week before you came to Mulberry Street.

Pizer: I was staying at a common lodging-house called the Round House, in the Holloway Road.

Coroner: Did you sleep the night there?

Pizer: Yes.

Coroner: At what time did you go in?

Pizer: On the night of the London Dock fire I went in about two or a quarter-past. It was on the Friday morning.

Coroner: When did you leave the lodging-house?

Pizer: At 11am on the same day. I saw on the placards, 'Another Horrible Murder.'

Coroner: Where were you before two o'clock on Friday morning?

Pizer: At 11pm on Thursday I had my supper at the Round House.

Coroner: Did you go out?

Pizer: Yes, as far as the Seven Sisters Road, and then returned towards Highgate way, down the Holloway Road. Turning, I saw the reflection of a fire. Coming as far as the church in the Holloway Road I saw two constables and the lodging housekeeper talking together. There might have been one or two constables. I cannot say which. I asked a constable where the fire was, and he said it was a long way off. I asked him where he thought it was, and he replied: 'Down by the Albert Docks.' It was then about half-past one, to the best of my recollection. I went as far as Highbury Railway Station on the same side of the way, returned, and then went into the lodging-house.

Coroner: Did anyone speak to you about being so late?

Pizer: No: I paid the night watchman. I asked him if my bed was let, and he said: 'They are let by eleven o'clock. You don't think they are to let to this hour.' I paid him 4d for another bed. I stayed up smoking on the form of the kitchen, on the right hand side near the fireplace, and then went to bed.

Coroner: You got up at eleven o'clock?

Pizer: Yes. The day man came, and told us to get up, as he wanted to make the bed. I got up and dressed, and went down into the kitchen.

Coroner: Is there anything else you want to say?

Pizer: Nothing.

Coroner: When you said the West End of town did you mean Holloway?

Pizer: No; another lodging-house in Peter Street, Westminster.

Coroner: It is only fair to say that the witness's statements can be corroborated.

[Detective Sergeant] William Thicke: Knowing that 'Leather Apron' was suspected of being concerned in the murder, on Monday morning I arrested Pizer at 22, Mulberry Street. I have known him by the name of 'Leather Apron' for many years.

Coroner: When people in the neighbourhood speak of the 'Leather Apron' do they mean Pizer?

Thicke: They do.

Coroner: He has been released from custody?

Thicke: He was released last night at 9.30pm.

John Richardson (recalled) produced the knife, a much worn dessert knife, with which he had cut his boot. He added that as it was not sharp enough he had borrowed another one at the market. ...

Day Three: Thursday, 13 September 1888

Inspector Joseph Chandler (H Division): On Saturday morning, at ten minutes past six, I was on duty in Commercial Street. At the corner of Hanbury Street I saw several men running. I beckoned to them. One of them said, 'Another woman has been murdered.' I at once went with him to 29, Hanbury Street, and through the passage into the yard. There was no one in the yard. I saw the body of a woman lying on the ground on her back. Her head was towards the back wall of the house, nearly two feet from the wall, at the bottom of the steps, but six or nine inches away from them. The face was turned to the right side, and the left arm was resting on the left breast.

The right hand was lying down the right side. Deceased's legs were drawn up, and the clothing was above the knees. A portion of the intestines, still connected with the body, were lying above the right shoulder, with some pieces of skin. There were also some pieces of skin on the left shoulder. The body was lying parallel with the fencing dividing the two yards. I remained there and sent for the divisional surgeon, Mr Phillips, and to the police station for the ambulance and for further assistance. When the constables arrived I cleared the passage of people, and saw that no one touched the body until the doctor arrived. I obtained some sacking to cover it before the arrival of the surgeon, who came at about half-past six o'clock, and he, having examined the body, directed that it should be removed to the mortuary. After the body had been taken away I examined the yard, and found a piece of coarse muslin, a small toothcomb, and a pocket hair comb in a case. They were lying near the feet of the woman. A portion of an envelope was found near her head, which contained two pills.

Coroner: What was on the envelope?

Inspector Chandler: On the back there was a seal with the words, embossed in blue, 'Sussex Regiment.' The other part was torn away. On the other side there was a letter 'M' in writing.

Coroner: A man's handwriting?

Inspector Chandler: I should imagine so.

Coroner: Any postage stamp?

Inspector Chandler: No. There was a postal stamp 'London, August 3rd, 1888.' That was in red. There was another black stamp, which was indistinct.

Coroner: Any other marks on the envelope?

Inspector Chandler: There were also the letters 'Sp' lower down, as if someone had written 'Spitalfields.' The other part was gone. There were no other marks.

Coroner: Did you find anything else in the yard?

Inspector Chandler: There was a leather apron, lying in the yard, saturated with water. It was about two feet from the water tap.

Coroner: Was it shown to the doctor?

Inspector Chandler: Yes. There was also a box, such as is commonly used by casemakers for holding nails. It was empty. There was also a piece of steel, flat, which has since been identified by Mrs Richardson as the spring of her son's leggings.

Coroner: Where was that found? It was close to where the body had been. The apron and nail box have also been identified by her as her property. The yard was paved roughly with stones in parts; in other places it was earth.

Coroner: Was there any appearance of a struggle there?

Inspector Chandler: No.

Coroner: Are the palings strongly erected?

Inspector Chandler: No; to the contrary.

Coroner: Could they support the weight of a man getting over them?

Inspector Chandler: No doubt they might.

Coroner: Is there any evidence of anybody having got over them?

Inspector Chandler: No. Some of them in the adjoining yard have been broken since. They were not broken then.

Coroner: You have examined the adjoining yard?

Inspector Chandler: Yes.

Coroner: Was there any staining as of blood on any of the palings?

Inspector Chandler: Yes, near the body.

Coroner: Was it on any of the other yards?

Inspector Chandler: No.

Coroner: Were there no other marks?

Inspector Chandler: There were marks discovered on the wall of No. 25. They were noticed on Tuesday afternoon. They have been seen by Dr Phillips.

Coroner: Were there any drops of blood outside the yard of No. 29?

Inspector Chandler: No; every possible examination has been made, but we could find no trace of them. The bloodstains at No. 29 were in the immediate neighbourhood of the body only. There were also a few spots of blood on the back wall, near the head of the deceased, 2ft from the ground. The largest spot was of the size of a sixpence. They were all close together. I assisted in the preparation of the plan produced, which is correct.

Coroner: Did you search the body?

Inspector Chandler: I searched the clothing at the mortuary. The outside jacket, a long black one, which came down to the knees, had bloodstains round the neck, both upon the inside and out, and two or three spots on the left arm. The jacket was hooked at the top, and buttoned down the front. By the appearance of the garment there did not seem to have been any struggle. A large pocket was worn under the skirt (attached by strings), which I produce. It was torn down the front and also at the side, and it was empty. Deceased wore a black skirt. There was a little blood on the outside. The two petticoats were stained very little; the two bodices were stained with blood round the neck, but they had not been damaged. There was no cut in the clothing at all. The boots were on the feet of deceased. They were old. No part of the clothing was torn. The stockings were not bloodstained.

Coroner: Did you see John Richardson?

Inspector Chandler: I saw him about a quarter to seven o'clock. He told me he had been to the house that morning about a quarter to five. He said he came to the back door and looked down to the cellar, to see if all was right, and then went away to his work.

Coroner: Did he say anything about cutting his boot?

Inspector Chandler: No.

Coroner: Did he say that he was sure the woman was not there at that time?

Inspector Chandler: Yes. …

Foreman of the jury: Reference has been made to the Sussex Regiment and the pensioner. Are you going to produce the man Stanley?

Inspector Chandler: We have not been able to find him as yet. … There is nobody that can give us the least idea where he is. The parties were requested to communicate with the police if he came back. Every inquiry has been made, but nobody seems to know anything about him.

Coroner: I should think if that pensioner knows his own business he will come forward himself.

Sergeant Badham, 31 H, stated that he conveyed the body of the deceased to the mortuary on the ambulance.

Coroner: Are you sure that you took every portion of the body away with you?

Sergeant Badham: Yes.

Coroner: Where did you deposit the body?

Sergeant Badham: In the shed, still on the ambulance. I remained with it until Inspector Chandler arrived. Detective Sergeant Thicke viewed the body, and I took down the description. There were present two women, who came to identify the body, and they described the clothing. They came from 35, Dorset Street.

Coroner: Who touched the clothing?

Sergeant Badham: Sergeant Thicke. I did not see the women touch the clothing nor the body. I did not see Sergeant Thicke touch the body.

Inspector Chandler, recalled, said he reached the mortuary a few minutes after seven. The body did not appear to have been disturbed. He did not stay until the doctor arrived. Police constable 376 H was left in charge, with the mortuary keeper. Robert Marne, the mortuary keeper and an inmate of the Whitechapel Union Workhouse, said he received the body at seven o'clock on Saturday morning. He remained at the mortuary until Dr Phillips came. The door of the mortuary was locked except when two nurses from an infirmary came and undressed the body. No one else touched the corpse. He gave the key into the hands of the police. …

Timothy Donovan, the deputy of the lodging-house, 35, Dorset Street, was recalled.

Coroner: You have seen that handkerchief?

Donovan: I recognise it as one, which the deceased used to wear. She bought it off a lodger, and she was wearing it when she left the lodging-house. She was wearing it three-corner ways, placed round her neck, with a black woollen scarf underneath. It was tied in front with one knot.

Foreman of the jury: Would you recognise Ted Stanley, the pensioner?

A juror: Stanley is not the pensioner.

Coroner (to Donovan): Do you know the name of Stanley?

Donovan: No.

Foreman of the jury: He has been mentioned, and also 'Harry the Hawker.'

Donovan: I know 'Harry the Hawker.'

Coroner (having referred to the evidence): It may be an inference, there is no actual evidence that the pensioner was called Ted Stanley.

The Foreman said he referred to the man who came to see the deceased regularly. The man ought to be produced.

Coroner (to Donovan): Would you recognise the pensioner?

Donovan: Yes.

Coroner: When did you see him last?

Donovan: On Saturday.

Coroner: Why did you not then send him to the police?

Donovan: Because he would not stop.

Foreman of the jury: What was he like?

Donovan: He had a soldierly appearance. He dressed differently at times – sometimes gentlemanly.

A juror: He is not Ted Stanley.

George Bagster Phillips (divisional surgeon, H Division, Metropolitan Police): On Saturday last I was called by the police at 6.20 am to 29, Hanbury Street, and arrived at half-past six. I found the body of the deceased lying in the yard on her back, on the left hand of the steps that lead from the passage. The head was about 6 inches in front of the level of the bottom step, and the feet were towards a shed at the end of the yard. The left arm was across the left breast, and the legs were drawn up, the feet resting on the ground, and the knees turned outwards.

The face was swollen and turned on the right side, and the tongue protruded between the front teeth, but not beyond the lips; it was much swollen. The small intestines and other portions were lying on the right side of the body on the ground above the right shoulder, but attached. There was a large quantity of blood, with a part of the stomach above the left shoulder. I searched the yard and found a small piece of coarse muslin, a small toothcomb, and a pocket comb, in a paper case, near the railing. They had apparently been arranged there. I also discovered various other articles, which I handed to the police. The body was cold, except that there was a certain remaining heat, under the intestines, in the body. Stiffness of the limbs was not marked, but it was commencing. The throat was dissevered deeply. I noticed that the incision of the skin was jagged, and reached right round the neck. On the back wall of the house, between the steps and the palings, on the left side, about 18 inches from the ground, there were about six patches of blood, varying in size from a sixpenny piece to a small point, and on the wooden fence there were smears of blood, corresponding to where the head of the deceased laid, and immediately above the part where the blood had mainly flowed from the neck, which was well clotted. Having received instructions soon after two o'clock on Saturday afternoon, I went to the labour yard of the Whitechapel Union for the purpose of further examining the body and making the usual post-mortem investigation. I was surprised to find that the body had been stripped and was lying ready on the table. It was under great disadvantage I made my examination. As on many occasions I have met with the same difficulty, I now raise my protest, as I have before, that members of my profession should be called upon to perform their duties under these inadequate circumstances. ...

The body had been attended to since its removal to the mortuary, and probably partially washed. I noticed a bruise over the right temple. There was a bruise under the clavicle, and there were two distinct bruises, each the size of a man's thumb, on the fore part of the chest. The stiffness of the limbs was then well marked. The fingernails were turgid. There was an old scar of long standing on the left of the frontal bone. On the left side the stiffness was more noticeable, and especially in the fingers, which were partly closed. There was an abrasion over the bend of the first joint of the ring finger, and there were distinct markings of a ring or rings – probably the latter. There were small sores on the fingers. The head being opened showed that the membranes of the brain were opaque and the veins loaded with blood of a dark character. There was a large quantity of fluid between the membranes and the substance of the brain. The brain substance was unusually firm, and its cavities also contained a large amount of fluid. The throat had been severed. The incisions of the skin indicated that they had been made from the left side of the neck on a line with the angle of the jaw, carried entirely round and again in front of the neck, and ending at a point about midway between the jaw and the sternum or breast bone on the right hand. There were two distinct clean cuts on the body of the vertebrae on the left side of the spine. They were parallel to each other, and separated by about half an inch. The muscular structures between the side processes of bone of the vertebrae had an appearance as if an attempt had been made to separate the bones of the neck. There are various other mutilations of the body, but I am of opinion that they occurred subsequently to the death of the woman and to the large escape of blood from the neck. [Phillips paused] I am entirely in your hands, sir, but is it necessary that I should describe the further mutilations? From what I have said I can state the cause of death.

Coroner: The object of the inquiry is not only to ascertain the cause of death, but the means by which it occurred. Any mutilation, which took place afterwards, may suggest the character of the man who did it. Possibly you can give us the conclusions to which you have come respecting the instrument used.

Dr Phillips: You don't wish for details. I think if it were possible to escape the details it would be advisable. The cause of death is visible from injuries I have described.

Coroner: You have kept a record of them?

Dr Phillips: I have.

Coroner: Supposing anyone is charged with the offence, they would have to come out then, and it might be a matter of comment that the same evidence was not given at the inquest.

Dr Phillips: I am entirely in your hands.

Coroner: We will postpone that for the present. You can give your opinion as to how the death was caused.

Dr Phillips: From these appearances I am of opinion that the breathing was interfered with previous to death, and that death arose from syncope, or failure of the heart's action, in consequence of the loss of blood caused by the severance of the throat.

Coroner: Was the instrument used at the throat the same as that used at the abdomen?

Dr Phillips: Very probably. It must have been a very sharp knife, probably with a thin, narrow blade, and at least six to eight inches in length, and perhaps longer.

Coroner: Is it possible that any instrument used by a military man, such as a bayonet, would have done it?

Dr Phillips: No; it would not be a bayonet.

Coroner: Would it have been such an instrument as a medical man uses for post-mortem examinations?

Dr Phillips: The ordinary post-mortem case perhaps does not contain such a weapon.

Coroner: Would any instrument that slaughterers employ have caused the injuries?

Dr Phillips: Yes; well ground down.

Coroner: Would the knife of a cobbler or of any person in the leather trades have done?

Dr Phillips: I think the knife used in those trades would not be long enough in the blade.

Coroner: Was there any anatomical knowledge displayed?

Dr Phillips: I think there was. There were indications of it. My own impression is that that anatomical knowledge was only less displayed or indicated in consequence of haste. The person evidently was hindered from making a more complete dissection in consequence of the haste.

Coroner: Was the whole of the body there?

Dr Phillips: No; the absent portions being from the abdomen.

Coroner: Are those portions such as would require anatomical knowledge to extract?

Dr Phillips: I think the mode in which they were extracted did show some anatomical knowledge.

Coroner: You do not think they could have been lost accidentally in the transit of the body to the mortuary?

Dr Phillips: I was not present at the transit. I carefully closed up the clothes of the woman. Some portions had been excised.

Coroner: How long had the deceased been dead when you saw her?

Dr Phillips: I should say at least two hours, and probably more; but it is right to say that it was a fairly cold morning, and that the body would be more apt to cool rapidly from its having lost the greater portion of its blood.

Coroner: Was there any evidence of any struggle?

Dr Phillips: No; not about the body of the woman. You do not forget the smearing of blood about the palings.

Coroner: In your opinion did she enter the yard alive?

Dr Phillips: I am positive of it. I made a thorough search of the passage, and I saw no trace of blood, which must have been visible had she been taken into the yard.

Coroner: You were shown the apron?

Dr Phillips: I saw it myself. There was no blood upon it. It had the appearance of not having been unfolded recently.

Coroner: You were shown some staining on the wall of No. 25, Hanbury Street?

Dr Phillips: Yes; that was yesterday morning. To the eye of a novice I have no doubt it looks like blood. I have not been able to trace any signs of it. I have not been able to finish my investigation. I am almost convinced I shall not find any blood.

Coroner: We have not had any result of your examination of the internal organs. Was there any disease?

Dr Phillips: Yes. It was not important as regards the cause of death. Disease of the lungs was of long standing, and there was disease of the membranes of the brain. The stomach contained a little food.

Coroner: Was there any appearance of the deceased having taken much alcohol?

Dr Phillips: No. There were probably signs of great

privation. I am convinced she had not taken any strong alcohol for some hours before her death.

Coroner: Were any of these injuries self-inflicted?

Dr Phillips: The injuries, which were the immediate cause of death, were not self-inflicted.

Coroner: Was the bruising you mentioned recent?

Dr Phillips: The marks on the face were recent, especially about the chin and sides of the jaw. The bruise upon the temple and the bruises in front of the chest were of longer standing, probably of days. I am of opinion that the person who cut the deceased's throat took hold of her by the chin, and then commenced the incision from left to right.

Coroner: Could that be done so instantaneously that a person could not cry out?

Dr Phillips: By pressure on the throat no doubt it would be possible.

Foreman of the jury: There would probably be suffocation.

Coroner: The thickening of the tongue would be one of the signs of suffocation?

Dr Phillips: Yes. My impression is that she was partially strangled. (Witness added that the handkerchief produced was, when found amongst the clothing, saturated with blood. A similar article was round the throat of the deceased when he saw her early in the morning at Hanbury Street.)

Coroner: It had not the appearance of having been tied on afterwards?

Dr Phillips: No. Sarah Simonds, a resident nurse at the Whitechapel Infirmary, stated that, in company of the senior nurse, she went to the mortuary on Saturday, and found the body of the deceased on the ambulance in the yard. It was afterwards taken into the shed, and placed on the table. She was directed by Inspector Chandler to undress it, and she placed the clothes in a corner. She left the handkerchief round the neck. She was sure of this. They washed stains of blood from the body. It seemed to have run down from the throat. She found the pocket tied round the waist. The strings were not torn. There were no tears or cuts in the clothes.

Inspector Chandler: I did not instruct the nurses to undress the body and to wash it.

Day Four: Wednesday, 19 September 1888
Eliza Cooper: I am a hawker, and lodge in Dorset Street, Spitalfields. Have done so for the last five months. I knew the deceased, and had a quarrel with her on the Tuesday before she was murdered. The quarrel arose in this way: On the previous Saturday she brought Mr Stanley into the house where I lodged in Dorset Street, and coming into the kitchen asked the people to give her some soap. They told her to ask 'Liza' – meaning me. She came to me, and I opened the locker and gave her some. She gave it to Stanley, who went outside and washed himself in the lavatory. When she came back I asked for the soap, but she did not return it. She said, 'I will see you by and bye.' Mr Stanley gave her two shillings, and paid for her bed for two nights. I saw no more of her that night. On the following Tuesday I saw her in the kitchen of the lodging-house. I said, 'Perhaps you will return my soap.' She threw a halfpenny on the table, and said, 'Go and get a halfpennyworth of soap.' We got quarrelling over this piece of soap, and we went out to the Ringers public house and continued the quarrel. She slapped my face, and said, 'Think yourself lucky I don't do more.' I struck her in the

left eye, I believe, and then in the chest. I afterwards saw that the blow I gave her had marked her face.

Coroner: When was the last time you saw her alive?

Cooper: On the Thursday night, in the Ringers.

Coroner: Was she wearing rings?

Cooper: Yes, she was wearing three rings on the middle finger of the left hand. They were all brass.

Coroner: Had she ever a gold wedding ring to your knowledge?

Cooper: No, not since I have known her. I have known her about fifteen months. I know she associated with Stanley, 'Harry the Hawker,' and several others.

Foreman of the jury: Are there any of those with whom she associated missing?

Cooper: I could not tell.

A juror: Was she on the same relations with them as she was with Stanley?

Cooper: No, sir. She used to bring them casually into the lodging-house....

Coroner: ...Whatever may be your opinion and objections, it appears to me necessary that all the evidence that you ascertained from the post-mortem examination should be on the records of the Court for various reasons, which I need not enumerate. However painful it may be, it is necessary in the interests of justice.

Dr Phillips: I have not had any notice of that. I should have been glad if notice had been given me, because I should have been better prepared to give the evidence; however, I will do my best.

Coroner: Would you like to postpone it?

Dr Phillips: Oh, no. I will do my best. I still think that it is a very great pity to make this evidence public. Of course, I bow to your decision; but there are matters, which have come to light now which show the wisdom of the course pursued on the last occasion, and I cannot help reiterating my regret that you have come to a different conclusion. On the last occasion, just before I left the court, I mentioned to you that there were reasons why I thought the perpetrator of the act upon the woman's throat had caught hold of her chin. These reasons were that just below the lobe of the left ear were three scratches, and there was also a bruise on the right cheek. When I come to speak of the wounds on the lower part of the body I must again repeat my opinion that it is highly injudicious to make the results of my examination public. These details are fit only for yourself, sir, and the jury, but to make them public would simply be disgusting.

Coroner: We are here in the interests of justice, and must have all the evidence before us. I see, however, that there are several ladies and boys in the room, and I think they might retire. (Two ladies and a number of newspaper messenger boys accordingly left the court.)

Dr Phillips (raising an objection to the evidence): In giving these details to the public I believe you are thwarting the ends of justice.

Coroner: We are bound to take all the evidence in the case, and whether it be made public or not is a matter for the responsibility of the press.

Foreman of the jury: We are of opinion that the evidence the doctor on the last occasion wished to keep back should be heard. (Several Jurymen: Hear, hear.)

Coroner: I have carefully considered the matter and have never before heard of any evidence requested being kept back. ...

Dr Phillips: I am of opinion that what I am about to describe took place after death, so that it could not affect the cause of death, which you are inquiring into.

Coroner: That is only your opinion, and might be repudiated by other medical opinion.

Dr Phillips: Very well. I will give you the results of my post-mortem examination.

Witness then detailed the terrible wounds, which had been inflicted upon the woman, and described the parts of the body which the perpetrator of the murder had carried away with him. He added: I am of opinion that the length of the weapon with which the incisions were inflicted was at least five to six inches in length, probably more and must have been very sharp. The manner in which they had been done indicated a certain amount of anatomical knowledge.

Coroner: Can you give any idea how long it would take to perform the incisions found on the body?

Dr Phillips: I think I can guide you by saying that I myself could not have performed all the injuries I saw on that woman, and effect them, even without a struggle, under a quarter of an hour. If I had done it in a deliberate way, such as would fall to the duties of a surgeon, it would probably have taken me the best part of an hour. The whole inference seems to me that the operation was performed to enable the perpetrator to obtain possession of these parts of the body.

Coroner: Have you anything further to add with reference to the stains on the wall?

Dr Phillips: I have not been able to obtain any further traces of blood on the wall.

Foreman of the jury: Is there anything to indicate that

the crime in the case of the woman Nichols was perpetrated with the same object as this?

Coroner: There is a difference in this respect, at all events, that the medical expert is of opinion that, in the case of Nichols, the mutilations were made first.

Foreman of the jury: Was any photograph of the eyes of the deceased taken, in case they should retain any impression of the murderer?

Dr Phillips: I have no particular opinion upon that point myself. I was asked about it very early in the inquiry, and I gave my opinion that the operation would be useless, especially in this case. The use of a bloodhound was also suggested. It may be my ignorance, but the blood around was that of the murdered woman, and it would be more likely to be traced than the murderer. The police submitted these questions to me very early. I think within twenty-four hours of the murder of the woman.

Coroner: Were the injuries to the face and neck such as might have produced insensibility?

Dr Phillips: Yes; they were consistent with partial suffocation.

Mrs Elizabeth Long: I live in Church-row, Whitechapel, and my husband, James Long, is a cart minder. On Saturday, Sept. 8, about half-past five o'clock in the morning, I was passing down Hanbury Street, from home, on my way to Spitalfields Market. I knew the time, because I heard the brewer's clock strike half-past five just before I got to the street. I passed 29, Hanbury Street. On the right-hand side, the same side as the house, I saw a man and a woman standing on the pavement talking. The man's back was turned towards Brick-lane, and the woman's was towards the market.

They were standing only a few yards nearer Brick-lane from 29, Hanbury Street. I saw the woman's face. Have seen the deceased in the mortuary, and I am sure the woman that I saw in Hanbury Street was the deceased. I did not see the man's face, but I noticed that he was dark. He was wearing a brown low-crowned felt hat. I think he had on a dark coat, though I am not certain. By the look of him he seemed to me a man over forty years of age. He appeared to me to be a little taller than the deceased.

Coroner: Did he look like a working man, or what?

Long: He looked like a foreigner.

Coroner: Did he look like a dock labourer, or a workman, or what?

Long: I should say he looked like what I should call shabby-genteel.

Coroner: Were they talking loudly?

Long: They were talking pretty loudly. I overheard him say to her 'Will you?' and she replied, 'Yes.' That is all I heard, and I heard this as I passed. I left them standing there, and I did not look back, so I cannot say where they went to.

Coroner: Did they appear to be sober?

Long: I saw nothing to indicate that either of them was the worse for drink.

Coroner: Was it not an unusual thing to see a man and a woman standing there talking?

Long: Oh no. I see lots of them standing there in the morning.

Coroner: At that hour of the day?

Long: Yes; that is why I did not take much notice of them.

Coroner: You are certain about the time?

Long: Quite.

Coroner: What time did you leave home?

Long: I got out about five o'clock, and I reached the Spitalfields Market a few minutes after half-past five.

Foreman of the jury: What brewer's clock did you hear strike half-past five?

Long: The brewer's in Brick-lane.

Edward Stanley (of Osborn Place, Osborn Street, Spitalfields): I am a bricklayer's labourer.

Coroner: Are you known by the name of the pensioner?

Stanley: Yes.

Coroner: Did you know the deceased?

Stanley: I did.

Coroner: And you sometimes visited her?

Stanley: Yes.

Coroner: At 35, Dorset Street?

Stanley: About once there, or twice, something like that. Other times I have met her elsewhere.

Coroner: When did you last see her alive?

Stanley: On Sunday, Sept. 2, between one and three o'clock in the afternoon.

Coroner: Was she wearing rings when you saw her?

Stanley: Yes, I believe two. I could not say on which finger, but they were on one of her fingers.

Coroner: What sort of rings were they – what was the metal?

Stanley: Brass, I should think, by the look of them.

Coroner: Do you know anyone she was on bad terms with?

Stanley: No one, so far as I know. The last time I saw her she had some bruises on her face – a slight black eye, which some other woman had given her. I did not take much notice of it. She told me something about having had a quarrel. It is possible that I may have seen deceased after September 2nd, as I was doing nothing all that week. If I did see her I only casually met her, and we might have had a glass of beer together. My memory is rather confused about it.

Coroner: The deputy of the lodging-house said he was told not to let the bed to the deceased with any other man but you?

Stanley: It was not from me he received those orders. I have seen it described that the man used to come on the Saturday night, and remain until the Monday morning. I have never done so.

Foreman of the jury: You were supposed to be the pensioner.

Coroner: It must be some other man?

Stanley: I cannot say; I am only speaking for myself.

Coroner: Are you a pensioner?

Stanley: Can I object to answer that question, sir? It does not touch on anything here.

Coroner: It was said the man was with her on one occasion when going to receive his pension?

Stanley: Then it could not have been me. It has been stated all over Europe that it was me, but it was not.

Coroner: It will affect your financial position all over Europe when it is known that you are not a pensioner?

Stanley: It will affect my financial position in this way, sir, in that I am a loser by having to come here for nothing, and may get discharged for not being at my work.

Coroner: Were you ever in the Royal Sussex Regiment?

Stanley: Never, sir. I am a law-abiding man, sir, and interfere with no person who does not interfere with me.

Coroner: Call the deputy.

Timothy Donovan, deputy of the lodging-house, who gave evidence on a previous occasion, was then recalled.

Coroner: Did ever you see that man (pointing to Stanley) before?
Donovan: Yes.
Coroner: Is he the man you call 'the pensioner'?
Donovan: Yes.
Coroner: Was it he who used to come with the deceased on Saturday and stay till Monday?
Donovan: Yes.
Coroner: Was it he who told you not to let the bed to the deceased with any other man?
Donovan: Yes; on the second Saturday he told me.
Coroner: How many times have you seen him there?
Donovan: I should think five or six Saturdays.
Coroner: When was he last there?
Donovan: On the Saturday before the woman's death. He stayed until Monday. He paid for one night, and the woman afterwards came down and paid for the other.
Coroner: What have you got to say to that, Mr Stanley?
Stanley: You can cross it all out, sir.
Coroner: Cross your evidence out, you mean?
Stanley: Oh, no; not mine, but his. It is all wrong. I went to Gosport on August 6th and remained there until Sept. 1st.
Coroner: Probably the deputy has made a mistake.
A juror (to Stanley): Had you known deceased at Windsor at all?
Stanley: No; she told me she knew some one about Windsor, and that she once lived there.
Juror: You did not know her there?
Stanley: No; I have only known her about two years. I have never been to Windsor.

Juror: Did you call at Dorset Street on Saturday, the 8th, after the murder?

Stanley: Yes; I was told by a shoeblack it was she who was murdered, and I went to the lodging-house to ask if it was the fact. I was surprised, and went away.

Juror: Did you not give any information to the police that you knew her? You might have volunteered evidence, you know?

Stanley: I did volunteer evidence. I went voluntarily to Commercial Street Police Station, and told them what I knew.

Coroner: They did not tell you that the police wanted you?

Stanley: Not on the 8th, but afterwards. They told me the police wanted to see me after I had been to the police.

Albert Cadoch: I live at 27, Hanbury Street, and am a carpenter. 27 is next door to 29, Hanbury Street. On Saturday, September 8th, I got up about a quarter-past five in the morning, and went into the yard. It was then about twenty minutes past five, I should think. As I returned towards the back door I heard a voice say 'No' just as I was going through the door. It was not in our yard, but I should think it came from the yard of No. 29. I, however, cannot say which side it came from. I went indoors, but returned to the yard about three or four minutes afterwards. While coming back I heard a sort of a fall against the fence, which divides my yard from that of 29. It seemed as if something touched the fence suddenly.

Coroner: Did you look to see what it was?

Cadoch: No.

Coroner: Had you heard any noise while you were at the end of your yard?

Cadoch: No.

Coroner: Any rustling of clothes?

Cadoch: No. I then went into the house, and from there into the street to go to my work. It was about two minutes after half-past five as I passed Spitalfields Church.

Coroner: Do you ever hear people in these yards?

Cadoch: Now and then, but not often. ...

Foreman of the jury: What height are the palings?

Cadoch: About 5 ft. 6 in. to 6 ft. high.

Coroner: And you had not the curiosity to look over?

Cadoch: No, I had not.

Coroner: It is not usual to hear thumps against the palings?

Cadoch: They are packing-case makers, and now and then there is a great case goes up against the palings. I was thinking about my work, and not that there was anything the matter, otherwise most likely I would have been curious enough to look over.

Foreman of the jury: It's a pity you did not.

William Stevens (of 35 Dorset Street): I am a painter. I knew the deceased. I last saw her alive at twenty minutes past twelve on the morning of Saturday, Sept. 8. She was in the kitchen. She was not the worse for drink.

Coroner: Had she got any rings on her fingers?

Stevens: Yes.

Witness was shown a piece of an envelope, witness said he believed it was the same as she picked up near the fireplace. Did not notice a crest, but it was about that size, and it had a red postmark on it. She left the kitchen, and witness thought she was going to bed. Never saw her again. Did not know any one that she was on bad terms with. This was all the evidence obtainable. ...

Coroner: As far as we know, the case is complete.

Foreman of the jury: It seems to be a case of murder against some person or persons unknown.

Day Five: Wednesday, 26 September 1888

... **Coroner** (to jury): I congratulate you that your labours are now nearly completed. Although up to the present they have not resulted in the detection of any criminal, I have no doubt that if the perpetrator of this foul murder is eventually discovered, our efforts will not have been useless. The evidence is now on the records of this court, and could be used even if the witnesses were not forthcoming; while the publicity given has already elicited further information, which I shall presently have to mention, and which, I hope I am not sanguine in believing, may perhaps be of the utmost importance. We shall do well to recall the important facts. The deceased was a widow, forty-seven years of age, named Annie Chapman. Her husband was a coachman living at Windsor. For three or four years before his death she had lived apart from her husband, who allowed her 10s a week until his death at Christmas, 1886. Evidently she had lived an immoral life for some time, and her habits and surroundings had become worse since her means had failed. Her relations were no longer visited by her, and her brother had not seen her for five months, when she borrowed a small sum from him. She lived principally in the common lodging-houses in the neighbourhood of Spitalfields, where such as she herd like cattle, and she showed signs of great deprivation, as if she had been badly fed. The glimpses of life in these dens which the evidence in this case discloses is sufficient to make us feel that there is much in the nineteenth century civilisation of which we have small reason to be proud; but you who are constantly called together to hear the sad tale of starvation, or semi-starvation, of misery, immorality, and wickedness which some of the occupants of the 5,000 beds in this district have every week to relate to coroner's inquests, do not require to be reminded of what life in a Spitalfields lodging-house means. It was in one of these that the older bruises found on the temple and in front of the chest of the deceased were received, in a trumpery quarrel, a week before her death. It was in one of these that she was seen a few hours before her mangled remains were discovered. On the afternoon and evening of Friday, Sept. 7, she divided her time partly in such a place at 35, Dorset Street, and partly in the Ringers public house, where she spent whatever money she had; so that between one and two on the morning of Saturday, when the money for her bed is demanded, she is obliged to admit that she is without means, and at once turns out into the street to find it. She leaves there at 1.45 am, is seen off the premises by the night watchman, and is observed to turn down Little Paternoster Row into Brushfield Street, and not in the more direct route to Hanbury Street. On her wedding finger she was wearing two or three rings, which appear to have been palpably of base metal, as the witnesses are all clear about their material and value. We now lose sight of her for about four hours, but at half-past five, Mrs Long is in Hanbury Street on her way from home in Church Street, Whitechapel, to Spitalfields Market. She walked on the northern side of the road going westward, and remembers having seen a man and woman standing a few yards from the place where the deceased is afterwards found. And, although she did not know Annie Chapman, she is positive that that woman was deceased. The two were talking loudly, but not sufficiently so to arouse her suspicions that there was anything wrong. Such words as she overheard were not calculated to do so. The laconic inquiry of the man, 'Will you?' and the simple assent of the woman, viewed in the light of subsequent events, can be easily translated and explained. Mrs Long passed on her way, and neither saw nor heard anything more of her, and this is the last time she is known to have been alive. There is some conflict in the evidence about the time at which the deceased was despatched. It is not unusual to find inaccuracy in such details, but this variation is not very great or very important. She was found dead about six o'clock. She was not in the yard when Richardson was there at 4.50 am She was talking outside the house at half-past five when Mrs Long passed them. Cadoch says it was about 5.20am when he was in the back yard of the adjoining house, and heard a voice say 'No,' and three or four minutes afterwards a fall against the fence; but if he is out of his reckoning but a quarter of an hour, the discrepancy in the evidence of fact vanishes, and he may be mistaken, for he admits that he did not get up till a quarter-past five, and that it was after the half-hour when he passed Spitalfields clock. It is true that Dr Phillips thinks that when he saw the body at 6.30am the deceased had been dead at least two hours, but he admits that the coldness of the morning and the great loss of blood may affect his opinion; and if the evidence of the other witnesses be correct, Dr Phillips has miscalculated the effect of those forces. But many minutes after Mrs Long passed the man and woman cannot have elapsed before the deceased became a mutilated corpse in the yard of 29, Hanbury Street, close by where she was last seen by any witness. This place is a fair sample of a large number of houses in the neighbourhood. It was built, like hundreds of others, for the Spitalfields weavers, and when handlooms were driven out by steam and power, these were converted into dwellings for the poor. Its size is about such as a superior artisan would occupy in the country, but its condition is such as would to a certainty leave it without a tenant. In this place seventeen persons were living, from a woman and her son sleeping in a cat's meat shop on the ground floor to Davis and his wife and their three grown-up sons, all sleeping together in an attic. The street door and the yard door were never locked, and the passage and yard appear to have been constantly used by people who had no legitimate business there. There is little doubt that the deceased knew the place, for it was only 300 or 400 yards from where she lodged. If so, it is quite unnecessary to assume that her companion had any knowledge – in fact, it is easier to believe that he was ignorant both of the nest of living beings by whom he was surrounded, and of their occupations and habits. Some were on the move late at night, some were up long before the sun. A carman, named Thompson, left the house for his work as early as 3.50 am; an hour later John Richardson was paying the house a visit of inspection; shortly after 5.15 Cadoch, who lived in the next house, was in the adjoining yard twice. Davis, the carman, who occupied the third floor front, heard the church clock strike a quarter to six, got up, had a cup of tea, and went into the back yard, and was horrified to find the mangled body of deceased. It was then a little after six am. At ten minutes past the hour Inspector Chandler had been informed of the discovery while on duty in Commercial Street. There is nothing to suggest that the deceased was not fully conscious of what she was doing. It is true that she had passed through some stages of intoxication, for although she appeared perfectly sober to her friend who met her in Dorset Street at five o'clock the previous evening, she had been drinking afterwards; and when she left the lodging-house shortly before two o'clock the night watchman noticed that she was the worse for drink, but not badly so, while the deputy asserts that, though she had evidently been drinking, she could walk straight, and it was probably only malt liquor that she had taken, and its effects would pass off quicker than if she had taken spirits. Consequently it is not surprising to find that Mrs Long saw nothing to make her think that the deceased was the worse for drink. Moreover, it is unlikely that she could have had the opportunity of getting intoxicants. Again the post-mortem examination shows that while the stomach contained a meal of food there was no sign of fluid and no appearance of her having taken alcohol, and Dr Phillips is convinced that she had not taken any alcohol for some time. The deceased, therefore, entered the yard in full possession of her faculties; although with a very different object from her companion. From the evidence which the condition of the yard affords and the medical examination discloses, it appears that after the two had passed through the passage and opened the swing door at the end, they descended the three steps into the yard. On their left hand side there was a recess between those steps and the palings. Here a few feet from the house and a less distance from the paling they must have stood.

The wretch must have then seized the deceased, perhaps with Judas like approaches. He seized her by the chin. He pressed her throat, and while thus preventing the slightest cry, he at the same time produced insensibility and suffocation. There is no evidence of any struggle. The clothes are not torn. Even in these preliminaries, the wretch seems to have known how to carry out efficiently his nefarious work. The deceased was then lowered to the ground, and laid on her back; and although in doing so she may have fallen slightly against the fence, this movement was probably effected with care. Her throat was then cut in two places with savage determination, and the injuries to the abdomen commenced. All was done with cool impudence and reckless daring; but, perhaps, nothing is more noticeable than the emptying of her pockets, and the arrangement of their contents with business-like precision in order near her feet. The murder seems, like the Buck's Row case, to have been carried out without any cry. Sixteen people were in the house. The partitions of the different rooms are of wood. Davis was not asleep after three am, except for three-quarters of an hour, or less, between five and 5.45am. Mrs Richardson only dozed after 3am., and heard no noise during the night. Mrs Hardiman, who occupies the front ground-floor room, did not awake until the noise succeeding the finding of the body had commenced, and none of the occupants of the houses by which the yard is surrounded heard anything suspicious. The brute who committed the offence did not even take the trouble to cover up his ghastly work, but left the body exposed to the view of the first comer. This accords but little with the trouble taken with the rings, and suggests either that he had at length been disturbed, or that as the daylight broke a sudden fear suggested the danger of detection that he was running. There are two things missing. Her rings had been wrenched from her fingers and have not been found, and the uterus has been removed. The body has not been dissected, but someone who had considerable anatomical skill and knowledge has made the injuries. There are no meaningless cuts. One who knew where to find what he wanted, what difficulties he would have to contend against, and how he should use his knife, so as to abstract the organ without injury to it, did it. No unskilled person could have known where to find it, or have recognised it when it was found. For instance, no mere slaughterer of animals could have carried out these operations. It must have been someone accustomed to the post-mortem room. The conclusion that the desire was to possess the missing part seems overwhelming. If the object were robbery, these injuries were meaningless, for death had previously resulted from the loss of blood at the neck. Moreover, when we find an easily accomplished theft of some paltry brass rings and such an operation, after, at least, a quarter of an hour's work, and by a skilled person, we are driven to the deduction that the mutilation was the object, and the theft of the rings was only a thin-veiled blind, an attempt to prevent the real intention being discovered. Had not the medical examination been of a thorough and searching character, it might easily have been left unnoticed. The difficulty in believing that this was the real purport of the murderer is natural. It is abhorrent to our feelings to conclude that a life should be taken for so slight an object; but, when rightly considered, the reasons for most murders are altogether out of proportion to the guilt. It has been suggested that the criminal is a lunatic with morbid feelings. This may or may not be the case; but the object of the murderer appears palpably shown by the facts, and it is not necessary to assume lunacy, for it is clear that there is a market for the object of the murder. To show you this, I must mention a fact, which at the same time proves the assistance, which publicity and the newspaper press afford in the detection of crime. Within a few hours of the issue of the morning papers containing a report of the medical evidence given at the last sitting of the Court, I received a communication from an officer of one of our great medical schools, that they had information which might or might not have a distinct bearing on our inquiry. I attended at the first opportunity, and was told by the sub-curator of the Pathological Museum that some months ago an American had called on him, and asked him to procure a number of specimens of the organ that was missing in the deceased. He stated his willingness to give 20 shillings for each, and explained that his object was to issue an actual specimen with each copy of a publication on which he was then engaged. Although he was told that his wish was impossible to be complied with, he still urged his request. He desired them preserved, not in spirits of wine, the usual medium, but in glycerine, in order to preserve them in a flaccid condition, and he wished them sent to America direct. It is known that this request was repeated to another institution of a similar character. Now, is it not possible that the knowledge of this demand may have incited some abandoned wretch to possess himself of a specimen. It seems beyond belief that such inhuman wickedness could enter into the mind of any man, but unfortunately our criminal annals prove that every crime is possible. I need hardly say that I at once communicated my information to the Detective Department at Scotland Yard. Of course I do not know what use has been made of it, but I believe that publicity may possibly further elucidate this fact, and, therefore, I have not withheld from you my knowledge. By means of the press some further explanation may be forthcoming from America if not from here. I have endeavoured to suggest to you the object with which this offence was committed, and the class of person who must have perpetrated it. The greatest deterrent from crime is the conviction that detection and punishment will follow with rapidity and certainty, and it may be that the impunity with which Emma Smith and Martha Tabram were murdered suggested the possibility of such horrid crimes as those, which you and another jury have been recently considering. It is, therefore, a great misfortune that nearly three weeks have elapsed without the chief actor in this awful tragedy having been discovered. Surely, it is not too much even yet to hope that the ingenuity of our detective force will succeed in unearthing this monster. It is not as if there were no clue to the character of the criminal or the cause of his crime. His object is clearly divulged. His anatomical skill carries him out of the category of a common criminal, for his knowledge could only have been obtained by assisting at post-mortems, or by frequenting the post-mortem room. Thus the class in which search must be made, although a large one, is limited. Moreover it must have been a man who was from home, if not all night, at least during the early hours of September 8th. His hands were undoubtedly blood stained, for he did not stop to use the tap in the yard as the pan of clean water under it shows. If the theory of lunacy be correct, which I very much doubt, the class is still further limited, while, if Mrs Long's memory does not fail, and the assumption be correct that the man who was talking to the deceased at half-past five was the culprit, he is even more clearly defined. In addition to his former description, we should know that he was a foreigner of dark complexion, over forty years of age, a little taller than the deceased, of shabby genteel appearance, with a brown deer-stalker hat on his head, and a dark coat on his back. If your views accord with mine, you will be of opinion that we are confronted with a murder of no ordinary character, committed not from jealousy, revenge, or robbery, but from motives less adequate than the many, which still disgrace our civilisation, mar our progress, and blot the pages of our Christianity. I cannot conclude my remarks without thanking you for the attention you have given to the case, and the assistance you have rendered me in our efforts to elucidate the truth of this horrible tragedy.

Foreman of the jury: We can only find one verdict – that of wilful murder against some person or persons unknown. We were about to add a rider with respect to the condition of the mortuary, but that having been done by a previous jury it is unnecessary.

A verdict of wilful murder against a person or persons unknown was then entered.

Annie Chapman's murder shows that her killer was taking an

enormous risk, as people would have been moving about the streets and back yards at that time. If Albert Cadoch can be believed in saying he heard noises over the fence, the killer obviously would have heard him. Yet apparently he still went about his killing and mutilation, which would have taken him 15–20 minutes from start to finish. So, as well as being disorganised, the killer was now not scared to take risks to fulfil his grisly purpose.

Having studied all the facts of this murder, I find marked similarities between it and the killing of Mary Ann Nichols. The coroner in his summing up also highlighted these similarities:

- Both victims were street prostitutes in their mid-forties.
- Both murders were committed in the same locality and both in the early hours of the morning.
- In both cases the killer used a sharp, long-bladed knife.
- Both victims' throats were cut at some point and both had savage wounds to stomach and abdomen.
- Both victims may have been rendered unconscious before their throats were cut: Nichols by being hit and Chapman by being throttled or suffocated.

However, there are also marked differences which could point to the killer being a different person in the two cases. In the case of the previous victim, Polly Nichols, none of her internal organs or intestines appeared to have been removed. But it is documented that Annie Chapman's body was subjected to precise and specific removal and mutilations of her vital organs. Could the same killer, now grown in confidence, have committed Chapman's murder? If so, Dr Phillips's report on the time needed to remove the organs is interesting and again goes to show that the killer was disorganised and reckless, as the longer he remained with the body the more he risked being seen and possibly captured.

I have had great difficulty in accepting some of Dr Phillips's comments, not only on this murder but also on later ones on which he worked. In the Chapman case, he states that the killer must have had some anatomical knowledge to be able to remove the victim's organs as he did. Here we have a killer who takes a female into a back yard of a house in the early hours, while it is still dark. He kills her and supposedly disembowels her. Hospital surgeons normally require a great deal of light to locate the organs and either operate on or remove them. But in this murder the killer is supposed to have found them and cut them out in almost total darkness. We cannot disagree with Dr Phillips's finding that the organs were removed with precision. So could the killer have been a highly trained medical man? If he was, why savage and mutilate the body?

Could there be another explanation, overlooked all these years? I suggest there is.

In those days, the medical sciences were less advanced than they are now and many areas were being investigated. This research would have called for the use of organs and body parts, which were very difficult to acquire by conventional means. I suggest that Annie Chapman's organs were expertly removed, not at the scene by the murderer but after the body had been taken to the mortuary and before the post-mortem was carried out. This also applies to the later murder of Catherine Eddowes, discussed below.

Body parts were a valuable commodity and it would have been easy for a mortuary keeper, in particular, to provide these. He may well have had sufficient medical skill himself to remove organs from bodies in his care, although it is more likely that he allowed a medical researcher or a doctor to do so. In either case he, no doubt, would have received a substantial reward. Removal of organs would have been even easier in cases where the body had already been opened up, as with Chapman and Eddowes.

The findings of the post-mortem would, quite naturally, have left everyone thinking that the killer had removed the organs at the murder scene. Let's look at the timeline from the initial examination of Chapman's body at the murder scene to the post-mortem:

6.20am: Dr Phillips examines the body at the scene. No thorough examination is carried out to suggest organs were missing at that time.

7am: The body is taken by Inspector Chandler on an ambulance (handcart) to a shed at the workhouse that was used as a mortuary. No one stayed with the body, which initially was left outside on the ambulance. The mortuary keeper, an employee of the workhouse, stated at the inquest that he then locked the body in the shed and no one touched it. However, we know that two witnesses came to view the body, and as to whoever else came, and for whatever reason, we can only speculate.

2pm: Dr Phillips arrived to carry out the post-mortem. Later he reported that the body was already stripped and lying on the table, and it was only when he commenced the post-mortem that he found the organs were missing. I believe there is good reason to suggest that her organs were removed between 7am and 2pm, while the body was awaiting the doctor's arrival, and not by the killer at the murder scene.

Supportive of this theory is the fact that, in the later murder of Mary Kelly (discussed in Chapter Seven), although her body was mutilated and her organs removed, they were all left at the scene. There is no evidence to show that her organs were removed with any medical precision; quite the contrary.

You may be asking why, if Chapman's and Eddowes's organs were removed, as I suggest, weren't any removed from the other victims? The answer is simple: these were the only two victims who were savagely mutilated to the extent that their abdomens were ripped open and their intestines removed. The other victims were not mutilated to this degree, so it would have been impossible to remove the organs for fear of their absence being noted at the post-mortem.

Adding weight to this theory, the coroner in the Chapman inquest mentioned that an American recently trying to purchase organs had been prepared to pay a high price. Even more reason for a mortuary keeper or another to be a party to the theft of Chapman's and, later, Eddowes's organs.

CHAPTER FIVE

ELIZABETH STRIDE

A 45-year-old prostitute, Elizabeth Stride was the first victim of the so-called 'double event'. Her body was found in Dutfield's Yard, off Berner Street (now Henriques Street), at about 1am on the night of 30 September 1888 by a salesman returning with his pony and cart. He went to enter the yard, but his pony shied and hesitated as if something ahead was startling him.

Suspecting something was wrong, the salesman walked into the yard, but could not see as the yard was pitch-black. He probed his way with his whip and came into contact with the body of a female, whom he initially believed to be either drunk or asleep.

He entered the working men's club whose rear entrance opened into the yard, to get help in rousing the woman, and when he and two other men returned they discovered a woman later identified as Elizabeth Stride. She was dead and her throat had been cut. In her left hand she was clutching a packet of cachous – pills used by smokers to sweeten their breath – which suggested there had been no struggle.

It has been suggested that the salesman's untimely arrival frightened the killer, causing him to flee before he could perform any mutilation. The salesman stated that he believed the killer was still in the yard when he entered, because of the warm temperature of the woman's body and his pony's continuing odd behaviour. It remains unclear how the killer escaped, but one logical theory is that the salesman's leaving to seek help would have given him an ideal opportunity. Another theory is that the murderer jumped over the fence at the rear of the yard. A third is that Stride was attacked earlier and left to bleed to death.

Stride was last seen alive at about 12.35am. Her throat was gashed, but the body was otherwise unmutilated. Speculation at the time suggested that the killer was interrupted in his work.

Dr George Bagster Phillips, who had reported on Annie's Chapman murder and would later handle the Mary Kelly case, carried out the post-mortem. He was present at the murder scene and, after examining Stride's corpse there, he reported:

The body was lying on the near side, with the face turned toward the wall, the head up the yard and the feet toward the street. The left arm was extended and there was a packet of cachous in the left hand.

The right arm was over the belly; the back of the hand and wrist had on it clotted blood. The legs were drawn up with the feet close to the wall. The body and face were warm and the hand cold. The legs were quite warm.

The deceased had a silk handkerchief round her neck, and it appeared to be slightly torn. I have since ascertained it was cut. This corresponded with the right angle of the jaw. The throat was deeply gashed and there was an abrasion of the skin about one and a half inches in diameter, apparently stained with blood, under her right arm.

At three o'clock p.m. on Monday at St George's Mortuary, Dr Blackwell and I made a post-mortem examination. Rigor mortis was still thoroughly marked. There was mud on the left side of the face and it was matted in the head.

The body was fairly nourished. Over both shoulders, especially the right, and under the collarbone and in front of the chest there was a bluish discoloration, which I have watched and have seen on two occasions since.

There was a clear-cut incision on the neck. It was six inches in length and commenced two and a half inches in a straight line below the angle of the jaw, one half inch in over an undivided muscle, and then becoming deeper, dividing the sheath. The cut was very clean and deviated a little downwards. The arteries and other vessels contained in the sheath were all cut through.

The cut through the tissues on the right side was more superficial, and tailed off to about two inches below the right angle of the jaw. The deep vessels on that side were uninjured. From this it was evident that the haemorrhage was caused through the partial severance of the left carotid artery and a small bladed knife could have been used.

Decomposition had commenced in the skin. Dark brown spots were on the anterior surface of the left chin. There was a deformity in the bones of the right leg, which was not straight, but bowed forwards. There was no recent external injury save to the neck.

The body being washed more thoroughly I could see some healing sores. The lobe of the left ear was torn as if from the removal or wearing through of an earring, but it was thoroughly healed. On removing the scalp there was no sign of extravasation of blood.

The heart was small, the left ventricle firmly contracted, and the right slightly so. There was no clot in the pulmonary artery, but the right ventricle was full of dark clot. The left was firmly contracted as to be absolutely empty.

The stomach was large and the mucous membrane only congested. It contained partly digested food, apparently consisting of cheese, potato, and farinaceous powder. All the teeth on the lower left jaw were absent.

The inquest into the death of Elizabeth Stride was presided over by Mr Wynne E. Baxter, Coroner for the South-East Division of Middlessex. From the report:

Day One: Monday, 1 October 1888
At the outset of the inquiry the deceased was described as Elizabeth Stride, but it subsequently transpired that she had not yet been really identified. ...

William West: I reside at No. 2, William-street, Cannon Street Road, and am overseer in the printing office attached to No. 40, Berner Street, Commercial Road, which premises are in the occupation of the International Working Men's Education Society, whose club is carried on there. ...

On Saturday last I was in the printing office during the day and in the club during the evening. From nine to half-past ten at night I was away seeing an English friend home, but I was in the club again till a quarter-past midnight. A discussion was proceeding in the lecture-room, which has three windows overlooking the courtyard. From ninety to 100 persons attended the discussion, which terminated soon after half-past eleven, when the bulk of the members left, using the street door, the most convenient exit. From twenty to thirty members remained, some staying in the lecture-room and the others going downstairs. Of those upstairs a few continued the discussion, while the rest were singing. The windows of the lecture-room were partly open.

Coroner: How do you know that you finally left at a quarter-past twelve o'clock?

West: Because of the time when I reached my lodgings. Before leaving I went into the yard, and thence to the printing office, in order to leave some literature there, and on returning to the yard I observed that the double door at the entrance was open. There is no lamp in the yard, and none of the street lamps light it, so that the yard is only lit by the lights through the windows at the side of the club and of the tenements opposite. As to the tenements, I only observed lights in two first-floor windows. There was also a light in the printing office, the editor being in his room reading.

Coroner: Was there much noise in the club?

West: Not exactly much noise; but I could hear the singing when I was in the yard.

Coroner: Did you look towards the yard gates?

West: Not so much to the gates as to the ground, but nothing unusual attracted my attention.

Coroner: Can you say that there was no object on the ground?

West: I could not say that.

Coroner: Do you think it possible that anything can have been there without your observing it?

West: It was dark, and I am a little shortsighted, so that it is possible. The distance from the gates to the kitchen door is 18 ft.

Coroner: What made you look towards the gates at all?

West: Simply because they were open. I went into the

club, and called my brother, and we left together by the front door.

Coroner: On leaving did you see anybody as you passed the yard?

West: No.

Coroner: Or did you meet anyone in the street?

West: Not that I recollect. I generally go home between twelve and one o'clock.

Coroner: Do low women frequent Berner Street?

West: I have seen men and women standing about and talking to each other in Fairclough Street.

Coroner: But have you observed them nearer the club?

West: No.

Coroner: Or in the club yard?

West: I did once, at eleven o'clock at night, about a year ago. They were chatting near the gates. That is the only time I have noticed such a thing, nor have I heard of it....

Day Two: Tuesday, 2 October 1888

Constable Henry Lamb (H Division): Last Sunday morning, shortly before one o'clock, I was on duty in Commercial Road, between Christian Street and Batty Street, when two men came running towards me and shouting. I went to meet them, and they called out, 'Come on, there has been another murder.' I asked where, and as they got to the corner of Berner Street they pointed down and said, 'There.' I saw people moving some distance down the street. I ran, followed by another constable – 426 H. Arriving at the gateway of No. 40 I observed something dark lying on the ground on the right-hand side. I turned my light on, when I found that the object was a woman, with her throat cut and apparently dead. I sent the other constable for the nearest doctor, and a young man who was standing by I despatched to the police station to inform the inspector what had occurred. On my arrival there were about thirty people in the yard, and others followed me in. No one was nearer than a yard to the body. As I was examining the deceased the crowd gathered round, but I begged them to keep back, otherwise they might have their clothes soiled with blood, and thus get into trouble.

Coroner: Up to this time had you touched the body?

Constable Lamb: I had put my hand on the face.

Coroner: Was it warm?

Constable Lamb: Slightly. I felt the wrist, but could not discern any movement of the pulse. I then blew my whistle for assistance.

Coroner: Did you observe how the deceased was lying?

Constable Lamb: She was lying on her left side, with her left hand on the ground.

Coroner: Was there anything in that hand?

Constable Lamb: I did not notice anything. The right arm was across the breast. Her face was not more than five or six inches away from the club wall.

Coroner: Were her clothes disturbed?

Constable Lamb: No.

Coroner: Only her boots visible?

Constable Lamb: Yes, and only the soles of them. There were no signs of a struggle. Some of the blood was in a liquid state, and had run towards the kitchen door of the club. A little, that nearest to her on the ground, was slightly congealed. I can hardly say whether any was still flowing from the throat. Dr Blackwell was the first doctor to arrive; he came ten or twelve minutes after myself, but I had no watch with me.

Coroner: Did anyone of the crowd say whether the body had been touched before your arrival?

Constable Lamb: No. Dr Blackwell examined the body and its surroundings. Dr Phillips came ten minutes later. Inspector Pinhorn arrived directly after Dr Blackwell. When I blew my whistle other constables came, and I had the entrance of the yard closed. This was while Dr Blackwell was looking at the body. Before that the doors were wide open. The feet of the deceased extended just to the swing of the gate, so that the barrier could be closed without disturbing the body. I entered the club and left a constable at the gate to prevent any one passing in or out. I examined the hands and clothes of all the members of the club. There were from fifteen to twenty present, and they were on the ground floor.

Coroner: Did you discover traces of blood anywhere in the club?

Constable Lamb: No.

Coroner: Was the steward present?

Constable Lamb: Yes.

Coroner: Did you ask him to lock the front door?

Constable Lamb: I did not. There was a great deal of commotion. That was done afterwards.

Coroner: But time is the essence of the thing.

Constable Lamb: I did not see any person leave. I did not try the front door of the club to see if it was locked. I afterwards went over the cottages, the occupants of which were in bed. Men, who came down partly dressed, admitted me, all the other people were undressed. As to the water closets in the yard, one was locked and the other unlocked, but no one was there. There is a recess near the dustbin.

Coroner: Did you go there?

Constable Lamb: Yes, afterwards, with Dr Phillips.

Coroner: But I am speaking of at the time.

Constable Lamb: I did it subsequently. I do not recollect looking over the wooden partition. I, however, examined the store belonging to Messrs. Hindley, sack manufacturers, but I saw nothing there.

Coroner: How long were the cottagers in opening their doors?

Constable Lamb: Only a few minutes, and they seemed frightened. When I returned Dr Phillips and Chief Inspector West had arrived.

Coroner: Was there anything to prevent a man escaping while you were examining the body?

Constable Lamb: Several people were inside and outside the gates, and I should think that they would be sure to observe a man who had marks of blood.

Coroner: But supposing he had no marks of blood?

Constable Lamb: It was quite possible, of course, for a person to escape while I was examining the corpse. Everyone was more or less looking towards the body. There was much confusion.

Coroner: Do you think that a person might have got away before you arrived?

Constable Lamb: I think he is more likely to have escaped before than after.

Detective Inspector Reid: How long before had you passed this place?

Constable Lamb: I am not on the Berner Street beat, but I passed the end of the street in Commercial Road six or seven minutes before.

Coroner: When you were found what direction were you going in?

Constable Lamb: I was coming towards Berner Street. A constable named Smith was on the Berner Street beat. He did not accompany me, but the constable who was on fixed point duty between Grove Street and Christian Street in Commercial Road. Constables at fixed-points leave duty at one in the morning. I believe that is the practice nearly all over London.

Coroner: I think this is important. The Hanbury Street murder was discovered just as the night police were going off duty. (To witness): Did you see anything suspicious?

Constable Lamb: I did not at any time. There were squabbles and rows in the streets, but nothing more.

Foreman of the jury: Was there light sufficient to enable you to see, as you were going down Berner Street, whether any person was running away from No. 40?

Constable Lamb: It was rather dark, but I think there was light enough for that, though the person would be somewhat indistinct from Commercial Road. ...

Edward Spooner: I live at No. 26, Fairclough Street, and am a horse keeper with Messrs. Meredith, biscuit bakers. On Sunday morning, between half-past twelve and one o'clock, I was standing outside the Beehive public house, at the corner of Christian Street, with my young woman. We had left a public house in Commercial Road at closing time, midnight, and walked quietly to the point named. We stood outside the Beehive about twenty-five minutes, when two Jews came running along, calling out 'Murder' and 'Police.' They ran as far as Grove Street, and then turned back. I stopped them and asked what was the matter, and they replied that a woman had been murdered. I thereupon proceeded down Berner Street and into Dutfield's Yard, adjoining the International

Workmen's Club House, and there saw a woman lying just inside the gate.

Coroner: Was anyone with her?

Spooner: There were about fifteen people in the yard.

Coroner: Was anyone near her?

Spooner: They were all standing round.

Coroner: Were they touching her?

Spooner: No. One man struck a match, but I could see the woman before the match was struck. I put my hand under her chin when the match was alight.

Coroner: Was the chin warm?

Spooner: Slightly.

Coroner: Was any blood coming from the throat?

Spooner: Yes; it was still flowing. I noticed that she had a piece of paper doubled up in her right hand, and some red and white flowers pinned on her breast. I did not feel the body, nor did I alter the position of the head. I am sure of that. Her face was turned towards the club wall.

Coroner: Did you notice whether the blood was still moving on the ground?

Spooner: It was running down the gutter. I stood by the side of the body for four or five minutes, until the last witness arrived.

Coroner: Did you notice anyone leave the yard while you were there?

Spooner: No.

Coroner: Could anyone have left without your observing it?

Spooner: I cannot say, but I think there were too many people about. I believe it was twenty-five minutes to one o'clock when I arrived in the yard.

Coroner: Have you formed any opinion as to whether the people had moved the body before you came?

Spooner: No.

Foreman of the jury: As a rule, Jews do not care to touch dead bodies.

Spooner: The legs of the deceased were drawn up, but her clothes were not disturbed. When Police Constable Lamb came I helped him to close the gates of the yard, and I left through the club.

Inspector Reid: I believe that was after you had given your name and address to the police?

Spooner: Yes.

Inspector Reid: And had been searched?

Spooner: Yes.

Inspector Reid: And examined by Dr Phillips?

Spooner: Yes.

Coroner: Was there no blood on your hands?

Spooner: No.

Coroner: Then there was no blood on the chin of the deceased?

Spooner: No. ...

Mary Malcolm: I live at No. 50, Eagle Street, Red Lion Square, Holborn, and am married. My husband, Andrew Malcolm, is a tailor. I have seen the body at the mortuary. I saw it once on Sunday and twice yesterday.

Coroner: Who is it?

Malcolm: It is the body of my sister, Elizabeth Watts.

Coroner: You have no doubt about that?

Malcolm: Not the slightest. ...

Dr Frederick William Blackwell: I reside at No. 100, Commercial Road, and am a physician and surgeon. On Sunday morning last, at ten minutes past one o'clock, I was called to Berner Street by a policeman. My assistant,

Mr Johnston, went back with the constable, and I followed immediately I was dressed. I consulted my watch on my arrival, and it was 1.16 am. The deceased was lying on her left side obliquely across the passage, her face looking towards the right wall. Her legs were drawn up, her feet close against the wall of the right side of the passage. Her head was resting beyond the carriage wheel rut, the neck lying over the rut. Her feet were three yards from the gateway. Her dress was unfastened at the neck. The neck and chest were quite warm, as were also the legs, and the face was slightly warm. The hands were cold. The right hand was open and on the chest, and was smeared with blood. The left hand, lying on the ground, was partially closed, and contained a small packet of cachous wrapped in tissue paper. There were no rings, nor marks of rings, on her hands. The appearance of the face was quite placid. The mouth was slightly open. The deceased had round her neck a check silk scarf, the bow of which was turned to the left and pulled very tight. In the neck there was a long incision, which exactly corresponded with the lower border of the scarf. The border was slightly frayed, as if by a sharp knife. The incision in the neck commenced on the left side, 2 inches below the angle of the jaw, and almost in a direct line with it, nearly severing the vessels on that side, cutting the windpipe completely in two, and terminating on the opposite side 1 inch below the angle of the right jaw, but without severing the vessels on that side. I could not ascertain whether the bloody hand had been moved. The blood was running down the gutter into the drain in the opposite direction from the feet. There was about 1lb of clotted blood close by the body, and a stream all the way from there to the back door of the club.

Coroner: Were there no spots of blood about?

Dr Blackwell: No; only some marks of blood which had been trodden in.

Coroner: Was there any blood on the soles of the deceased's boots?

Dr Blackwell: No.

Coroner: No splashing of blood on the wall?

Dr Blackwell: No, it was very dark, and what I saw was by the aid of a policeman's lantern. I have not examined the place since. I examined the clothes, but found no blood on any part of them. The bonnet of the deceased was lying on the ground a few inches from the head. Her dress was unbuttoned at the top.

Coroner: Can you say whether the injuries could have been self-inflicted?

Dr Blackwell: It is impossible that they could have been.

Coroner: Did you form any opinion as to how long the deceased had been dead?

Dr Blackwell: From twenty minutes to half an hour when I arrived. The clothes were not wet with rain. She would have bled to death comparatively slowly on account of vessels on one side only of the neck being cut and the artery not completely severed.

Coroner: After the infliction of the injuries was there any possibility of any cry being uttered by the deceased?

Dr Blackwell: None whatever. Dr Phillips came about twenty minutes to half an hour after my arrival. The double doors of the yard were closed when I arrived, so that the previous witness must have made a mistake on that point.

A juror: Can you say whether the throat was cut before or after the deceased fell to the ground?

Dr Blackwell: I formed the opinion that the murderer

probably caught hold of the silk scarf, which was tight and knotted, and pulled the deceased backwards, cutting her throat in that way. The throat might have been cut as she was falling, or when she was on the ground. The blood would have spurted about if the act had been committed while she was standing up.

Coroner: Was the silk scarf tight enough to prevent her calling out?

Dr Blackwell: I could not say that.

Coroner: A hand might have been put on her nose and mouth?

Dr Blackwell: Yes, and the cut on the throat was probably instantaneous.

Day Three: Monday, 3 October 1888

Elizabeth Tanner: I am deputy of the common lodging-house, No. 32, Flower and Dean Street, and am a widow. I have seen the body of the deceased at St George's Mortuary, and recognise it as that of a woman who has lodged in our house, on and off, for the last six years.

Coroner: Who is she?

Tanner: She was known by the nickname of 'Long Liz.'

Coroner: Do you know her right name?

Tanner: No.

Coroner: Was she an English woman?

Tanner: She used to say that she was a Swedish woman. She never told me where she was born. She said that she was married, and that her husband and children were drowned in the *Princess Alice*. ...

Coroner: You are quite certain it is the body of the same woman?

Tanner: Quite sure. I recognise, beside the features, the roof of her mouth is missing. Deceased accounted for this by stating that she was in the *Princess Alice* when it went down, and that her mouth was injured. ...

Coroner: What sort of a woman was she?

Tanner: Very quiet.

Coroner: A sober woman?

Tanner: Yes. ...

Coroner: Do you recognise her clothes?

Tanner: Yes. I recognise the long cloak, which is hanging up in the mortuary. The other clothes she had on last Saturday. ...

Coroner: What made you go to the mortuary, then?

Tanner: Because I was sent for. I do not recollect at what hour she came to the lodging-house last Thursday. She was wearing the long cloak then. ...

Catherine Lane: I live in Flower and Dean Street, and am a charwoman and married. My husband is a dock labourer, and is living with me at the lodging-house of which the last witness [Elizabeth Tanner] is deputy. I have been there since last February. I have seen the body of the deceased at the mortuary.

Coroner: Did you recognise it?

Lane: Yes, as the body of Long Liz, who lived occasionally in the lodging-house. She came there last Thursday. ...

Coroner: Have you heard her mention any person but this man she was living with?

Lane: No. I have heard her say she was a Swede, and that at one time she lived in Devonshire Street, Commercial Road, never in Poplar.

Coroner: Did you ever hear her speak of her husband?

Lane: She said he was dead. She never said that she was afraid, or that anyone had threatened her life. I am satisfied the deceased is the same woman. ...

Michael Kidney: I live at No. 38, Dorset Street, Spitalfields, and am a waterside labourer. I have seen the body of the deceased at the mortuary.

Coroner: Is it the woman you have been living with?

Kidney: Yes.

Coroner: You have no doubt about it?

Kidney: No doubt whatever.

Coroner: What was her name?

Kidney: Elizabeth Stride.

Coroner: How long have you known her?

Kidney: About three years.

Coroner: How long has she been living with you?

Kidney: Nearly all that time.

Coroner: What was her age?

Kidney: Between thirty-six and thirty-eight years....

Coroner: You had a quarrel with her on Thursday?

Kidney: I did not see her on Thursday.

Coroner: When did you last see her?

Kidney: On the Tuesday, and I then left her on friendly terms in Commercial Street. That was between nine and ten o'clock at night, as I was coming from work.

Coroner: Did you expect her home?

Kidney: I expected her home half an hour afterwards. I subsequently ascertained that she had been in and had gone out again, and I did not see her again alive.

Coroner: Can you account for her sudden disappearance? Was she the worse for drink when you last saw her?

Kidney: She was perfectly sober.

Coroner: You can assign no reason whatever for her going away so suddenly?

Kidney: She would occasionally go away.

Coroner: Oh, she has left you before?

Kidney: During the three years I have known her she has been away from me about five months altogether.

Coroner: Without any reason?

Kidney: Not to my knowledge. I treated her the same as I would a wife.

Coroner: Do you know whether she had picked up with anyone?

Kidney: I have seen the address of the brother of the gentleman with whom she lived as a servant, somewhere near Hyde Park, but I cannot find it now.

Coroner: Did she have any reason for going away?

Kidney: It was drink that made her go on previous occasions. She always came back again. I think she liked me better than any other man. I do not believe she left me on Tuesday to take up with any other man.

Coroner: Had she any money?

Kidney: I do not think she was without a shilling when she left me. From what I used to give her I fancy she must either have had money or spent it in drink.

Coroner: You know of nobody whom she was likely to have complications with or fall foul of?

Kidney: No. ...

Dr George Bagster Phillips: I live at No. 2, Spital Square, and am surgeon of the H Division of police. I was called on Sunday morning last at twenty past one to Leman Street Police-station, and was sent on to Berner Street, to a yard at the side of what proved to be a clubhouse. I found Inspector Pinhorn and Acting-Superintendent West in possession of a body, which had already been seen by Dr Blackwell, who had arrived some time before me. The body was lying on its left side, the face being turned towards the wall, the head towards the yard, and the feet toward the street. The left arm was extended from elbow, and a packet of cachous was in the hand. Similar ones were in the gutter. I took them from the hand and gave them to Dr Blackwell. The right arm was lying over the body, and the back of the hand and wrist had on them clotted blood. The legs were drawn up, feet close to wall, body still warm, face warm, hands cold, legs quite warm, silk handkerchief round throat, slightly torn (so is my note, but I since find it is cut). I produce the handkerchief. This corresponded to the right angle of the jaw. The throat was deeply gashed, and there was an abrasion of the skin, about an inch and a quarter in diameter, under the right clavicle. On Oct. 1, at three p.m., at St George's Mortuary, present Dr Blackwell and for part of the time Dr Reigate and Dr Blackwell's assistant; temperature being about 55 degrees, Dr Blackwell and I made a post-mortem examination, Dr Blackwell kindly consenting to make the dissection, and I took the following note: 'Rigor mortis still firmly marked. Mud on face and left side of the head. Matted on the hair and left side. We removed the clothes. We found the body fairly nourished. Over both shoulders, especially the right, from the front aspect under collarbones and in front of chest there is a bluish discolouration, which I have watched and seen on two occasions since. On neck, from left to right, there is a clean cut incision six inches in length; incision commencing two and a half inches in a straight line below the angle of the jaw. Three quarters of an inch over undivided muscle, then becoming deeper, about an inch dividing sheath and the vessels, ascending a little, and then grazing the muscle outside the cartilages on the left side of the neck. The carotid artery on the left side and the other vessels contained in the sheath were all cut through, save the posterior portion of the carotid, to a line about 1-12th of an inch in extent, which prevented the separation of the upper and lower portion of the artery. The cut through the tissues on the right side of the cartilages is more superficial, and tails off to about two inches below the right angle of the jaw. It is evident that the haemorrhage, which produced death, was caused through the partial severance of the left carotid artery. There is a deformity in the lower fifth of the bones of the right leg, which are not straight, but bow forward; there is a thickening above the left ankle. The bones are here straighter. No recent external injury save to neck. The lower lobe of the ear was torn, as if by the forcible removing or wearing through of an earring, but it was thoroughly healed. The right ear was pierced for an earring, but had not been so injured, and the earring was wanting. On removing the scalp there was no sign of bruising or extravasation of blood between it and the skullcap. The skull was about one sixth of an inch in thickness, and dense in texture. The brain was fairly normal. Both lungs were unusually pale. The heart was small; left ventricle firmly contracted, right less so. The right ventricle was full of dark clot; left absolutely empty. Partly digested food, apparently consisting of cheese, potato, and farinaceous edibles. Teeth on left lower jaw absent.' On Tuesday, at the mortuary, I found the total circumference of the neck 12 inches. I found in the pocket of the underskirt of the deceased a key, as of a padlock, a small piece of lead pencil, a comb, a broken piece of comb, a metal spoon, half a dozen large and one small button, a hook, as if off a dress, a piece of muslin, and one or two small pieces of paper. Examining her jacket I found that although there was a slight amount of mud on the right side, the left was well plastered with mud.

A juror: You have not mentioned anything about the roof of the mouth? One witness said part of the roof of the mouth was gone.

Dr Phillips: That was not noticed.

Coroner: What was the cause of death?

Dr Phillips: Undoubtedly the loss of blood from the left carotid artery and the division of the windpipe.

Coroner: Did you examine the blood at Berner Street carefully, as to its direction and so forth?

Dr Phillips: Yes.

Coroner: The blood near to the neck and a few inches to the left side was well clotted, and it had run down the waterway to within a few inches of the side entrance to the clubhouse.

Coroner: Were there any spots of blood anywhere else?

Dr Phillips: I could trace none except that which I considered had been transplanted – if I may use the term – from the original flow from the neck. Roughly estimating it, I should say there was an unusual flow of blood, considering the stature and the nourishment of the body. …

Day Four: Monday, 5 October 1888

Dr Phillips: On the last occasion I was requested to make a re-examination of the body of the deceased, especially with regard to the palate, and I have since done so at the mortuary, along with Dr Blackwell and Dr Gordon Brown. I did not find any injury to, or absence of, any part of either the hard or the soft palate. The Coroner also desired me to examine the two handkerchiefs, which were found on the deceased. I did not discover any blood on them, and I believe that the stains on the larger handkerchief are those of fruit. Neither on the hands nor about the body of the deceased did I find grapes, or connection with them. I am convinced that the deceased had not swallowed either the skin or seed of a grape within many hours of her death. I have stated that the neckerchief, which she had on, was not torn, but cut. The abrasion, which I spoke of on the right side of the neck, was only apparently an abrasion, for on washing it it was removed, and the skin found to be uninjured. The knife produced on the last occasion was delivered to me, properly secured, by a constable, and on examination I found it to be such a knife as is used in a chandler's shop, and is called a slicing knife. It has blood upon it, which has characteristics similar to the blood of a human being. It has been recently blunted, and its edge apparently turned by rubbing on a stone such as a kerbstone. It evidently was before a very sharp knife.

Coroner: Is it such as knife as could have caused the injuries, which were inflicted upon the deceased?

Dr Phillips: Such a knife could have produced the incision and injuries to the neck, but it is not such a weapon as I should have fixed upon as having caused the injuries in this case; and if my opinion as regards the position of the body is correct, the knife in question would become an improbable instrument as having caused the incision.

Coroner: What is your idea as to the position the body was in when the crime was committed?

Dr Phillips: I have come to a conclusion as to the position of both the murderer and the victim, and I

POLICE · BUDGET · EDITION   EDITED · BY HAROLD FURNISS

FAMOUS CRIMES

PAST AND PRESENT   ONE · PENNY

HOW THE "RIPPER'S" VICTIMS WENT TO THEIR DEATH.

Vol. II.—No. 17.

A newspaper illustration shows how victims were allegedly lured to their deaths.

The back of the Hanbury Street building where Annie Chapman was found between the steps and the fence.

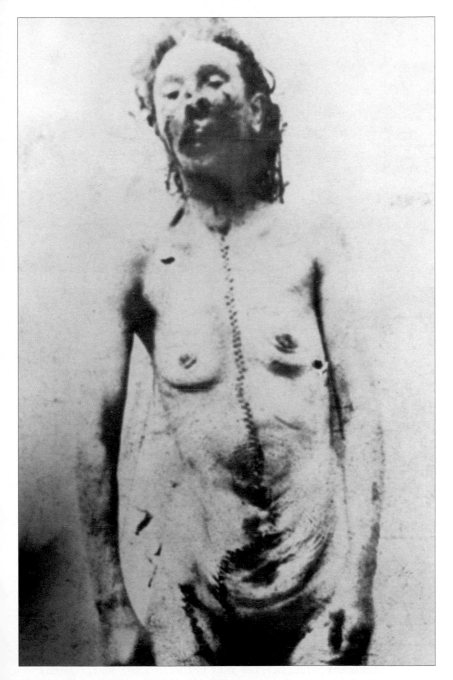

The mutilated body of Catherine Eddowes.

Top: A crime-scene photograph of Mary Kelly.

Bottom: Middlesex Street Market, now Petticoat Lane, where James Maybrick was reputed to have once rented a room.

An example of what was believed to have been the handwriting of Jack the Ripper (*top*) and a knife, the type of which the Ripper may have used to murder and mutilate his victims with (*bottom*).

Prince Albert Victor, the Duke of Clarence, was among the suspects.

Suspects included James Maybrick.

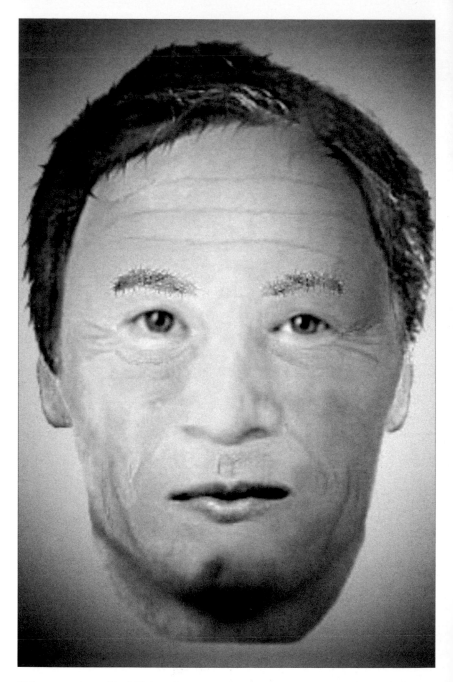

Prime suspect: Carl Feigenbaum.

opine that the latter was seized by the shoulders and placed on the ground, and that the murderer was on her right side when he inflicted the cut. I am of opinion that the cut was made from the left to the right side of the deceased, and taking into account the position of the incision it is unlikely that such a long knife inflicted the wound in the neck.

Coroner: The knife produced on the last occasion was not sharp pointed, was it?

Dr Phillips: No, it was rounded at the tip, which was about an inch across. The blade was wider at the base.

Coroner: Was there anything to indicate that the cut on the neck of the deceased was made with a pointed knife?

Dr Phillips: Nothing.

Coroner: Have you formed any opinion as to the manner in which the deceased's right hand became stained with blood?

Dr Phillips: It is a mystery. There were small oblong clots on the back of the hand. I may say that I am taking it as a fact that after death the hand always remained in the position in which I found it – across the body.

Coroner: How long had the woman been dead when you arrived at the scene of the murder, do you think?

Dr Phillips: Within an hour she had been alive.

Coroner: Would the injury take long to inflict?

Dr Phillips: Only a few seconds – it might be done in two seconds.

Coroner: Does the presence of the cachous in the left hand indicate that the murder was committed very suddenly and without any struggle?

Dr Phillips: Some of the cachous were scattered about the yard.

Foreman of the jury: Do you not think that the woman

would have dropped the packet of cachous altogether if she had been thrown to the ground before the injuries were inflicted?

Dr Phillips: That is an inference, which the jury would be perfectly entitled to draw.

Coroner: I assume that the injuries were not self-inflicted?

Dr Phillips: I have seen several self-inflicted wounds more extensive than this one, but then they have not usually involved the carotid artery. In this case, as in some others, there seems to have been some knowledge where to cut the throat to cause a fatal result.

Coroner: Is there any similarity between this case and Annie Chapman's case?

Dr Phillips: There is very great dissimilarity between the two. In Chapman's case the neck was severed all round down to the vertebral column, the vertebral bones being marked with two sharp cuts, and there had been an evident attempt to separate the bones.

Coroner: From the position you assume the perpetrator to have been in, would he have been likely to get bloodstained?

Dr Phillips: Not necessarily, for the commencement of the wound and the injury to the vessels would be away from him, and the stream of blood – for stream it was – would be directed away from him, and towards the gutter in the yard.

Coroner: Was there any appearance of an opiate or any smell of chloroform?

Dr Phillips: There was no perceptible trace of any anaesthetic or narcotic. The absence of noise is a difficult question under the circumstances of this case to account for, but it must not be taken for granted that there was not any noise. If there was an absence of noise I cannot account for it.

Foreman of the jury: That means that the woman might cry out after the cut?

Dr Phillips: Not after the cut.

Coroner: But why did she not cry out while she was being put on the ground?

Dr Phillips: She was in a yard, and in a locality where she might cry out very loudly and no notice be taken of her. It was possible for the woman to draw up her legs after the wound, but she could not have turned over. Drawing the knife across the throat inflicted the wound. A short knife, such as a shoemaker's well-ground knife, would do the same thing. My reason for believing that deceased was injured when on the ground was partly on account of the absence of blood anywhere on the left side of the body and between it and the wall.

A juror: Was there any trace of malt liquor in the stomach?

Dr Phillips: There was no trace.

Dr Blackwell (who assisted in making the post-mortem examination): I can confirm Dr Phillips as to the appearances at the mortuary. I may add that I removed the cachous from the left hand of the deceased, which was nearly open. The packet was lodged between the thumb and the first finger, and was partially hidden from view. It was I who spilt them in removing them from the hand. My impression is that the hand gradually relaxed while the woman was dying, she dying in a fainting condition from the loss of blood. I do not think that I made myself quite clear as to whether it was possible for this to have been a case of suicide. What I meant to say was that, taking all the facts into consideration, more especially the absence of any instrument in the hand, it was impossible to have been a suicide. I have myself seen many equally severe wounds self-inflicted. With respect to the knife, which was found, I should like to say that I concur with Dr Phillips in his opinion that, although it might possibly have inflicted the injury, it is an extremely unlikely instrument to have been used. It appears to me that a murderer, in using a round pointed instrument, would seriously handicap him, as he would be only able to use it in one particular way. I am told that slaughterers always use a sharp pointed instrument.

Coroner: No one has suggested that this crime was committed by a slaughterer.

Dr Blackwell: I simply intended to point out the inconvenience that might arise from using a blunt-pointed weapon.

Foreman of the jury: Did you notice any marks or bruises about the shoulders?

Dr Phillips: They were what we call pressure marks. At first they were very obscure, but subsequently they became very evident. They were not what are ordinarily called bruises; neither is there any abrasion. Each shoulder was about equally marked.

A juror: How recently might the marks have been caused?

Dr Phillips: That is rather difficult to say.

Coroner: Did you perceive any grapes near the body in the yard?

Dr Phillips: No.

Coroner: Did you hear any person say that they had seen grapes there?

Dr Phillips: I did not. ...

William Marshall: I reside at No. 64, Berner Street, and am a labourer at an indigo warehouse. I have seen the body at the mortuary. I saw the deceased on Saturday night last.

Coroner: Where?

Marshall: In our street, three doors from my house, about a quarter to twelve o'clock. She was on the pavement, opposite No. 58, between Fairclough Street and Boyd Street.

Coroner: What was she doing?

Marshall: She was standing talking to a man.

Coroner: How do you know this was the same woman?

Marshall: I recognise her both by her face and dress. She did not then have a flower in her breast.

Coroner: Were the man and woman whom you saw talking quietly?

Marshall: They were talking together.

Coroner: Can you describe the man at all?

Marshall: There was no gas lamp near. The nearest was at the corner, about twenty feet off. I did not see the face of the man distinctly.

Coroner: Did you notice how he was dressed?

Marshall: In a black cut-away coat and dark trousers.

Coroner: Was he young or old?

Marshall: Middle-aged he seemed to be.

Coroner: Was he wearing a hat?

Marshall: No, a cap.

Coroner: What sort of a cap?

Marshall: A round cap, with a small peak. It was something like what a sailor would wear.

Coroner: What height was he?

Marshall: About 5ft. 6in.

Coroner: Was he thin or stout?

Marshall: Rather stout.

Coroner: Did he look well dressed?

Marshall: Decently dressed.

Coroner: What class of man did he appear to be?

Marshall: I should say he was in business, and did nothing like hard work.

Coroner: Not like a dock labourer?

Marshall: No.

Coroner: Nor a sailor?

Marshall: No.

Coroner: Nor a butcher?

Marshall: No.

Coroner: A clerk?

Marshall: He had more the appearance of a clerk.

Coroner: Is that the best suggestion you can make?

Marshall: It is.

Coroner: You did not see his face. Had he any whiskers?

Marshall: I cannot say. I do not think he had.

Coroner: Was he wearing gloves?

Marshall: No.

Coroner: Was he carrying a stick or umbrella in his hands?

Marshall: He had nothing in his hands that I am aware of.

Coroner: You are quite sure that the deceased is the woman you saw?

Marshall: Quite. I did not take much notice whether she was carrying anything in her hands.

Coroner: What first attracted your attention to the couple?

Marshall: By their standing there for some time, and he was kissing her.

Coroner: Did you overhear anything they said?

Marshall: I heard him say; 'You would say anything but your prayers.'

Coroner: Different people talk in a different tone and in a different way. Did his voice give you the idea of a clerk?

Marshall: Yes, he was mild speaking.

Coroner: Did he speak like an educated man?

Marshall: I thought so. I did not hear them say anything more. They went away after that. I did not hear the woman say anything, but after the man made that observation she laughed. They went away down the street, towards Ellen Street. They would not then pass No. 40 (the club).

Coroner: How was the woman dressed?

Marshall: In a black jacket and skirt.

Coroner: Was either the worse for drink?

Marshall: No, I thought not.

Coroner: When did you go indoors?

Marshall: About twelve o'clock.

Coroner: Did you hear anything more that night?

Marshall: Not till I heard that the murder had taken place, just after one o'clock. While I was standing at my door, from half-past eleven to twelve, there was no rain at all. The deceased had on a small black bonnet. The couple were standing between my house and the club for about ten minutes.

Detective Inspector Reid: Then they passed you?

Marshall: Yes.

A juror: Did you not see the man's face as he passed?

Marshall: No; he was looking towards the woman, and had his arm round her neck. There is a gas lamp at the corner of Boyd Street. It was not closing time when they passed me.

James Brown: I live in Fairclough Street, and am a dock labourer. I have seen the body in the mortuary. I did not know deceased, but I saw her about a quarter to one on Sunday morning last.

Coroner: Where were you?

Brown: I was going from my house to the chandler's shop at the corner of Berner Street and Fairclough Street, to get some supper. I stayed there three or four minutes, and then went back home, when I saw a man and woman standing at the corner of the Board School. I was in the road just by the kerb, and they were near the wall.

Coroner: Did you see enough to make you certain that the deceased was the woman?

Brown: I am almost certain.

Coroner: Did you notice any flower in her dress?

Brown: No.

Coroner: What were they doing?

Brown: He was standing with his arm against the wall; she was inclined towards his arm, facing him, and with her back to the wall.

Coroner: Did you notice the man?

Brown: I saw that he had a long dark coat on.

Coroner: An overcoat?

Brown: Yes; it seemed so.

Coroner: Had he a hat or a cap on?

Brown: I cannot say.

Coroner: You are sure it was not her dress that you chiefly noticed?

Brown: Yes. I saw nothing light in colour about either of them.

Coroner: Was it raining at the time?

Brown: No. I went on.

Coroner: Did you hear anything more?

Brown: When I had nearly finished my supper I heard screams of 'Murder' and 'Police.' This was a quarter of an hour after I had got home. I did not look at any clock at the chandler's shop. I arrived home first at ten minutes past twelve o'clock, and I believe it was not raining then.

Coroner: Did you notice the height of the man?

Brown: I should think he was 5ft. 7in.

Coroner: Was he thin or stout?

Brown: He was of average build.

Coroner: Did either of them seem the worse for drink?

Brown: No.

Coroner: Did you notice whether either spoke with a foreign accent?

Brown: I did not notice any. When I heard screams I opened my window, but could not see anybody. The cries were of moving people going in the direction of Grove-street. Shortly afterwards I saw a policeman standing at the corner of Christian Street, and a man called him to Berner Street.

Constable William Smith (H Division): On Saturday last I went on duty at ten p.m. My beat was past Berner Street, and would take me twenty-five minutes or half an hour to go round. I was in Berner Street about half-past twelve or twenty-five minutes to one o'clock, and having gone round my beat, was at the Commercial Road corner of Berner Street again at one o'clock. I was not called. I saw a crowd outside the gates of No. 40, Berner Street. I heard no cries of 'Police.' When I came to the spot two constables had already arrived. The gates at the side of the club were not then closed. I do not remember that I passed any person on my way down. I saw that the woman was dead, and I went to the police station for the ambulance, leaving the other constables in charge of the body. Dr Blackwell's assistant arrived just as I was going away.

Coroner: Had you noticed any man or woman in Berner Street when you were there before?

Constable Smith: Yes, talking together.

Coroner: Was the woman anything like the deceased?

Constable Smith: Yes. I saw her face, and I think the body at the mortuary is that of the same woman.

Coroner: Are you certain?

Constable Smith: I feel certain. She stood on the pavement a few yards from where the body was found, but on the opposite side of the street.

Coroner: Did you look at the man at all?

Constable Smith: Yes.

Coroner: What did you notice about him?

Constable Smith: He had a parcel wrapped in a newspaper in his hand. The parcel was about 18in. long and 6in. to 8in. broad.

Coroner: Did you notice his height?

Constable Smith: He was about 5ft. 7in.

Coroner: His hat?

Constable Smith: He wore a dark felt deerstalker's hat.

Coroner: Clothes?

Constable Smith: His clothes were dark. The coat was a cutaway coat.

Coroner: Did you overhear any conversation?

Constable Smith: No.

Coroner: Did they seem to be sober?

Constable Smith: Yes, both.

Coroner: Did you see the man's face?

Constable Smith: He had no whiskers, but I did not notice him much. I should say he was twenty-eight years of age. He was of respectable appearance, but I could not state what he was. The woman had a flower in her breast. It rained very little after eleven o'clock. There were but few about in the bye streets. When I saw the body at the mortuary I recognised it at once. ...

Detective Inspector Edmund Reid (H Division): I received a telegram at 1.25am on Sunday morning last at Commercial Street Police office. I at once proceeded to No. 40, Berner Street, where I saw several police officers, Drs Phillips and Blackwell, and a number of residents in the yard and persons who had come there and been shut in by the police. At that time Drs Phillips and Blackwell were examining the throat of the deceased. A thorough search was made by the police of the yard, and the houses in it, but no trace could be found of any person who might have committed the murder. As soon as the search was over the whole of the persons who had come into the yard and the members of the club were interrogated, their names and addresses taken, their pockets searched by the police, and their clothes and hands examined by the doctors. The people were twenty-eight in numbers. Each was dealt with separately, and they properly accounted for themselves. The houses were inspected a second time and the occupants examined and their rooms searched. A loft close by was searched, but no trace could be found of the murderer. A description was taken of the body, and circulated by wire around the stations. Inquiries were made at the different houses in the street, but no person could be found who had heard screams or disturbance during the night. I examined the wall near where the body was found, but could detect no spots of blood. About half-past four the body was removed to the mortuary. Having given information of the murder to the coroner I returned to the yard and made another examination and found that the blood had been removed.

It being daylight I searched the walls thoroughly, but could discover no marks of their having been scaled. I then went to the mortuary and took a description of the deceased and her clothing as follows: Aged forty-two; length 5ft. 2in; complexion pale; hair dark brown and curly; eyes light grey; front upper teeth gone. The deceased had on an old black skirt, dark-brown velvet body, a long black jacket trimmed with black fur, fastened on the right side, with a red rose backed by a maidenhair fern. She had two light serge petticoats, white stockings, and white chemise with insertion, side spring boots, and black crape bonnet. In her jacket pocket were two handkerchiefs, a thimble, and a piece of wool on a card. That description was circulated. Since then the police have made a house-to-house inquiry in the immediate neighbourhood, with the result that we have been able to produce the witnesses who have appeared before the Court. The investigation is still going on. Every endeavour is being made to arrest the assassin, but up to the present without success.

Day Five: Tuesday, 23 October 1888
… The Coroner, in summing up, said the jury would probably agree with him that it would be unreasonable to adjourn this inquiry again on the chance of something further being ascertained to elucidate the mysterious case on which they had devoted so much time. The first difficulty, which presented itself, was the identification of the deceased. That was not an unimportant matter. Their trouble was principally occasioned by Mrs Malcolm who, after some hesitation and after having had two further opportunities of viewing again the body, positively swore that the deceased was her sister – Mrs Elizabeth Watts of

Bath. It had since been clearly proved that she was mistaken, notwithstanding the visions, which were simultaneously vouchsafed at the hour of the death to her and her husband. If her evidence was correct, there were points of resemblance between the deceased and Elizabeth Watts which almost reminded one of the Comedy of Errors. Both had been courted by policemen; they both bore the same Christian name, and were of the same age; both lived with sailors; both at one time kept coffee-houses at Poplar; both were nick-named 'Long Liz;' both were said to have had children in charge of their husbands' friends; both were given to drink; both lived in East End common lodging-houses; both had been charged at the Thames Police-court; both had escaped punishment on the ground that they were subject to epileptic fits, although the friends of both were certain that this was a fraud; both had lost their front teeth, and both had been leading very questionable lives. Whatever might be the true explanation of this marvellous similarity, it appeared to be pretty satisfactorily proved that the deceased was Elizabeth Stride, and that about the year 1869 she was married to a carpenter named John Thomas Stride. Unlike the other victims in the series of crimes in this neighbourhood – a district teeming with representatives of all nations – she was not an Englishwoman. She was born in Sweden in the year 1843, but, having resided in this country for upwards of 22 years, she could speak English fluently and without much foreign accent. At one time the deceased and her husband kept a coffee house in Poplar. At another time she was staying in Devonshire-street, Commercial Road, supporting herself, it was said, by sewing and charring. On and off for the last six years she lived in a common lodging-house in the notorious lane called Flower and Dean Street. She was there known only by the nickname of 'Long Liz,' and often told a tale, which might have been apocryphal, of her husband and children having gone down with the *Princess Alice*. The deputy of the lodging-house stated that while with her she was a quiet and sober woman, although she used at times to stay out late at night – an offence very venial, he suspected, among those who frequented the establishment. For the last two years the deceased had been living at a common lodging-house in Dorset Street, Spitalfields, with Michael Kidney, a waterside labourer, belonging to the Army Reserve. But at intervals during that period, amounting altogether to about five months, she left him without any apparent reason, except a desire to be free from the restraint even of that connexion, and to obtain greater opportunity of indulging her drinking habits. She was last seen alive by Kidney in Commercial Street on the evening of Tuesday, September 25. She was sober, but never returned home that night. She alleged that she had some words with her paramour, but this he denied. The next day she called during his absence, and took away some things, but, with this exception, they did not know what became of her until the following Thursday, when she made her appearance at her old quarters in Flower and Dean Street. Here she remained until Saturday, September 29. On that day she cleaned the deputy's rooms, and received a small remuneration for her trouble. Between 6 and 7 o'clock on that evening she was in the kitchen wearing the jacket, bonnet, and striped silk neckerchief, which afterwards was found on her. She had at least 6 pence in her possession, which was possibly spent during the evening. Before leaving she gave a piece of velvet to a friend to take care of until her return, but she said neither where she was going nor when she would return. She had not paid for her lodgings, although she was in a position to do so. They knew nothing of her movements during the next four or five hours at least – possibly not till the finding of her lifeless body. But three witnesses spoke to having seen a woman that they identified as the deceased with more or less certainty, and at times within an hour and a quarter of the period when, and at places within 100 yards of the spot where she was ultimately found. William Marshall, who lived at 64, Berner Street, was standing at his doorway from half-past 11 till midnight. About a quarter to 12 o'clock he saw the deceased talking to a man between Fairclough Street and Boyd Street. There was every demonstration of affection by the man during the ten minutes they stood together, and when last seen, strolling down the road towards Ellen Street, his arms were round her neck. At 12 30 p.m. the constable on the beat (William Smith) saw the deceased in Berner Street standing on the pavement a few yards from Commercial Street, and he observed she was wearing a flower in her dress. A quarter of an hour afterwards James Brown, of Fairclough Street, passed the deceased close to the Board School. A man was at her side leaning against the wall, and the deceased was heard to say, 'Not to-night, but some other night.' Now, if this evidence was to be relied on, it would appear that the deceased was in the company of a man for upwards of an hour immediately before her death, and that within a quarter of an hour of her being found a corpse she was refusing her companion something in the immediate neighbourhood of where she met her death. But was this the deceased? And even if it were, was it one and the same man who was seen in her company on three different occasions? With regard to the identity of the woman, Marshall had the opportunity of watching her for ten minutes while standing talking in the street at a short distance from him, and she afterwards passed close to him. The constable feels certain that the woman he observed was the deceased, and when he afterwards was called to the scene of the crime he at once recognised her and made a statement; while Brown was almost certain that the deceased was the woman to whom his attention was attracted. It might be thought that the frequency of the occurrence of men and women being seen together under similar circumstances might have led to mistaken identity; but the police stated, and several of the witnesses corroborated the statement, that although many couples are to be seen at night in the Commercial Road, it was exceptional to meet them in Berner Street. With regard to the man seen, there were many points of similarity, but some of dissimilarity, in the descriptions of the three witnesses; but these discrepancies did not conclusively prove that there was more than one man in the company of the deceased, for every day's experience showed how facts were differently observed and differently described by honest and intelligent witnesses. Brown, who saw least in consequence of the darkness of the spot at which the two were standing, agreed with Smith that his clothes were dark and that his height was about 5ft. 7in., but he appeared to him to be wearing an overcoat nearly down to his heels; while the description of Marshall accorded with that of Smith in every respect but two. They agreed that he was respectably dressed in a black cut-away coat and dark trousers, and that he was of middle age and without whiskers. On the other hand, they differed with regard to what he was wearing on his head. Smith stated he wore a hard felt deerstalker of dark colour; Marshall that he was wearing a round cap with a small peak, like a sailor's. They also differed as to whether he had anything in his hand. Marshall stated that he observed nothing. Smith was very precise, and stated that he was carrying a parcel, done up in a newspaper, about 18in. in length and 6in. to 8in. in width. These differences suggested either that the woman was, during the evening, in the company of more than one man – a not very improbable supposition – or that the witness had been mistaken in detail. If they were correct in assuming that the man seen in the company of deceased by the three was one and the same person it followed that he must have spent much time and trouble to induce her to place herself in his diabolical clutches. They last saw her alive at the corner of Fairclough Street and Berner Street, saying 'Not to-night, but some other night.' Within a quarter of an hour her lifeless body was found at a spot only a few yards from where she was last seen alive. It was late, and there were few people about, but the place to which the two repaired could not have been selected on account of it's being quiet or unfrequented. It had only the merit of darkness. It was the passageway leading into a court in which several families resided. Adjoining the passage and court there was a club of Socialists, who, having finished their debate, were singing and making merry. The deceased and her companion must have seen the lights of the clubroom, and the kitchen, and of the printing office. They must have heard the music and dancing, for the windows were open. There were persons in the yard but a short time previous to their arrival. ... At 1 o'clock the manager of the club found the body. He had been out all day, and returned at the time. He was in a 2-wheeled barrow drawn by a pony, and as he entered the gateway his pony shied at some object on his right. There was no lamp in the yard, and having just come out of the street it was too dark to see what the object was and he passed on further down the yard. He returned on foot, and on searching found the body of deceased with her throat cut. If he had not actually disturbed the wretch in the very act, at least he must have been close on his heels; possibly the man was alarmed by the sound of the approaching cart, for the death had only just taken place. He did not inspect the body himself with any care, but blood was flowing from the throat, even when Spooner reached the spot some few minutes afterwards, and although the bleeding had stopped when Dr Blackwell's assistant arrived, the whole of her body and the limbs, except her hands, were warm, and even at 16 minutes past 1 am Dr Blackwell found her face slightly warm, and her chest and legs quite warm. In this case, as in other similar cases, which had occurred in this neighbourhood, no call for assistance was noticed. Although there might have been some noise in the club, it seemed very unlikely that any cry could have been raised without its being heard by some one of those near. The editor of a Socialist paper was quietly at work in a shed down the yard, which was used as a printing office. There were several families in the cottages in the court only a few yards distant, and there were 20 persons in the different rooms of the club. But if there was no cry, how did the deceased meet with her death? The appearance of the injury to her throat was not in itself inconsistent with that of a self-inflicted wound. Both Dr Phillips and Dr Blackwell have seen self-inflicted wounds more extensive and severe, but those have not usually involved the carotid artery. Had some sharp instrument been found near the right hand of the deceased this case might have had very much the appearance of a determined suicide. But no such instrument was found, and its absence made suicide impossibility. The death was, therefore, one by homicide, and it seemed impossible to imagine circumstances which would fit in with the known facts of the case, and which would reduce the crime to manslaughter. There were no signs of any struggle; the clothes were neither torn nor disturbed. It was true that there were marks over both shoulders, produced by pressure of two hands, but the position of the body suggested either that she was willingly placed or placed herself where she was found. Only the soles of her boots were visible. She was still holding in her left hand a packet of cachous, and there was a bunch of flowers still pinned to her dress front. If she had been forcibly placed on the ground, as Dr Phillips opines, it was difficult to understand how she failed to attract attention, as it was clear from the appearance of the blood on the ground that the throat was not cut until after she was actually on her back. There were no marks of gagging, no bruises on the face, and no trace of any anaesthetic or narcotic in the stomach; while the presence of the cachous in her hand showed that she did not make use of it in self-defence. Possibly the pressure marks may have had a less tragical origin, as Dr Blackwell says it was difficult to say how recently they were produced. There was one particular, which was not easy to explain. When seen by Dr Blackwell her right hand was lying on the chest, smeared inside and out with blood. Dr Phillips was unable to make any suggestion how the hand became soiled. There was no injury to the hand; such as they would expect if it had been raised in self-defence while her throat was being cut. Was it done intentionally by her assassin? Or accidentally by those who were early on the spot? The evidence afforded no clue. Unfortunately the murderer had disappeared without leaving the slightest trace. Even the cachous were wrapped up in unmarked paper, so that there was nothing to show where they were bought. The cut in the throat might have been effected in such a manner that bloodstains on the hands and clothes of the operator were avoided, while the domestic history of the deed suggested the strong probability that her destroyer was a stranger to her. There was no one among her associates to whom any suspicion had attached. They had not heard that she had had a quarrel with anyone unless they magnified the fact that she had recently left the man with whom she generally cohabited; but this diversion was of so frequent an occurrence that neither a breach of the peace ensued, nor, so far as they knew, even hard words. There was therefore in the evidence no clue to the murderer and no suggested motive for the murder. The deceased was not in possession of any valuables. She was only known to have had a few pence in her pocket at the beginning of the evening. Those who knew her best were unaware of anyone likely to injure her. She never accused anyone of having threatened her. She never expressed any fear of anyone, and, although she had outbursts of drunkenness, she was generally a quiet woman. The ordinary motives of murder – revenge, jealousy, theft, and passion – appeared, therefore, to be absent from this case; while it was clear from the accounts of all who saw her that night, as well as from the post-mortem examination, that she was not otherwise than sober at the time of her death. In the absence of motive, the age and class of woman selected as victim, and the place and time of the crime, there was a similarity between this case and those mysteries, which had recently occurred in that neighbourhood. There had been no skilful mutilation as in the cases of Nichols and Chapman, and no unskilful injuries as in the case in Mitre Square – possibly the work of an imitator; but there had been the same skill exhibited in the way in which the victim had been entrapped, and the injuries inflicted, so as to cause instant death and prevent blood from soiling the operator, and the same daring defiance of immediate detection, which, unfortunately for the peace of the inhabitants and trade of the neighbourhood, had hitherto been only too successful. He himself was sorry that the time and attention which the jury had given to the case had not produced a result that would be a perceptible relief to the metropolis – the detection of the criminal; but he was sure that all had used their utmost effort to accomplish this object, and while he desired to thank the gentlemen of the jury for their kind assistance, he was bound to acknowledge the great attention which Inspector Reid and the police had given to the case. He left it to the jury to say, how, when, and by what means the deceased came by her death.

The jury, after a short deliberation, returned a verdict of 'Wilful murder against some person or persons unknown.'

The day after the murder, a mob formed outside Berner Street protesting about the continuation of the murders and the seemingly slipshod work of the police to catch the Ripper. From now on the Ripper was public enemy number one, and the Home Office began to consider offering rewards for his capture and arrest. This led to the formation of the Whitechapel Vigilance Committee.

For me the crucial question in the Stride murder is: was she a victim of the Ripper or simply an unconnected victim?

It would be foolhardy to dismiss any possibility lightly, so let us return to the murder of Annie Chapman and the description of a man seen with her (he was said to be shabbily dressed, over 40 years of age, with a dark complexion, possibly of foreign appearance, and wearing a brown deerstalker hat and what was believed to have been a dark overcoat.) As the inquest report shows, a police officer on duty on the night of the Stride murder stated that he saw her at about 12.35am in Berner Street, opposite the International Working Men's Educational Club, in company with a man about 28 years old, wearing a dark coat and a deerstalker hat. He was carrying, wrapped in newspaper, a parcel about 6–8 inches wide and 18 inches long. While there was a considerable difference in witnesses' estimates of the man's age, the descriptions of what he was wearing are similar. However, this could just be coincidence as deerstalker hats and dark overcoats were both common attire at that time. In any event, the coroner emphasised that the various descriptions were not accurate, so it is not safe to rely totally on them.

My conclusion is that Liz Stride's murder was not connected to any of either the previous or the later murders and she was not a Ripper victim. My reasons are:

- She was the only victim of the five canonical Ripper victims to have been killed south of Whitechapel Road.
- She was the only victim who was not subjected to stabbing or mutilation.
- The police doctor stated that he believed her murder to be unconnected to the previous murders.
- The area immediately around the murder site was well lit, very public and close to a busy drinking club, whereas the other Ripper murders occurred in

  locations where the killer (or killers) must have believed
  he (they) would not be interrupted.

- There was no evidence of the victim being knocked or throttled unconscious, as there was with other victims.
- The police doctor suggested that a small knife with a round tip was used to kill Stride. In the earlier murders of Chapman and Nichols and the later murders of Eddowes and Kelly a long-bladed knife was used. It is also suggested that Stride used to carry a small knife for her own protection. I pondered whether she could have been killed with this after luring a client into the yard and trying to rob him. However, I have been unable to find any direct evidence that she carried a knife.

Another theory is that Stride was a victim of a domestic dispute with her long-time boyfriend, Michael Kidney. I cannot rule this out and there are a number of issues about their relationship over her last few days that need closer scrutiny.

Stride stated to two different people that she had left Kidney, after they had argued, on the Thursday before she was murdered. Kidney stated that he last saw her on the Tuesday and they had not been arguing. Having studied the inquest reports, I find certain issues problematic. Why, apparently, was he never questioned about his whereabouts at the time of the murder? I find it very hard to believe that he wasn't asked this. With regard to his inquest testimony, was he trying to remove suspicion that he had a motive or murder? It is suggested that Stride had a torrid and violent relationship with him over the three years they were living together. Obviously Kidney was interviewed about her murder by the police, but it seems they could neither prove nor disprove his involvement.

CHAPTER SIX

CATHERINE EDDOWES

The second victim of the bloody night of 30 September was Catherine Eddowes, known as Kate, a prostitute aged 46. At 1.45am she was found brutally murdered in a dark corner of Mitre Square, which borders Whitechapel but falls under the control of the City of London Police.

Mitre Square is about 12 minutes' walk from Berner Street, the scene of Elizabeth Stride's murder, and Eddowes's body was found approximately 45 minutes after Stride's. The square could be entered by three passageways: from the east by Church Passage, from the west from Mitre Street or from the north by St James's Passage. At about 1.40am Police Constable Harvey passed along Church Passage and looked into Mitre Square, but he did not enter. Had he done so, he surely would have stumbled across the murderer. Four minutes later PC Watkins entered the square from Mitre Street and came across the body of Kate Eddowes lying on the pavement in the south-west corner. Yet neither Watkins nor Harvey reported seeing a man pass him or leaving the square hurriedly around the time of the murder. Therefore, presumably, the only route the killer could have taken was the northern passage, leading towards the City.

Eddowes was last seen alive at 1.35am in the company of a man described as aged 30, five feet seven inches tall, of medium build and with a fair complexion and moustache. He wore a pepper-and-salt-coloured jacket which fitted loosely, a grey cloth cap with a peak of the same colour and a reddish handkerchief knotted around his neck. He had the appearance of being a sailor.

Eddowes's head, like that of Polly Nichols, had been almost severed. Her body was gashed open from breastbone to stomach and her intestines had been cut out and placed over her right shoulder. The post-mortem showed that her kidney and uterus had been removed. Her face had been brutally mutilated. Was this savagery the Ripper compensating himself for having been interrupted in Berner Street, as some experts suggest?

Dr Frederick Gordon Brown, the London police surgeon called to the murder, arrived at Mitre Square around 2am. I have included his report as it reveals important findings that he did not give in his inquest testimony.

The body was on its back, the head turned to left shoulder. The arms by the side of the body as if they had fallen there. Both palms upwards, the fingers slightly bent. The left leg extended in a line with the body. The abdomen was exposed. Right leg bent at the thigh and knee. The throat cut across.

The intestines were drawn out to a large extent and placed over the right shoulder – they were smeared over with some feculent matter. A piece of about two feet was quite detached from the body and placed between the body and the left arm, apparently by design. The lobe and auricle of the right ear were cut obliquely through.

There was a quantity of clotted blood on the pavement on the left side of the neck round the shoulder and upper part of arm, and fluid blood-coloured serum which had flowed under the neck to the right shoulder, the pavement sloping in that direction.

Body was quite warm. No death stiffening had taken place. She must have been dead most likely within the half hour. We looked for superficial bruises and saw none. No blood on the skin of the abdomen or secretion of any kind on the thighs. No spurting of blood on the bricks or pavement around. No marks of blood below the middle of the body. Several buttons were found in the clotted blood after the body was removed. There was no blood on the front of the clothes. There were no traces of recent connexion.

When the body arrived at Golden Lane, some of the blood was dispersed through the removal of the body to the mortuary. The clothes were taken off carefully from the body. A piece of deceased's ear dropped from the clothing.

I made a post mortem examination at half-past two on Sunday afternoon. Rigor mortis was well marked; body not quite cold. There was a green discoloration over the abdomen.

After washing the left hand carefully, a bruise the size of a sixpence, recent and red, was discovered on the back of the left hand between the thumb and first finger. A few small bruises on right shin of older date. The hands and arms were bronzed. No bruises on the scalp, the back of the body, or the elbows.

The face was very much mutilated. There was a cut about a quarter of an inch through the lower left eyelid, dividing the structures completely through. The upper eyelid on that side, there was a scratch through the skin on the left upper eyelid, near to the angle of the nose. The right eyelid was cut through to about half an inch.

There was a deep cut over the bridge of the nose,

extending from the left border of the nasal bone down near the angle of the jaw on the right side of the cheek. This cut went into the bone and divided all the structures of the cheek except the mucous membrane of the mouth.

The tip of the nose was quite detached by an oblique cut from the bottom of the nasal bone to where the wings of the nose join on to the face. A cut from this divided the upper lip and extended through the substance of the gum over the right upper lateral incisor tooth.

About half an inch from the top of the nose was another oblique cut. There was a cut on the right angle of the mouth as if the cut of·a point of a knife. The cut extended an inch and a half, parallel with the lower lip.

There was on each side of cheek a cut, which peeled up the skin, forming a triangular flap about an inch and a half. On the left cheek there were two abrasions of the epithelium under the left ear.

The throat was cut across to the extent of about six or seven inches. A superficial cut commenced about an inch and a half below the lobe below, and about two and a half inches behind the left ear, and extended across the throat to about three inches below the lobe of the right ear.

The big muscle across the throat was divided through on the left side. The large vessels on the left side of the neck were severed. The larynx was severed below the vocal cord. All the deep structures were severed to the bone, the knife marking intervertebral cartilages. The sheath of the vessels on the right side was just opened.

The carotid artery had a fine hole or opening, the internal jugular vein was opened about an inch and a half – not divided. The blood vessels contained clot. All these injuries were performed by a sharp instrument like a knife, and pointed. The cause of death was haemorrhage from the left common carotid artery. The death was immediate and the mutilations were inflicted after death.

We examined the abdomen. The front walls were laid open from the breastbone to the pubes. The cut commenced opposite the enciform cartilage. The incision went upwards, not penetrating the skin that was over the sternum. It then divided the enciform cartilage. The knife must have cut obliquely at the expense of that cartilage.

Behind this, the liver was stabbed as if by the point of a sharp instrument. Below this was another incision into the liver of about two and a half inches, and below this the left lobe of the liver was slit through by a vertical cut. A jagging of the skin on the left side showed two cuts.

The abdominal walls were divided in the middle line to within a quarter of an inch of the navel. The cut then took a horizontal course for two inches and a half towards the right side. It then divided round the navel on the left side, and made a parallel incision to the former horizontal incision, leaving the navel on a tongue of skin. Attached to the navel was two and a half inches of the lower part of the rectus muscle on the left side of the abdomen. The incision then took an oblique direction to the right and was shelving. The incision went down the right side of the vagina and rectum for half an inch behind the rectum.

There was a stab of about an inch on the left groin. This was done by a pointed instrument. Below this was a cut of three inches going through all tissues making a wound of the peritoneum about the same extent.

An inch below the crease of the thigh was a cut extending from the anterior spine of the ilium obliquely down the inner side of the left thigh and separating the left labium, forming a flap of skin up to the groin. The left rectus muscle was not detached.

There was a flap of skin formed by the right thigh, attaching the right labium, and extending up to the spine of the ilium. The muscles on the right side inserted into the frontal ligaments were cut through.

The skin was retracted through the whole of the cut through the abdomen, but the vessels were not clotted. Nor had there been any appreciable bleeding from the vessels. I draw the conclusion that the act was made after death, and there would not have been much blood on the murderer. The cut was made by someone on the right side of the body, kneeling below the middle of the body.

I removed the content of the stomach and placed it in a jar for further examination. There seemed very little in it in the way of food or fluid, but from the cut end partly digested farinaceous food escaped.

The intestines had been detached to a large extent from the mesentery. About two feet of the colon was cut away. The sigmoid flexure was invaginated into the rectum very tightly.

Right kidney was pale, bloodless with slight congestion of the base of the pyramids.

There was a cut from the upper part of the slit on the under surface of the liver to the left side, and another cut at right angles to this, which were about an inch and a half deep and two and a half inches long. Liver itself was healthy.

The gall bladder contained bile. The pancreas was cut, but not through, on the left side of the spinal column. Three and a half inches of the lower border of the spleen by half an inch was attached only to the peritoneum.

The peritoneal lining was cut through on the left side and the left kidney carefully taken out and removed. The left renal artery was cut through. I would say that someone who knew the position of the kidney must have done it.

The lining membrane over the uterus was cut through. The womb was cut through horizontally, leaving a stump of three quarters of an inch. The rest of the womb had been taken away with some of the ligaments. The vagina and cervix of the womb was uninjured.

The bladder was healthy and uninjured, and contained three or four ounces of water. There was a tongue-like cut through the anterior wall of the abdominal aorta. The other organs were healthy. There were no indications of connexion.

I believe the wound in the throat was first inflicted. I believe she must have been lying on the ground.

The wounds on the face and abdomen prove that they were inflicted by a sharp, pointed knife, and that in the abdomen by one six inches or longer.

I believe the perpetrator of the act must have had considerable knowledge of the position of the organs in the abdominal cavity and the way of removing them. It required a great deal of medical knowledge to have removed the kidney and to know where it was placed.

I think the perpetrator of this act had sufficient time, or he would not have nicked the lower eyelids. It would take at least five minutes.

I cannot assign any reason for the parts being taken away. I feel sure that there was no struggle, and believe it was the act of one person.

The throat had been so instantly severed that no noise could have been emitted. I should not expect much blood to have been found on the person who had inflicted these wounds. The wounds could not have been self-inflicted.

My attention was called to the apron, particularly the corner of the apron with a string attached. The blood spots were of recent origin. I have seen the portion of an apron produced by Dr Phillips and stated to have been found in Goulston Street. It is impossible to say that it is human blood on the apron. I fitted the piece of apron, which had a new piece of material on it (which had evidently been sewn on to the piece I have), the seams of the borders of the two actually correspond. Some blood and apparently faecal matter was found on the portion that was found in Goulston Street.

The inquest into the death of Catherine Eddowes (or Conway or Kelly) was presided over by Mr S. F. Langham, Coroner for the City of London.

Day One: Thursday, 4 October 1888
Mr Crawford, City solicitor, appeared on behalf of the Corporation [of London], as responsible for the police ...

Crawford: I appear here as representing the City police in this matter, for the purpose of rendering you every possible assistance, and if I should consider it desirable, in the course of the inquiry, to put any questions to witnesses, probably I shall have your permission when you have finished with them.
Coroner: Oh, certainly. ...

Eliza Gold: I live at 6, Thrawl Street, Spitalfields. I have been married, but my husband is dead. I recognise the deceased as my poor sister (witness here commenced to weep very much, and for a few moments she was unable to proceed with her story). Her name was Catherine Eddowes. I cannot exactly tell where she was living. She was staying with a gentleman, but she was not married to him. Her age last birthday was about 43 years, as far as I can remember. She has been living for some years with Mr Kelly. He is in court. I last saw her alive about four or five months ago. She used to go out hawking for a living, and was a woman of sober habits. Before she went to live with Kelly, she had lived with a man named Conway for several years, and had two children by him. I cannot tell how many years she lived with Conway. I do not know whether Conway is still living. He was a pensioner from the army, and used to go out hawking also. I do not know on what terms he parted from my sister. I do not know whether she had ever seen him from the time they parted. I am quite certain that the body I have seen is my sister. ...

Coroner: Was she living on friendly terms with Kelly?

Gold: I cannot say. Three or four weeks ago I saw them together, and they were then on happy terms. I cannot fix the time when I last saw them. They were living at 55, Flower and Dean Street, a lodging-house. My sister when staying there came to see me when I was very ill. From that time, until I saw her in the mortuary, I have not seen her. ...

John Kelly (labourer): I live at a lodging-house, 55, Flower and Dean Street. Have seen the deceased and recognise her as Catherine Conway. I have been living with her for seven years. She hawked a few things about the streets and lived with me at a common lodging-house in Flower and Dean Street. The lodging-house is known as Cooney's. I last saw her alive about two o'clock in the afternoon of Saturday in Houndsditch. We parted on very good terms. She told me she was going over to Bermondsey to try and find her daughter Annie. Those were the last words she spoke to me. Annie was a daughter whom I believe she had had by Conway. She promised me before we parted that she would be back by four o'clock, and no later. She did not return.

Coroner: Did you make any inquiry after her?

Kelly: I heard she had been locked up at Bishopsgate Street on Saturday afternoon. An old woman who works in the lane told me she saw her in the hands of the police.

Coroner: Did you make any inquiry into the truth of this?

Kelly: I made no further inquiries. I knew that she would be out on Sunday morning, being in the City.

Coroner: Did you know why she was locked up?

Kelly: Yes, for drink; she had had a drop of drink, so I was told. I never knew she went out for any immoral purpose. She occasionally drank, but not to excess. When I left her she had no money about her. ...

Frederick William Wilkinson: I am deputy of the lodging-house at Flower and Dean Street. I have known the deceased and Kelly during the last seven years. They passed as man and wife, and lived on very good terms. They had a quarrel now and then, but not violent. They sometimes had a few words when Kate was in drink, but they were not serious. I believe she got her living by hawking about the streets and cleaning amongst the Jews in Whitechapel. Kelly paid me pretty regularly. Kate was not often in drink. She was a very jolly woman, always singing. Kelly was not in the habit of drinking, and I never saw him the worse for drink. ...

Coroner: Did you know she was in the habit of walking the streets at night?

Wilkinson: No; she generally used to return between nine and ten o'clock. I never knew her to be intimate with any particular individual except Kelly; and never heard of such a thing. ...

Constable Edward Watkins (City of London Police): I was on duty at Mitre Square on Saturday night. I have been in the force seventeen years. I went on duty at 9.45pm upon my regular beat. That extends from Duke Street, Aldgate, through Heneage Lane, a portion of Bury Street, through Cree Lane, into Leadenhall Street, along eastward into Mitre Street, then into Mitre Square, round the square again into Mitre Street, then into King Street to St James's Place, round the place, then into Duke Street, where I started from. That beat takes twelve or fourteen minutes. I had been patrolling the beat continually from ten o'clock at night until one o'clock on Sunday morning.

Coroner: Had anything excited your attention during those hours?

Watkins: No.

Coroner: Or any person?

Watkins: No. I passed through Mitre Square at 1.30am on the Sunday morning. I had my lantern alight and on – fixed to my belt. According to my usual practice, I looked at the different passages and corners.

Coroner: At half-past one did anything excite your attention?

Watkins: No.

Coroner: Did you see anyone about?

Watkins: No.

Coroner: Could any people have been about that portion of the square without your seeing them?

Watkins: No. I next came into Mitre Square at 1.40am, when I discovered the body lying on the right as I entered the square. The woman was on her back, with her feet towards the square. Her clothes were thrown up. I saw her throat was cut and the stomach ripped open. She was lying in a pool of blood. I did not touch the body. I ran across to Kearley and Long's [Tonge's] warehouse. The door was ajar, and I pushed it open, and called on the watchman Morris, who was inside. He came out. I remained with the body until the arrival of Police Constable Holland. No one else was there before that but myself. Holland was followed by Dr Sequeira. Inspector Collard arrived about two o'clock, and also Dr Brown, surgeon to the police force.

Coroner: When you first saw the body did you hear any footsteps as if anybody were running away?

Watkins: No. The door of the warehouse to which I went was ajar, because the watchman was working about. It was no unusual thing for the door to be ajar at that hour of the morning.

[Replying to questioning by Crawford]: I was continually patrolling my beat from ten o'clock up to half-past one. I noticed nothing unusual up till 1.44am, when I saw the body. …

Frederick William Foster, of 26, Old Jewry, architect and surveyor, produced a plan, which he had made of the place where the body was found, and the district. From Berner Street to Mitre Street is three-quarters of a mile, and a man could walk the distance in twelve minutes.

Inspector Collard (City Police): At five minutes before two o'clock on Sunday morning last I received information at Bishopsgate Street Police Station that a woman had been murdered in Mitre Square. Information was at once telegraphed to headquarters. I dispatched a constable to Dr Gordon Brown, informing him, and proceeded myself to Mitre Square, arriving there about two or three minutes past two. I there found Dr Sequeira, two or three police officers, and the deceased person lying in the southwest corner of the square, in the position described by Constable Watkins. The body was not touched until the arrival shortly afterwards of Dr Brown. The medical gentlemen examined the body, and in my presence Sergeant Jones picked up from the foot way by the left side of the deceased three small black buttons, such as are generally used for boots, a small metal button, a common metal thimble, and a small penny mustard tin containing two pawn-tickets. They were handed to me. The doctors remained until the arrival of the ambulance, and saw the body placed in the conveyance. It was then taken to the mortuary, and stripped by Mr Davis, the mortuary keeper, in presence of the two doctors and myself. I have a list of articles of clothing more or less stained with blood and cut.

Coroner: Was there any money about her?

Inspector Collard: No; no money whatever was found. A piece of cloth was found in Goulston Street, corresponding with the apron worn by the deceased. When I got to the square I took immediate steps to have the neighbourhood searched for the person who committed the murder. Mr McWilliams, chief of the Detective Department, on arriving shortly afterwards sent men to search in all directions in Spitalfields, both in streets and lodging-houses. Several men were stopped and searched in the streets, without any good result. I have had a house-to-house inquiry made in the vicinity of Mitre Square as to any noises or whether persons were seen in the place; but I have not been able to find any beyond the witnesses who saw a man and woman talking together.

Coroner: When you arrived was the deceased in a pool of blood?

Inspector Collard: The head, neck, and, I imagine, the shoulders were lying in a pool of blood when she was first found, but there was no blood in front. I did not touch the body myself, but the doctor said it was warm.

Coroner: Was there any sign of a struggle having taken place?

Inspector Collard: None whatever. I made a careful inspection of the ground all round. There was no trace whatever of any struggle. There was nothing in the appearance of the woman, or of the clothes, to lead to the idea that there had been any struggle. From the fact that the blood was in a liquid state I conjectured that the murder had not been long previously committed. In my opinion the body had not been there more than a quarter of an hour. I endeavoured to trace footsteps, but could find no trace whatever. The backs of the empty houses adjoining were searched, but nothing was found.

Dr Frederick Gordon Brown: I am surgeon to the City of London Police. I was called shortly after two o'clock on Sunday morning, and reached the place of the murder about twenty minutes past two. My attention was directed to the body of the deceased. It was lying in the position described by Watkins, on its back, the head turned to the left shoulder, the arms by the side of the body, as if they had fallen there. Both palms were upwards, the fingers slightly bent. A thimble was lying near. The clothes were thrown up. The bonnet was at the back of the head. There was great disfigurement of the face. The throat was cut across. Below the cut was a neckerchief. The upper part of the dress had been torn open. The body had been mutilated, and was quite warm – no rigor mortis. The crime must have been committed within half an hour, or certainly within forty minutes from the time when I saw the body. There were no stains of blood on the bricks or pavement around. ...

Before we removed the body Dr Phillips was sent for, as I wished him to see the wounds, he having been engaged in a case of a similar kind previously. He saw the body at the mortuary. The clothes were removed from the deceased carefully. I made a post-mortem examination on Sunday afternoon. There was a bruise on the back of the left hand, and one on the right shin, but this had nothing to do with the crime. There were no bruises on the elbows or the back of the head. The face was very much mutilated, the eyelids, the nose, the jaw, the cheeks, the lips, and the mouth all bore cuts. There were abrasions under the left ear. The throat was cut across to the extent of six or seven inches.

Coroner: Can you tell us what was the cause of death?

Dr Brown: The cause of death was haemorrhage from the throat. Death must have been immediate.

Coroner: There were other wounds on the lower part of the body?

Dr Brown: Yes; deep wounds, which were inflicted after death.

(Witness here described in detail the terrible mutilation of the deceased's body.)

Crawford: I understand that you found certain portions of the body removed?

Dr Brown: Yes. The uterus was cut away with the exception of a small portion, and the left kidney was also cut out. Both these organs were absent, and have not been found.

Coroner: Have you any opinion as to what position the woman was in when the wounds were inflicted?

Dr Brown: In my opinion the woman must have been lying down. The way in which the kidney was cut out showed that it was done by somebody who knew what he was about.

Coroner: Does the nature of the wounds lead you to any conclusion as to the instrument that was used?

Dr Brown: It must have been a sharp-pointed knife, and I should say at least 6 inches long.

Coroner: Would you consider that the person who inflicted the wounds possessed anatomical skill?

Dr Brown: He must have had a good deal of knowledge as to the position of the abdominal organs, and the way to remove them.

Coroner: Would the parts removed be of any use for professional purposes?

Dr Brown: None whatever.

Coroner: Would the removal of the kidney, for example, require special knowledge?

Dr Brown: It would require a good deal of knowledge as to its position, because it is apt to be overlooked, being covered by a membrane.

Coroner: Would such a knowledge be likely to be possessed by someone accustomed to cutting up animals?

Dr Brown: Yes.

Coroner: Have you been able to form any opinion as to whether the perpetrator of this act was disturbed?

Dr Brown: I think he had sufficient time, but it was in all probability done in a hurry.

Coroner: How long would it take to make the wounds?

Dr Brown: It might be done in five minutes. It might take him longer; but that is the least time it could be done in.

Coroner: Can you, as a professional man, ascribe any reason for the taking away of the parts you have mentioned?

Dr Brown: I cannot give any reason whatever.

Coroner: Have you any doubt in your own mind whether there was a struggle?

Dr Brown: I feel sure there was no struggle. I see no reason to doubt that it was the work of one man.

Coroner: Would any noise be heard, do you think?

Dr Brown: I presume the throat was instantly severed, in which case there would not be time to emit any sound.

Coroner: Does it surprise you that no sound was heard?

Dr Brown: No.

Coroner: Would you expect to find much blood on the person inflicting these wounds?

Dr Brown: No, I should not. I would say that the abdominal wounds were inflicted by a person kneeling at the right side of the body. The wounds could not possibly have been self-inflicted.

Coroner: Was your attention called to the portion of the apron that was found in Goulston Street?

Dr Brown: Yes. I fitted that portion which was spotted with blood to the remaining portion, which was still attached by the strings to the body.

Coroner: Have you formed any opinion as to the motive for the mutilation of the face?

Dr Brown: It was to disfigure the corpse, I should imagine.

A juror: Was there any evidence of a drug having been used?

Dr Brown: I have not examined the stomach as to that. The contents of the stomach have been preserved for analysis. ...

Day Two: Thursday, 11 October 1888
... **Dr G.W. Sequeira** (surgeon, of No. 34, Jewry Street, Aldgate): On the morning of Sept. 30th I was called to Mitre Square, and I arrived at five minutes to two o'clock, being the first medical man on the scene of the murder. I saw the position of the body, and I entirely agree with the evidence of Dr Gordon Brown in that respect.

[Replying to questioning by Crawford]: I am well acquainted with the locality and the position of the lamps in the square. Where the murder was committed was probably the darkest part of the square, but there was sufficient light to enable the miscreant to perpetrate the deed. I think that the murderer had no design on any particular organ of the body. He was not possessed of any great anatomical skill.

Coroner: Can you account for the absence of noise?

Dr Sequeira: The death must have been instantaneous after the severance of the windpipe and the blood vessels.

Coroner: Would you have expected the murderer to be bespattered with blood?

Dr Sequeira: Not necessarily.

Coroner: How long do you believe life had been extinct when you arrived?

Dr Sequeira: Very few minutes – probably not more than a quarter of an hour.

William Sedgwick Saunders (medical officer of health for the City): I received the stomach of the deceased from Dr Gordon Brown, carefully sealed, and I made an analysis of the contents, which had not been interfered with in any way. I looked more particularly for poisons of the narcotic class, but with negative results, there being not the faintest trace of any of those or any other poisons. ...

Crawford: The theory has been put forward that it was possible for the deceased to have been murdered elsewhere, and her body brought to where it was found. I should like to ask Dr Gordon Brown, who is present, what his opinion is about that.

Dr Brown: I do not think there is any foundation for such a theory. The blood on the left side was clotted, and must have fallen at the time the throat was cut. I do not think that the deceased moved the least bit after that.

Coroner: The body could not have been carried to where it was found?

Dr Brown: Oh, no.

Constable Lewis Robinson: At half-past eight, on the night of Saturday, Sept. 29, while on duty in High Street, Aldgate, I saw a crowd of persons outside No. 29, surrounding a woman whom I have since recognised as the deceased.

Coroner: What state was she in?

Constable Robinson: Drunk.

Coroner: Lying on the footway?

Constable Robinson: Yes. I asked the crowd if any of them knew her or where she lived, but got no answer. I then picked her up and sat her against the shutters, but she fell down sideways. With the aid of a fellow-constable I took her to Bishopsgate Police Station. There she was asked her name, and she replied 'Nothing.' She was then put into a cell. ...

George James Morris (night watchman at Messrs. Kearley and Tonge's tea warehouse, Mitre Square): On Saturday, Sept. 29, I went on duty at seven o'clock in the evening. I occupied most of my time in cleaning the offices and looking about the warehouse.

Coroner: What happened about a quarter to two in the morning?

Morris: Constable Watkins, who was on the Mitre Square beat, knocked at my door, which was slightly ajar at the time. I was then sweeping the steps down towards the door. The door was pushed when I was about two yards off. I turned round and opened the door wide. The constable said, 'For God's sake, mate, come to my assistance.' I said, 'Stop till I get my lamp. What is the matter?' 'Oh, dear,' he exclaimed, 'here is another woman cut to pieces.' I asked where, and he replied, 'In the corner.' I went into the corner of the square and turned my light on the body. I agree with the previous witnesses as to the position of the body. I ran up Mitre Street into Aldgate, blowing my whistle all the while.

Coroner: Did you see any suspicious persons about?

Morris: No. Two constables came up and asked what was the matter. I told them to go down to Mitre Square, as there was another terrible murder. They went, and I followed and took charge of my own premises again. ...

Constable James Harvey (City of London Police): On the night of Saturday, Sept. 29th, I was on duty in the neighbourhood of Houndsditch, and Aldgate. I was there at the time of the murder, but did not see any one nor hear any cry. When I got into Aldgate, returning towards Duke Street, I heard a whistle and saw the witness Morris with a lamp. I asked him what was the matter, and he told me that a woman had been ripped up in Mitre Square. Together with Constable Hollins I went to Mitre Square, where Watkins was by the side of the body of the deceased. Hollins went for Dr Sequeira, and a private individual was despatched for other constables, who arrived almost immediately, having heard the whistle. I waited with Watkins, and information was sent to the inspector. ...

Joseph Lawende: I reside at No. 45, Norfolk Road, Dalston, and am a commercial traveller. On the night of Sept. 29th, I was at the Imperial Club, Duke Street, together with Mr Joseph Levy and Mr Harry Harris. It was raining, and we sat in the club till half-past one o'clock, when we left. I observed a man and woman together at the corner of Church Passage, Duke Street, leading to Mitre Square.
Coroner: Were they talking?
Lawende: The woman was standing with her face towards the man, and I only saw her back. She had one hand on his breast. He was the taller. She had on a black jacket and bonnet. I have seen the articles at the police station, and believe them to be those the deceased was wearing.
Coroner: What sort of man was this?
Lawende: He had on a cloth cap with a peak of the same. ...
Crawford: You have given a description of the man to the police?
Lawende: Yes.

Coroner: Would you know him again?

Lawende: I doubt it. The man and woman were about nine or ten feet away from me. I have no doubt it was half-past one o'clock when we rose to leave the club, so that it would be twenty-five minutes to two o'clock when we passed the man and woman.

Coroner: Did you overhear anything that either said?

Lawende: No.

Coroner: Did either appear in an angry mood?

Lawende: No.

Coroner: Did anything about their movements attract your attention?

Lawende: No. The man looked rather rough and shabby.

Coroner: When the woman placed her hand on the man's breast, did she do it as if to push him away?

Lawende: No; it was done very quietly.

Coroner: You were not curious enough to look back and see where they went?

Lawende: No. ...

Constable Alfred Long (Metropolitan Police): I was on duty in Goulston Street, Whitechapel, on Sunday morning, September 30th and about five minutes to three o'clock I found a portion of a white apron (produced). There were recent stains of blood on it. The apron was lying in the passage leading to the staircase of Nos. 106 to 119, a model dwelling house. Above on the wall was written in chalk, 'The Jews are the men that will not be blamed for nothing.' I at once searched the staircase and areas of the building, but did not find anything else. I took the apron to Commercial Road Police station and reported to the inspector on duty.

Coroner: Had you been past that spot previously to your discovering the apron?

Constable Long: I passed about twenty minutes past two o'clock.

Coroner: Are you able to say whether the apron was there then?

Constable Long: It was not.

Crawford: As to the writing on the wall, have you not put a 'not' in the wrong place? Were not the words, 'The Jews are not the men that will be blamed for nothing'?

Constable Long: I believe the words were as I have stated.

Coroner: Was not the word 'Jews' spelt 'Juwes'?

Constable Long: It may have been.

Coroner: Yet you did not tell us that in the first place. Did you make an entry of the words at the time?

Constable Long: Yes, in my pocket book.

Coroner: Is it possible that you have put the 'not' in the wrong place?

Constable Long: It is possible, but I do not think that I have.

Coroner: Which did you notice first – the piece of apron or the writing on the wall?

Constable Long: The piece of apron, one corner of which was wet with blood.

Coroner: How came you to observe the writing on the wall?

Constable Long: I saw it while trying to discover whether there were any marks of blood about.

Coroner: Did the writing appear to have been recently done?

Constable Long: I could not form an opinion.

Coroner: Do I understand that you made a search in the model dwelling house?

Constable Long: I went into the staircases.

Coroner: Did you not make inquiries in the house itself?

Constable Long: No.

Foreman of the jury: Where is the pocket book in which you made the entry of the writing?

Constable Long: At Westminster.

Coroner: Is it possible to get it at once?

Constable Long: I dare say.

Crawford: I will ask the coroner to direct that the book be fetched.

Coroner: Let that be done.

Detective Constable Daniel Halse (City of London Police): On Saturday, Sept. 29, pursuant to instructions received at the central office in Old Jewry, I directed a number of police in plain clothes to patrol the streets of the City all night. At two minutes to two o'clock on the Sunday morning, when near Aldgate Church, in company with Detectives Outram and Marriott, I heard that a woman had been found murdered in Mitre Square. We ran to the spot, and I at once gave instructions for the neighbourhood to be searched and every man stopped and examined. I myself went by way of Middlesex Street into Wentworth Street, where I stopped two men, who, however, gave a satisfactory account of themselves. I came through Goulston Street about twenty minutes past two, and then returned to Mitre Square, subsequently going to the mortuary. I saw the deceased, and noticed that a portion of her apron was missing. I accompanied Major Smith back to Mitre Square, when we heard that a piece of apron had been found in Goulston Street. After visiting Leman Street police station, I proceeded to Goulston Street, where I saw some chalk writing on the black facia of the wall. Instructions were given to have the writing photographed, but before it could be done the Metropolitan police stated that they thought the writing might cause a riot or outbreak against the Jews, and it was decided to have it rubbed out, as the people were already bringing out their stalls into the street. When Detective Hunt returned inquiry was made at every door of every tenement of the model dwelling house, but we gained no tidings of anyone who was likely to have been the murderer.

[Replying to questioning by Crawford]: At twenty minutes past two o'clock I passed over the spot where the piece of apron was found, but did not notice anything then. I should not necessarily have seen the piece of apron.

Coroner: As to the writing on the wall, did you hear anybody suggest that the word 'Jews' should be rubbed out and the other words left?

Detective Constable Halse: I did. The fear on the part of the Metropolitan police that the writing might cause A riot was the sole reason why it was rubbed out. I took a copy of it, and what I wrote down was as follows: 'The Juwes are not the men who will be blamed for nothing.'

Coroner: Did the writing have the appearance of having been recently done?

Detective Constable Halse: Yes. It was written with white chalk on a black facia.

Foreman of the jury: Why was the writing really rubbed out?

Detective Constable Halse: The Metropolitan police said it might create a riot, and it was their ground.

Crawford: I am obliged to ask this question. Did you protest against the writing being rubbed out?

Detective Constable Halse: I did. I asked that it might, at all events, be allowed to remain until Major Smith had seen it.

Crawford: Why do you say that it seemed to have been recently written?

Detective Constable Halse: It looked fresh, and if it had been done long before it could have been rubbed out by people passing. I did not notice whether there was any powdered chalk on the ground, though I did look about to see if a knife could be found. There were three lines of writing in a good schoolboy's round hand. The size of the capital letters would be about 3/4 in, and the other letters were in proportion. The writing was on the black bricks, which formed a kind of dado, the bricks above being white. ...

A juror: It seems surprising that a policeman should have found the piece of apron in the passage of the buildings, and yet made no inquiries in the buildings themselves. There was a clue up to that point, and then it was altogether lost.

Crawford: As to the premises being searched, I have in court members of the City police who did make diligent search in every part of the tenements the moment the matter came to their knowledge. But unfortunately it did not come to their knowledge until two hours after. There was thus delay, and the man who discovered the piece of apron is a member of the Metropolitan police.

A juror: It is the man belonging to the Metropolitan police that I am complaining of.

At this point Constable Long returned, and produced the pocket book containing the entry which he made at the time concerning the discovery of the writing on the wall.

Crawford: What is the entry?

Constable Long: The words are, 'The Jews are the men that will not be blamed for nothing.'

Coroner: Both here and in your inspector's report the word 'Jews' is spelt correctly?

Constable Long: Yes; but the inspector remarked that the word was spelt 'Juwes'.

Coroner: Why did you write 'Jews' then?

Constable Long: I made my entry before the inspector made the remark.

Coroner: But why did the inspector write 'Jews'?

Constable Long: I cannot say.

Coroner: At all events, there is a discrepancy?

Constable Long: It would seem so.

Coroner: What did you do when you found the piece of apron?

Constable Long: I at once searched the staircases leading to the buildings.

Coroner: Did you make inquiry in any of the tenements of the buildings?

Constable Long: No.

Coroner: How many staircases are there?

Constable Long: Six or seven.

Coroner: And you searched every staircase?

Constable Long: Every staircase to the top.

Coroner: You found no trace of blood or of recent footmarks?

Constable Long: No.

Coroner: About what time was that?

Constable Long: Three o'clock.

Coroner: Having examined the staircases, what did you next do?

Constable Long: I proceeded to the station.

Coroner: Before going did you hear that a murder had been committed?

Constable Long: Yes. It is common knowledge that two murders have been perpetrated.

Coroner: Which did you hear of?

Constable Long: I heard of the murder in the City. There were rumours of another, but not certain.

Coroner: When you went away did you leave anybody in charge?

Constable Long: Yes; the constable on the next beat – 190, H Division – but I do not know his name.

Coroner: Did you give him instructions as to what he was to do?

Constable Long: I told him to keep observation on the dwelling house, and see if anyone entered or left.

Coroner: When did you return?

Constable Long: About five o'clock.

Coroner: Had the writing been rubbed out then?

Constable Long: No; it was rubbed out in my presence at half-past five.

Coroner: Did you hear anyone object to its being rubbed out?

Constable Long: No. It was nearly daylight when it was rubbed out.

A juror: Having examined the apron and the writing, did it not occur to you that it would be wise to search the dwelling?

Constable Long: I did what I thought was right under the circumstances.

The juror: I do not wish to say anything to reflect upon you, because I consider that altogether the evidence of the police redounds to their credit; but it does seem strange that this clue was not followed up.

Constable Long: I thought the best thing to do was to proceed to the station and report to the inspector on duty.

The juror: I am sure you did what you deemed best.

Crawford: I suppose you thought it more likely to find the body there than the murderer?

Constable Long: Witness: Yes, and I felt that the inspector would be better able to deal with the matter than I was.

Foreman of the jury: Was there any possibility of a stranger escaping from the house?

Constable Long: Not from the front.

Coroner: Did you not know about the back?

Constable Long: No, that was the first time I had been on duty there.

That being all the evidence forthcoming, the coroner said he considered a further adjournment unnecessary, and the better plan would be for the jury to return their verdict and then leave the matter in the hands of the police. ...

[He] presumed that the jury would return a verdict of wilful murder against some person or persons unknown. ...

On reflection, perhaps it would be sufficient to return a verdict of wilful murder against some person unknown, inasmuch as the medical evidence conclusively demonstrated that only one person could be implicated.

The jury at once returned a verdict accordingly. ...

Was the killer of Catherine Eddowes responsible for murdering any of the previous victims? I suggest he was.

Eddowes's murder is almost identical to those of Annie Chapman and Polly Nichols, the only significant difference being that these two victims were killed much later at night. The alleged removal of Eddowes's organs and the placing of her intestines on her shoulders mirror the Chapman murder, although whether Eddowes's organs were removed and taken away is now questionable.

Dr Frederick Gordon Brown stated in his report that the wounds and mutilations were committed after Eddowes died and while she was on the ground. Could she have been knocked out before her throat was cut? Owing to the severity of her facial and throat injuries, this theory cannot be proved or disproved; nor can the suggestion that she was strangled first. But neither possibility can be discounted.

Was the same killer responsible for killing Liz Stride earlier? I believe not, for the reasons previously stated.

Some experts suggest that the killer of these women lived in or near Whitechapel, and that his knowledge of the area would have made it easy for him to disappear into the backstreets and evade detection. While I do not entirely agree with this theory, it would be wrong for me as an investigator to disregard it.

When another murder, similar to the previous ones, was reported, I would have expected word of it to spread like wildfire, putting the whole East End on its guard and making it imperative for the murderer to get away as quickly as possible. In view of this, if he had already killed Stride, would he have remained in the area and searched out another victim within the hour? I suggest not.

I believe that the killer did not come from the area. A look at the map of the murder locations reveals that they are all on the edge of Whitechapel and all a few streets away from main roads that would have assisted the killer to get away quickly. As can be from previous paragraphs with regard to the finding of Eddowes, the killer, on foot, may well have made his escape towards the City and away from Whitechapel, or perhaps doubled back using a longer route; or perhaps he took a hansom cab to do either.

All of this could also explain the fact that at the height of these murders there was a huge police presence in Whitechapel, in both uniform and plainclothes. But all in the Whitechapel area. If the killer moved back and forth, away from Whitechapel towards the City, or returned using a different route, he would have avoided all the police activity.

In addition to flooding the area, the police used all their known informants and spoke to many types of local people in their quest to discover the killer's identity. The fact that no information of any substance appears to have been obtained again suggests that the killer did not come from Whitechapel.

Another point to consider is that if the killer was a man of good standing in society – and this would have showed in his style of dress – he would not have wanted to venture too far into the heart of Whitechapel for fear of being robbed or murdered himself. Prostitutes most likely realised that this caution among well-heeled clients meant that there was not much business for them in the crime-ridden backstreets of the heart of Whitechapel, so instead they plied their trade nearer to the more affluent edges of the area.

Eddowes's murder differs in a further respect from the previous murders described above. After her body was discovered, there came to the notice of the police two different pieces of 'evidence' which at the time were suggested as being material to the murder and have generally been accepted up until the present day. Both pieces of evidence were found in a stairwell leading to dwellings in Goulston Street. I suggest that perhaps the police and other experts have been wrong all this time about this evidence.

The first item of evidence was a piece of apron stained with blood. This was later examined closely and found also to have on it a smearing of faecal matter. The piece of fabric was later identified as coming from the apron of Catherine Eddowes, and was described as having been cleanly cut. The second item was writing found on a wall at the spot where the piece of apron was found. At the time the police believed that the killer might have written this.

How did these two pieces of evidence come to be discovered? And what is their significance?

After the discovery of Eddowes's body, Detective Constable Halse, who had been summoned to the murder site, ordered the whole area to be searched. He also undertook a search and, wanting to check the area as quickly as possible, found himself hurrying through the backstreets in search of the fugitive, despite having no description to go on.

At 2.20am, he passed along Goulston Street, apparently seeing nothing untoward. However, he later stated that he 'believed' the writing which we now know as 'The Juwes are the men that will not be blamed for nothing' had appeared on the wall after his search of Goulston Street, because he said that when he had initially examined the entrance to Wentworth Model Dwellings he had found nothing of interest. But was Halse too intent on looking for someone who was hiding to notice what was written on walls?

At 2.55am, PC Alfred Long did make a find. As he made his way along Goulston Street he stopped at the entrance to the same tenement block and made two discoveries: the writing on the wall and what he described at the time as a dirty, bloodstained piece of rag. Why he stopped and why he saw both pieces of evidence as worthy of reporting was never explained and remains a mystery within a mystery.

Why did he suspect that a few lines of writing on a wall and a discarded rag were of any importance? Graffiti was common in poor areas in those days and, besides, the words scrawled on the wall would surely have meant nothing to him at that time. As to the piece of fabric, casually discarded rubbish would have been a common sight on his beat, especially with a street market nearby. What significance could he have seen at that time in the 'rag', which he did not identify as coming from Eddowes's apron until some 12 hours later at the mortuary?

In any event, these finds were hastily reported and Sir Charles Warren, Commissioner of the Metropolitan Police, took it upon himself to attend Goulston Street despite the fact that this murder was under the jurisdiction of the City of London Police. There were many Jews in the area and, to prevent hostilities against them, Warren ordered the writing to be removed before the City Police could photograph it. However, before it was removed an officer from the City of London Police and one from the Metropolitan Police noted the writing in their pocket books. The two policemen took down different versions: 'The Juwes are Not the Men That Will be Blamed for Nothing' and, correctly: 'The Juwes are the Men That Will Not be Blamed for Nothing'.

Asked to put in writing to the Home Secretary his reasons for removing the graffito, Warren replied:

> 4 Whitehall Place, S.W.
> 6th November 1888
> Confidential
> The Under Secretary of State
> The Home Office
>
> Sir,
>
> In reply to your letter of the 5th instant, I enclose a report of the circumstances of the Mitre Square Murder so far as they have come under the notice of the Metropolitan Police, and I now give an account regarding the erasing the writing on the wall in Goulston Street which I have already partially explained to Mr Matthews verbally.
>
> On the 30th September on hearing of the Berner Street murder, after visiting Commercial Street Station I arrived at

Leman Street Station shortly before 5 AM and ascertained from the Superintendent Arnold all that was known there relative to the two murders.

The most pressing question at that moment was some writing on the wall in Goulston Street evidently written with the intention of inflaming the public mind against the Jews, and which Mr Arnold with a view to prevent serious disorder proposed to obliterate, and had sent down an Inspector with a sponge for that purpose, telling him to await his arrival.

I considered it desirable that I should decide the matter myself, as it was one involving so great a responsibility whether any action was taken or not.

I accordingly went down to Goulston Street at once before going to the scene of the murder: it was just getting light, the public would be in the streets in a few minutes, in a neighbourhood very much crowded on Sunday mornings by Jewish vendors and Christian purchasers from all parts of London.

There were several Police around the spot when I arrived, both Metropolitan and City.

The writing was on the jamb of the open archway or doorway visible in the street and could not be covered up without danger of the covering being torn off at once.

A discussion took place whether the writing could be left covered up or otherwise or whether any portion of it could be left for an hour until it could be photographed; but after taking into consideration the excited state of the population in London generally at the time, the strong feeling which had been excited against the Jews, and the fact that in a short time there would be a large concourse of the people in the streets, and having before me the Report that if it was left there the house was likely to be wrecked (in which from my own observation I entirely concurred) I considered it desirable to obliterate the writing at once, having taken a copy of which I enclose a duplicate.

After having been to the scene of the murder, I went on to the City Police Office and informed the Chief Superintendent of the reason why the writing had been obliterated.

I may mention that so great was the feeling with regard to the Jews that on the 13th ulto. the Acting Chief Rabbi wrote to me on the subject of the spelling of the word 'Jewes' on account of a newspaper asserting that this was Jewish spelling in the Yiddish dialect. He added 'in the present state of excitement it is dangerous to the safety of the poor Jews in the East [End] to allow such an assertion to remain uncontradicted. My community keenly appreciates your humane and vigilant action during this critical time.'

It may be realised therefore if the safety of the Jews in Whitechapel could be considered to be jeopardised 13 days after the murder by the question of the spelling of the word Jews, what might have happened to the Jews in that quarter had that writing been left intact.

I do not hesitate myself to say that if that writing had been left, there would have been an onslaught upon the Jews, property would have been wrecked, and lives would probably have been lost; and I was much gratified with the promptitude with which Superintendent Arnold was prepared to act in the matter if I had not been there.

I have no doubt myself whatever that one of the principal objects of the Reward offered by Mr Montagu was to show to the world that the Jews were desirous of having the Hanbury Street Murder [of Annie Chapman] cleared up, and thus to divert from them the very strong feeling which was then growing up.

I am, Sir,
Your most obedient Servant,
(signed) C. Warren

Does the writing on the wall have any relevance to the four murders? Before we can answer this, we must ask what message, if any, the writer was trying to convey. Whoever wrote the words may have been suggesting that the Jewish community was responsible, through the act of either an individual or a group, for something – but what?

Can we read anything into the spelling of 'Jews' as 'Juwes'? It can also be spelled 'Jewes', 'Jeuwes', 'Juwes', 'Jeuws', 'Juewes' or 'Juews'. A dictionary search on these variants will produce the same result in each case: the spelling 'Jews' and a definition referring to the group as a whole rather than to particular persons. I believe it was simply an unusual spelling.

Had the writing been put there before that night and could it have been dismissed by anyone passing as just another piece of graffito and only noticed when the fragment of apron was found? I see this as a distinct possibility, and, although the police conducted extensive enquiries in the building, they were never able to prove or disprove this. The officer who found the message stated that he believed it to have been written recently, but, how he deduced that, only he knew.

Does the writing have any connection with the Eddowes murder, any of the previous murders or any of the later murders? The answer is definitely no. This is the only writing ever found which has been suggested as being connected to any of the murders. However, it was not found at the scene of Eddowes's murder and the content does not refer to either this murder or any other murders before or after.

I am sure that a search of the area would have revealed countless other scrawlings on walls and in alleys, some of which would have had meaning for the writer alone, as this example may have done. But the idea that a killer making his escape would stop to write a message on a wall is unbelievable. He would have wanted to get away from the area as fast as possible, and if he had wanted to write a message I am sure he would have left it at the scene and referred to either himself or the killings.

Moving on to the piece of apron, later identified as having come from Eddowes's apron, several questions arise. When was it removed? By whom? For what reason? And how long had it been at the location where it was found?

At the time the police put forward several theories. One suggestion was that the killer had cut the piece from the apron to wipe away the blood from his hands and/or the knife, and that he may have even used it to carry her organs away. The police also believed the apron piece showed the direction in which the killer had escaped, regardless of whether he had deliberately left it or accidentally dropped it.

I disagree with all these suggestions and have my own theory based on my research. First, let us assume that, as I suggested earlier, he does not reside in Whitechapel. He kills Eddowes at a location on the edge of Whitechapel and then flees into the misty, murky, dimly lit streets of the City. If the police theory, which has been widely accepted, is correct, he then makes his way back almost into the centre of Whitechapel, where he either deposits or loses the piece of apron. Even if I am wrong and he did live in the heart of the area and decided to go to ground there, he was taking a huge risk in making his way back home knowing that there would be a large police presence in response to Eddowes's murder and Stride's a short time earlier. We are asked to believe he would have risked being stopped, searched and possibly apprehended.

I must also ask why the killer would have cut off a piece of the apron. Perhaps it was for the reasons the police suggested at the time. But there is no evidence of a similar act in any of the other murders. If it was to clean his knife with, he could have done that at the scene with one swift wipe across her clothing. If it was to clean his hands with, he could have done that at the scene without cutting off and taking away a piece of apron. Even if he did cut it off, surely he would have discarded it long before reaching Goulston Street. He would not have wanted to be seen walking down the road wiping his bloodstained hands. Besides, the killer may have worn gloves and not needed to clean his hands.

If we accept that the piece of apron was correctly identified as coming from Eddowes's apron but the killer did not cut it off, what other explanation could there be? I will put forward one which, I am sure, many experts will regard as unbelievable. However, as there is very little direct evidence it is unwise to dismiss anything which may add additional weight to existing evidence and, likewise, theories which could suggest earlier theories have been wrong all these years.

First, the apron piece. This was made of cotton and was wet when found; it was stained with what was described as blood and was smeared with faecal matter. It was found screwed up and lying in the stairwell of the tenement building. The immediate area was no doubt used as a short cut from one part of Whitechapel to another and could have been used by Eddowes at some time that day or after her release from police custody shortly before her death.

My theory revolves around matters of personal feminine hygiene which would account for the blood and faecal matter on the apron piece. In Victorian times women of the lower class, when menstruating, did not use sanitary towels as we know them today. If they bothered to use anything at all, it was a cotton rag. In addition the use of public toilets was unheard of among this class owing to the fact that a penny was required (hence the saying 'to spend a penny') and most could not afford this. When outdoors, they would relieve themselves wherever they could: waste ground, alleyways and stairwells, for example. How do we know that the piece of apron was not cut by Eddowes herself from her apron for this purpose and then discarded when totally soiled or when she used the stairwell in Goulston Street as a toilet while passing through at some time before her murder? After all, there was a six-hour gap from when she left home until her arrest for being drunk at approximately 8.30pm, and almost an hour after her release from police custody before her murder. She was in the area earlier that day, before being arrested for being drunk. The apron piece was in the stairwell, so if it had been raining it would not have become wet with the rain. Maybe the wetness was caused by Eddowes's urine.

Was she killed by the murderer who killed Chapman and Nichols? I say yes. So, at this point we have six murders, three of which, I suggest, were committed by the same killer – Jack the Ripper – and three possibly by three separate killers. However, Martha Tabram must not be discounted as a Ripper victim as she was found with her clothes up around her upper body. This was the same in the case of a later victim, Alice McKenzie, which I will discuss later.

As to when, in my opinion, Eddowes's organs were removed, the timeline is as follows:

2am: Dr Brown briefly examines the body at the scene, as does Dr Sequeira. From police officers' testimony in the inquest report we know the murder scene was described as being the darkest part of Mitre Square. This would have made it difficult for the killer to remove the kidney and uterus with precision, and he is hardly likely to have had a lamp in one hand and a six-inch knife in the other and still been able to perform precise excision of these organs.

No thorough examination of the body is conducted at the scene. So there is no evidence to corroborate the suggestion that the organs had been removed by that time. The body is then taken to the mortuary and handed over to the mortuary keeper. No police officials stay with the body.

2.30pm: Twelve hours later Dr Brown attends the mortuary to conduct a post-mortem. This allows more than ample time for someone to remove the organs before Dr Brown arrives.

It should also be noted that half of a human kidney was sent, purportedly by the Ripper, to a local official with a letter suggesting that it had been taken from Eddowes. The organ was examined and found to have a disease similar to that found in the remaining kidney of Eddowes, although I would imagine that half of the population of the East End could have been suffering from kidney complaints.

The gruesome package was believed at the time, and is still widely accepted, to have been a prank carried out by a morbid medical student who may even have had access to the mortuary and the body of Eddowes before the post-mortem. This lends further weight to my suggestion that the victim's organs could have been removed before the doctor's arrival.

CHAPTER SEVEN

MARY JANE KELLY

Twenty-five-year-old Mary Jane Kelly was, after Frances Coles, the second-youngest victim of the Whitechapel rampage, and the most savaged. Unlike the other prostitutes, who were killed on the streets where they worked, Kelly had a private room. She met her death on 8 November 1888, at 13 Miller's Court, off Dorset Street, where she was disembowelled, disfigured and dismembered in a fury of madness. The post-mortem found no defensive wounds nor any signs of a struggle. Kelly may even have been killed as she slept.

Her outer clothes were folded on a chair and she was lying on the bed wearing a light undergarment.

Kelly's last known movements are as follows:

> 2am: George Hutchinson, a resident of the Victoria Home in Commercial Street, has just returned to the area from Romford. He is walking along Commercial Street and passes a man at the corner of Thrawl Street but pays no attention to him. At the junction of Flower and Dean Street he meets Kelly, who asks him for money. They have known each other for some time.

'Mr Hutchinson, can you lend me sixpence?' Kelly asks.

'I can't,' Hutchinson replies, 'I spent all my money going down to Romford.'

'Good morning,' Kelly says. 'I must go and find some money.' Then she walks off in the direction of Thrawl Street.

She meets the man Hutchinson had passed earlier. The man puts his hand on Kelly's shoulder and says something at which they both laugh. Hutchinson hears Kelly say, 'All right' and the man say, 'You will be all right for what I have told you.' The man then puts his right hand on Kelly's shoulder and they begin to walk towards Dorset Street. Hutchinson notices that the man has a small parcel in his left hand.

Later Hutchinson will state that while standing under a streetlight outside the Queen's Head public house in Commercial Street he got a good look at the man with Mary Jane Kelly. He describes him as being of dark complexion, with a heavy, dark moustache, turned up at the corners, dark eyes and bushy eyebrows. He is, according to Hutchinson, 'Jewish looking'. The man is wearing a soft felt hat pulled down over his eyes, a long, dark coat trimmed with astrakhan and a white collar with a black necktie fixed with a horseshoe pin. He wears dark spats over light, button-over boots. On his waistcoat there is a massive gold chain with a large seal with a red stone hanging from it. He carries kid gloves in his right hand and a small package in his left. He is five feet six or seven tall and about 35 years old.

Kelly and the man cross Commercial Street and turn down Dorset Street. Hutchinson follows them. Kelly and the man stop outside Miller's Court and talk for about three minutes. Kelly is heard to say 'All right, my dear. Come along. You will be comfortable.' The man puts his arm around Kelly, who kisses him. 'I've lost my handkerchief,' she says. At this he hands her a red handkerchief. The couple then head into Miller's Court. Hutchinson waits until the clock strikes three, leaving as it does so. It should be noted that Hutchinson did not come forward at the time to give this account but waited until several days after the murder, and his testimony was never put before the coroner.

3am: Another local resident, Mrs Cox, returns home. It is raining hard. There is no sound or light coming from Kelly's room. Cox does not go out again but does not fall asleep. Occasionally throughout the night she hears men going in and out of Miller's Court. Later she will tell the inquest: 'I heard someone go out at a quarter to six. I do not know what house he went out of as I heard no door shut.'

10.45am: John McCarthy, owner of 'McCarthy's Rents', as Miller's Court was known, sends Thomas Bowyer to collect rent money from Mary Kelly. After Bowyer receives no response from knocking, and because the door is locked, he puts his hand through the broken window, pushes aside the curtain and peers inside. He sees the body of Mary Kelly. He informs McCarthy, who, after seeing the mutilated remains of Kelly for himself, runs to Commercial Road Police Station, where he informs the police, who return to Miller's Court with him.

The police break down the front door. On entering the room, they find Mary Kelly's clothes neatly folded on a chair. She was still wearing a chemise. Her boots are in front of the fireplace. They see her mutilated body lying on the bed.

Dr Thomas Bond, a distinguished police surgeon, was called. His report states:

> The body was lying naked in the middle of the bed, the shoulders flat but the axis of the body inclined to the left side of the bed. The head was turned on the left cheek. The left arm was close to the body with the forearm flexed at a right angle and lying across the abdomen.
>
> The right arm was slightly abducted from the body and rested on the mattress. The elbow was bent, the forearm supine with the fingers clenched. The legs were wide apart, the left thigh at right angles to the trunk and the right forming an obtuse angle with the pubes.
>
> The whole of the surface of the abdomen and thighs was removed and the abdominal cavity emptied of its viscera. The breasts were cut off, the arms mutilated by several jagged wounds and the face hacked beyond recognition of the features. The tissues of the neck were severed all round down to the bone.
>
> The viscera were found in various parts viz: the uterus and kidneys with one breast under the head, the other breast by the right foot, the liver between the feet, the intestines by the right side and the spleen by the left side of the body. The flaps removed from the abdomen and thighs were on a table.
>
> The bed clothing at the right corner was saturated with blood, and on the floor beneath was a pool of blood covering about two feet square. The wall by the right side of the bed and in a line with the neck was marked by blood, which had struck it in several places.
>
> The face was gashed in all directions, the nose, cheeks, eyebrows, and ears being partly removed. The lips were blanched and cut by several incisions running obliquely

down to the chin. There were also numerous cuts extending irregularly across all the features.

The neck was cut through the skin and other tissues right down to the vertebrae, the fifth and sixth being deeply notched. The skin cuts in the front of the neck showed distinct ecchymosis. The air passage was cut at the lower part of the larynx through the cricoid cartilage.

Both breasts were more or less removed by circular incisions, the muscle down to the ribs being attached to the breasts. The intercostals between the fourth, fifth, and sixth ribs were cut through and the contents of the thorax visible through the openings.

The skin and tissues of the abdomen from the costal arch to the pubes were removed in three large flaps. The right thigh was denuded in front to the bone, the flap of skin, including the external organs of generation, and part of the right buttock. The left thigh was stripped of skin fascia, and muscles as far as the knee.

The left calf showed a long gash through skin and tissues to the deep muscles and reaching from the knee to five inches above the ankle. Both arms and forearms had extensive jagged wounds.

The right thumb showed a small superficial incision about one inch long, with extravasation of blood in the skin, and there were several abrasions on the back of the hand moreover showing the same condition.

On opening the thorax it was found that the right lung was minimally adherent by old firm adhesions. The lower part of the lung was broken and torn away. The left lung was intact. It was adherent at the apex and there were a few adhesions over the side. In the substances of the lung there were several nodules of consolidation.

The pericardium was open below and the heart absent.

In the abdominal cavity there was some partly digested food of fish and potatoes, and similar food was found in the remains of the stomach attached to the intestines.

The inquest into Mary Jane Kelly's death was presided over by Dr Macdonald MP, Coroner for North East Middlesex.

Monday, 12 November 1888

... **Joseph Barnett**: I was a fish porter, and I work as a labourer and fruit porter. Until Saturday last I lived at 24, New Street, Bishopsgate, and have since stayed at my sister's, 21, Portpool Lane, Gray's Inn Road. I have lived with the deceased one year and eight months. Her name was Marie Jeanette Kelly with the French spelling as described to me. Kelly was her maiden name. I have seen the body, and I identify it by the ear and eyes, which are all that I can recognise; but I am positive it is the same woman I knew. I lived with her in No. 13 room, at Miller's Court for eight months. I separated from her on October 30th.

Coroner: Why did you leave her?

Barnett: Because she had a woman of bad character there, whom she took in out of compassion, and I objected to it. That was the only reason. I left her on the Tuesday between five and six p.m. I last saw her alive between half-past seven and a quarter to eight on Thursday night last, when I called upon her. I stayed there for a quarter of an hour.

Coroner: Were you on good terms?

Barnett: Yes, on friendly terms; but when we parted I told her I had no work, and had nothing to give her, for which I was very sorry.

Coroner: Did you drink together?

Barnett: No, sir. She was quite sober.

Coroner: Was she, generally speaking, of sober habits?

Barnett: When she was with me I found her of sober habits, but she has been drunk several times in my presence. ...

Coroner: Have you heard her speak of being afraid of anyone?

Barnett: Yes; several times. I bought newspapers, and I read to her everything about the murders, which she asked me about.

Coroner: Did she express fear of any particular individual?

Barnett: No, sir. Our own quarrels were very soon over. ...

Mary Ann Cox: I live at No. 5 Room, Miller's Court. It is the last house on the left hand side of the court. I am a widow, and get my living on the streets. I have known the deceased for eight or nine months as the occupant of No. 13 Room. She was called Mary Jane. I last saw her alive on Thursday night, at a quarter to twelve, very much intoxicated.

Coroner: Where was this?

Cox: In Dorset Street. She went up the court, a few steps in front of me.

Coroner: Was anybody with her?

Cox: A short, stout man shabbily dressed. He had on a longish coat, very shabby, and carried a pot of ale in his hand.

Coroner: What was the colour of the coat?

Cox: A dark coat.

Coroner: What hat had he?

Cox: A round hard billycock.

Coroner: Long or short hair?

Cox: I did not notice. He had a blotchy face, and full carrotty moustache.

Coroner: The chin was shaven?

Cox: Yes. A lamp faced the door.

Coroner: Did you see them go into her room?

Cox: Yes; I said 'Good night, Mary,' and she turned round and banged the door.

Coroner: Had he anything in his hands but the can?

Cox: No. ...

Coroner: What would you take the stout man's age to be?

Cox: Six-and-thirty.

Coroner: Did you notice the colour of his trousers?

Cox: All his clothes were dark. ...

Caroline Maxwell (of 14 Dorset Street): My husband is a lodging-house deputy. I knew the deceased for about four months. I believe she was an unfortunate. On two occasions I spoke to her.

Coroner: You must be very careful about your evidence, because it is different to other peoples. You say you saw her standing at the corner of the entry to the court?

Maxwell: Yes, on Friday morning, from eight to half-past eight. I fix the time by my husband's finishing work. When I came out of the lodging-house she was opposite.

Coroner: Did you speak to her?

Maxwell: Yes; it was an unusual thing to see her up. She was a young woman who never associated with anyone. I spoke across the street, 'What, Mary, brings you up so early?' She said, 'Oh, Carrie, I do feel so bad.'

Coroner: And yet you say you had only spoken to her twice previously; you knew her name and she knew yours?

Maxwell: Oh, yes, by being about in the lodging-house.

Coroner: What did she say?

Maxwell: She said, 'I've had a glass of beer, and I've brought it up again'; and it was in the road. I imagined she had been in the Britannia beer shop at the corner of the street. I left her, saying that I could pity her feelings. I went to Bishopsgate Street to get my husband's breakfast. Returning I saw her outside the Britannia public house, talking to a man.

Coroner: This would be about what time?

Maxwell: Between eight and nine o'clock. I was absent about half-an-hour. It was about a quarter to nine.

Coroner: What description can you give of this man?

Maxwell: I could not give you any, as they were at some distance.

Inspector Frederick G. Abberline (Criminal Investigation Department, Scotland Yard): The distance is about sixteen yards.

Maxwell: I am sure it was the deceased. I am willing to swear it.

Coroner: You are sworn now. Was he a tall man?

Maxwell: No; he was a little taller than me and stout.

Inspector Abberline: On consideration I should say the distance was twenty-five yards.

Coroner: What clothes had the man?

Maxwell: Dark clothes; he seemed to have a plaid coat on. I could not say what sort of hat he had. ...

Dr George Bagster Phillips: I was called by the police on Friday morning at eleven o'clock, and on proceeding to Miller's Court, which I entered at 11.15, I found a room, the door of which led out of the passage at the side of 26, Dorset Street, photographs of which I produce. It had two windows in the court. Two panes in the lesser window were broken, and as the door was locked I looked through the lower of the broken panes and satisfied myself that the mutilated corpse lying on the bed was not in need of any immediate attention from me, and I also came to the conclusion that there was nobody else upon the bed, or within view, to whom I could render any professional assistance. Having ascertained that probably it was advisable that no entrance should be made into the room at that time, I remained until about 1.30p.m., when the door was broken open by McCarthy, under the direction of Superintendent Arnold. On the door being opened it knocked against a table, which was close to the left-hand side of the bedstead, and the bedstead was close against the wooden partition. The mutilated remains of a woman were lying two thirds over, towards the edge of the bedstead, nearest the door. Deceased had only an linen under garment upon her, and by subsequent examination I am sure the body had been removed, after the injury which caused death, from that side of the bedstead which was nearest to the wooden partition previously mentioned. The large quantity of blood under the bedstead, the saturated condition of the palliasse, pillow, and sheet at the top corner of the bedstead nearest to the partition leads me to the conclusion that the severance of the right carotid artery, which was the immediate cause of death, was inflicted while the deceased was lying at the right side of the bedstead and her head and neck in the top right-hand corner. ...

Inspector Abberline: ... I arrived at Miller's Court about 11.30am on Friday morning. ... I agree with the medical evidence as to the condition of the room. I subsequently took an inventory of the contents of the room. There were traces of a large fire having been kept up in the grate, so much so that it had melted the spout of a kettle off. We have since gone through the ashes in the fireplace; there were remnants of clothing, a portion of a brim of a hat, and a skirt, and it appeared as if a large quantity of women's clothing had been burnt.

Coroner: Can you give any reason why they were burnt?

Inspector Abberline: I can only imagine that it was to make a light for the man to see what he was doing. There was only one small candle in the room, on the top of a broken wine glass. An impression has gone abroad that the murderer took away the key of the room. Barnett informs me that it has been missing some time, and since it has been lost they have put their hand through the broken window, and moved back the catch. It is quite easy. There was a man's clay pipe in the room, and Barnett informed me that he smoked it. ...

Coroner (to the jury): ... It is for you to say whether at an adjournment you will hear minutiae of the evidence, or whether you will think it is a matter to be dealt with in the police courts later on, and that, this woman having met with her death by the carotid artery having been cut, you will be satisfied to return a verdict to that effect. ...

The Foreman, having consulted with his colleagues, considered that the jury had had quite sufficient evidence before them upon which to give a verdict.

Coroner: What is the verdict?

Foreman of the jury: Wilful murder against some person or persons unknown.

If the killer had not removed the organs from the previous victims after being accused of this he perhaps decided to mutilate her body and try to remove them to add momentum to his crimes. Perhaps his thinking was, 'If I have been accused of removing the organs, I might as well try to remove them myself this time.'

Of all the Whitechapel murders I find Mary Jane Kelly's the most interesting as it both raises new theories and gives further food for thought about theories I have already advanced in this book.

Was Kelly murdered by the same hand as the other victims discussed so far? I would say that there is a strong possibility that they were all, except for Emma Smith, killed by the Ripper.

Let's look at the similarities that link Kelly's murder to those of all or some of the other victims.

- All the victims were prostitutes whose throats were cut.
- All the murders were committed within a short distance of one another and all occurred in the early hours of the morning.
- All the victims were killed with a knife and, except for Nichols and Tabram, savagely mutilated. One explanation for the lack of direct mutilation and the non-removal of organs in these two cases could be that they were early victims and the killer later performed far more savage mutilation as, with each murder, his confidence and grisly desires grew. This theory is supported by the ferocious savagery he inflicted on the body of Mary Kelly, the last of the five canonical Ripper victims.
- There are certain similarities in the wounds inflicted on Kelly and Eddowes, such as the cutting and nicking of the eyelids and the mutilation of the upper thighs. Also, in both cases (and in that of Nichols) internal organs were removed from the body, although in Kelly's case they were not taken away from the murder site.

- All the victims could have been rendered unconscious before being killed, although in Kelly's case she could have been asleep when killed, having drunk too much alcohol.
- All the victims appear to have been available for business when they encountered their killer. And, although all the previous victims were murdered outside in the street and Kelly in her own room, no great play should be made of this. I believe the killer was walking the streets looking for prostitutes and struck lucky in coming across Kelly. For she had a room to take him back to, where, with less chance of being disturbed, he could indulge in even greater savagery than with the previous victims.

However, there are a number of puzzling facts about Kelly's murder. The first is that she had obviously undressed before being murdered, which suggests sex was about to take place. With the exception of Martha Tabram, it is not evident that any of the other victims before Kelly had undressed. When the victims went with the killer they were presumably expecting sex, but that is as far as it appears to have got. Here we have a victim methodically undressing. Could she have known the killer? If so, she would have felt at ease in his presence. Was the killer a man of substance, as I suggested earlier, who had promised to pay her well? In any event, Kelly's murderer, for whatever reason, chose to let her undress and possibly even let her lie on the bed before killing her. This may suggest sexual activity linking some of the murders.

Another point to consider is the removal of the organs. We know that a person with anatomical knowledge removed organs from Eddowes and Nichols at some stage, despite both victims being savagely mutilated, as Mary Kelly was. But, in Kelly's case, although some of her organs were removed there was no evidence that this was done with anatomical knowledge, or that the organs were taken away from the murder scene. So what can be deduced from this?

The answer is that if I am correct about the other victims' organs being removed at the mortuary, we can say that the same killer was responsible for the murders of Kelly, Nichols, Chapman and Eddowes and possibly Tabram, but not Smith and Stride. If my theory is not correct, someone else killed Kelly and made it look like the work of the other killer.

Mary Jane Kelly is said to have been the last of the Ripper's victims. But my investigation uncovered several other murders of prostitutes in the Whitechapel area that are worthy of consideration in deciding whether the Ripper continued killing after Kelly.

CHAPTER EIGHT

ALICE MCKENZIE

Forty-year-old Alice McKenzie died in Castle Alley on 17 July 1889 of wounds to the left side of her neck. Her abdomen had also been mutilated. Her clothes were up around her chin. Had the Ripper struck again? She was last seen alive at 11.40pm and her body was found at 12.50am in the same alley that a police officer later stated he patrolled some 20 minutes before this time and saw nothing suspicious.

Dr George Bagster Phillips and Dr Thomas Bond, who carried out a medical examination, concurred that the cause of death was the severance of the left carotid artery. They noted the following wounds:

- Two stab wounds in the left side of the neck 'carried forward in the same skin wound'
- Bruising on chest
- Five bruises or marks on left side of abdomen
- A cut to the throat, made from left to right, apparently while the victim was on the ground
- A seven-inch 'but not unduly deep wound was visible from the bottom of the left breast to the navel'

- Seven or eight scratches, beginning at the navel, and pointing towards the genitalia (this could suggest the killer clawed at her clothing in an attempt to expose her body before mutilating it)
- A small cut on the mons veneris.

Dr Phillips believed the murderer would have needed some anatomical knowledge to have inflicted the atrocities on McKenzie.

The severing of the left carotid artery was consistent with previous Ripper murders, although four were murdered with much deeper and longer injuries, which cut down to the spinal column. McKenzie suffered only two jagged wounds on the left side, which were no longer than four inches each and had left the air passages untouched.

The bruises on the chest strongly suggested that the killer held her down on the ground with one hand while inflicting the wounds with the other.

The mutilations were mostly superficial, the deepest opening neither the abdominal cavity nor the muscular structure. Dr Phillips suggested that the five marks on the left side of the body were an imprint of the killer's right hand, which left only his left hand to cause the wounds. Dr Bond disagreed, claiming there was no evidence to support the theory that the marks were made in this way. However, he saw the body the day after the post-mortem and it had already begun to decompose.

However, the two doctors agreed that a 'sharp-pointed weapon' was used, but also that it could have been smaller than the one used in the previous killings.

Dr Phillips decided that McKenzie's death was not attributable to the Ripper: 'After careful and long deliberation, I cannot satisfy myself, on purely anatomical and professional grounds, that the perpetrator of all the "Wh Ch. murders" is our man. I am on the contrary impelled to a contrary conclusion in this noting the mode of procedure and the character of the mutilations and judging of motive in connection with the latter.'

Dr Bond came to the opposite conclusion: 'I see in this murder evidence of similar design to the former Whitechapel murders, viz. sudden onslaught on the prostrate woman, the throat skilfully and resolutely cut with subsequent mutilation, each mutilation indicating sexual thoughts and a desire to mutilate the abdomen and sexual organs. I am of the opinion that the same person who committed the former series of Whitechapel murders performed the murder.'

The Assistant Commissioner of the Metropolitan Police, Robert Anderson, disagreed, writing, 'I am here assuming that the murder of Alice McKenzie, on the 17th of July 1889, was by another hand. I was absent from London when it occurred, but the Chief Commissioner investigated the case on the spot and decided it was an ordinary murder, and not the work of a sexual maniac.'

However, a senior officer who was on duty during the investigation disagreed: 'I need not say that every effort will be made by the police to discover the murderer, who, I am inclined to believe, is identical with the notorious Jack the Ripper of last year.'

Indeed, on the day of the murder another senior officer, James Monro, deployed three sergeants and 39 constables to Whitechapel, increasing the force with 42 extra men.

The inquest into Alice McKenzie's death was presided over by Mr Wynne E. Baxter, Coroner for South East Middlesex. From the report:

Day One: Wednesday, 17 July 1889
... **John McCormack**: I live at 54, Gun Street, Spitalfields. It is a common lodging-house. I am a porter. I have seen the body in the mortuary, and recognise it as that of Alice McKenzie. I can't exactly tell her age, but it was about 40.

Coroner: Has she been living with you?

McCormack: Yes, for about six years. I recognise her by her thumb, which had been crushed at the top by a machine. The nail was half off.

Coroner: Did you recognise her face?

McCormack: Yes, Sir; by the scars on her forehead. I also recognised her clothes she was wearing, and also the boots. She told me she came from Peterborough. I did not know if she had any children. She worked very hard as a washerwoman and charwoman to the Jews.

Coroner: When did you last see her alive?

McCormack: Between 3 and 4 o'clock yesterday afternoon. She left me in bed at that time. She went from me with the intention of paying a night's rent – 8 pence.

Coroner: Did you give her the money?

McCormack: Of course I did. I gave her 1 Shilling and 8 pence altogether; to pay the rent, and to do what she liked with the remainder.

Coroner: You did not see her again?

McCormack: Not until I saw the body in the mortuary. The deputy told me that my old woman was lying dead in the mortuary, and I went and recognised her.

Coroner: Was she sober when she left you?

McCormack: Perfectly.

Coroner: How came you in bed at 4 o'clock?

McCormack: As soon as I come home I lie down; and, having a little drop of drink, I go and lie down. When I came home yesterday I went and lay down immediately.

Coroner: Had the deceased been to work on Tuesday?

McCormack: No; she told me she went to work on Monday, but I did not believe it. She came home about 7 o'clock on Monday evening, and she then went to bed.

Coroner: Why did you not believe she went to work?

McCormack: Because I know she did not.

Coroner: How do you know?

McCormack: Because others told me she did not go to work.

Coroner: Did she often come home late at night?

McCormack: Not to my knowledge. Deceased was usually at home at night.

Coroner: Did you have any words with the deceased yesterday?

McCormack: I had a few words and that upset her.

Coroner: Did she tell you she was going to walk the streets?

McCormack: She did not; she told me nothing. ...

Constable Joseph Allen (H Division): Last night I was in Castle Alley. It was then 20 minutes past 12 when I passed through. I was through the alley several times. I remained there for five minutes. I entered the alley through the archway in Whitechapel Road. I had something to eat under the lamp where the deceased was found. Having remained in the alley for five minutes, I went into Wentworth Street. There was neither man nor woman there. There were wagons in the alley, two right underneath the lamp.

Coroner: Would you swear there was no one in the wagons?

Constable Allen: I would not swear to that, as I did not look into them; one of the wagons was an open one. Everything was very quiet at the time. The backs of some of the houses in Newcastle Street faced the alley, and in some of the upper windows were lights. That was not an unusual thing at that time. I cannot say if any of the windows were open. No sounds came from those houses.

On leaving the alley I met Constable Walter Andrews, 272 H, in Wentworth Street. It was about 100 yards from the alley where I met Andrews. I spoke to Andrews, who then went towards Goulston Street.

Coroner: How did you fix the time?

Constable Allen: I looked at my watch. It was 12:30 when I left the alley. At the end is a public house, the Three Crowns, and as I passed the landlord was shutting up the house. After leaving Andrews I went towards Commercial Street and met Sergeant Badham 31 H, who told me a woman had been found murdered in Castle Alley, and he directed me to go to the station. When the sergeant spoke to me it was five minutes to 1, and 1 o'clock when I got to the station.

Constable Walter Andrews (H Division): About ten minutes to 1 this morning I saw Sergeant Badham at the corner of Old Castle Street, leading into Castle Alley. That was on the opposite corner of the public house. The sergeant said, 'All right,' and I said the same. I then proceeded up Castle Alley, and tried the doors on the west side of the alley. While doing so I noticed a woman lying on the pavement. Her head was lying eastward, and was on the edge of the kerbstone, with her feet towards the building, which was a wheelwright's shop and warehouse.

Coroner: Was the body touched before the doctor arrived?

Constable Andrews: Only by my touching the face to see if it was cold. It had not been disturbed.

Coroner: How far was it from the lamp?

Constable Andrews: Almost underneath. About 2 ft. from the lamp post.

Coroner: Was any wagon there?

Constable Andrews: Two; one was a scavenger's wagon, and the other a brewer's dray. They were on the same side of the way. The wagons hid the body from persons in the cottages opposite. The head was almost underneath the scavenger's wagon.

Coroner: Were her clothes up?

Constable Andrews: Yes, almost level to the chin. Her legs and body were exposed. I noticed that blood was running from the left side of the neck.

Coroner: You said you felt her?

Constable Andrews: I touched the abdomen. It was quite warm. I then blew my whistle, and between two and three minutes Sergeant Badham came up. The sergeant gave me orders to stay by the body and not touch it until the doctor arrived. The body was not touched until Dr Phillips arrived about five or ten minutes past 1.

Coroner: Had you seen anyone?

Constable Andrews: I had not. There was not a soul in the alley that I saw. After I saw the body lying on the pavement I heard a footstep coming from Old Castle Place, and I saw a young man, named Isaac Lewis Jacobs. I said, 'Where are you going?' He said, 'I am going to Wentworth Street to fetch something for my supper.' At the time he was carrying a plate in his hand. Jacobs came back with me and stayed there until the sergeant arrived.

Coroner: Had you been in the alley before?

Constable Andrews: Yes. Between 20 and 25 minutes past 12. I went into the alley after Allen. After he came out I went in some two or three minutes later. No one was in the alley then. After I left Allen I went into Goulston Street, then into Whitechapel High Street, down Middlesex Street into Wentworth Street again. It was there I saw the sergeant, as I have already stated.

Coroner: Did anyone attract your attention?

Constable Andrews: No, I saw no one in Goulston or Middlesex streets.

Foreman of the jury: Do you think deceased had been drawn to where you found her or murdered there?

Constable Andrews: I think she was killed there. I should think she had been standing up against the lamp post, and then pulled or dragged down. There was no trail of blood away from the body, and no splashes of blood. ...

Day Two: Thursday, 18 July 1889

Detective Inspector Edmund Reid (H Division): I received a call to Castle Alley about five minutes past 1 on the morning of the murder. I dressed and ran down at once. On arriving at Castle Alley I found the Wentworth Street end blocked by a policeman. On arriving at the back of the baths I saw the deceased woman. I saw she had a cut on the left side of the throat, and there was a quantity of blood under the head which was running into the gutter. The clothes were up and her face was slightly turned towards the road. She was lying on he back. I felt the face and body, and found they were warm. Dr Phillips arrived. At the time I arrived I ascertained the fact that the other end (Whitechapel) was blocked and search was being made through the alley and also in the immediate neighbourhood. The deputy superintendent and his wife at the baths were seen and stated they heard nothing unusual. After the body had been examined by the doctor it was placed on the police ambulance, underneath the body of the deceased was found the short clay pipe produced. The pipe was broken and there was blood on it, and in the bowl was some unburnt tobacco. I also found a bronze farthing underneath the clothes of the deceased. There was also blood on the farthing. I produce a rough plan of Castle Alley; A correct copy of which will be sent by the draughtsman. During the whole time from the finding of the body only one private person was present, except Lewis Jacobs, who was examined yesterday. Everything was done very quietly. The fence on the other side of the alley, to where the body was found, is about 10 ft. high. Along that was a row of barrows. Close to where the body was found were two barrows chained together. There was a lamp where the body was found; one outside the public house; one at the entrance to Old Castle Street; and one at the entrance to the passage leading into the alley. I do not think any stranger would go down there unless he was taken there. I did not go into the High Street, Whitechapel, within a few minutes of my arrival in the alley. There are people in High Street, Whitechapel, all night. Two constables are continually passing through the alley all night. It is hardly ever left alone for more than five minutes. Although it is called an alley it is really a broad turning, with two narrow entrances. Any person standing at the Wentworth Street end would look upon it as a blind street. No stranger would think he could pass through it, and none but foot passengers can. It was raining when the body was removed. It was raining when I arrived, but a very little. The spot under which the deceased was lying was dry except where there was blood. I searched the body at the mortuary and found nothing. There is no doubt about the name of the deceased. I have since made inquiries at 54, Gun Street, and have ascertained from the deputy, Ryder, that Mog Cheeks, the woman that was mentioned yesterday, stayed with her sister all night. I saw the deputy this morning, and she said she would try to get Mog Cheeks here. I have no doubt the deed was committed on the spot where the body was found. I should say she was lying down on the pavement when she was murdered, as if she had been standing up there would have been blood on the wall. She was lying along the pavement, her head being towards Whitechapel. No person, unless he went along the pathway, could have seen the body on account of the shadow of the lamp and the vans, which screened the body. Any person going along the road would have seen it. If I wanted to watch anyone I would stand under the lamp. The darkness was so great that it was necessary to use the constable's lamp to see that the throat was cut, although it was just under the lamp. I think the alley is sufficiently lighted; there are five lamps here. In another instance of this kind, the Hanbury Street murder, two similar farthings were found. The tobacco in the pipe had not been smoked. The pipe was a very old one and was what was termed in the lodging-house 'a nose warmer.'

Dr George Bagster Phillips, divisional surgeon of the H Division, said that he was called, and arrived at Castle Alley at 1.10am on Wednesday, when it was raining very hard. On his arrival in Castle Alley, at the back premises of the washhouses he found the body lying on the pavement in the position already described, as to which the witness gave full details. Having inspected the body, he had it removed to the shed used as a mortuary in the Pavilion Yard, Whitechapel. There he re-examined the body and left it in charge of the police. ... With several colleagues he made the examination at 2 o'clock, when rigor mortis was well marked. The witness then described the wounds, of which there were several, and these were most of them superficial cuts on the lower part of the body. There were several old scars and there was the loss of the top of the right thumb, apparently caused by some former injury. The wound in the neck was 4 in. long, reaching from the back part of the muscles, which were almost entirely divided. It reached to the fore part of the neck to a point 4 in. below the chin. There was a second incision, which must have commenced from behind and immediately below the first. The cause of death was syncope, arising from the loss of blood through the divided carotid vessels, and such death probably was almost instantaneous. ...

Day Three: Wednesday, 14 August 1889
... **Dr George Bagster Phillips**: On the occasion of my making the post-mortem examination, the attendants of the mortuary, on taking off the clothing of the deceased woman removed a short clay pipe, which one of them threw upon the ground, by which means it was broken. I had the broken pieces placed upon a ledge at the end of the post-mortem table; but it has disappeared, and although inquiry has been made about it, up to the present time it has not been forthcoming. The pipe had been used. It came from the woman's clothing. The attendants, whom I have often seen there before, are old workhouse men. There were five marks on the abdomen, and, with the exception of one, were on the left side of the abdomen. The largest one was the lowest, and the smallest one was the exceptional one mentioned, and was typical of a finger-nail mark. They were coloured, and in my opinion were caused by the fingernails and thumbnail of a hand. I have on a subsequent examination assured

myself of the correctness of this conclusion.

Coroner: When you first saw the body, how long should you say she had been dead?

Dr Phillips: Not more than half an hour, and very possibly a much shorter time. It was a wet and cold night. The deceased met her death, in my opinion, while lying on the ground on her back. The injuries to the abdomen were caused after death.

Coroner: In what position do you think the assailant was at the time?

Dr Phillips: The great probability is that he was on the right side of the body at the time he killed her, and that he cut her throat with a sharp instrument. I should think the latter had a shortish blade and was pointed. I cannot tell whether it was the first or second cut that terminated the woman's life. The first cut, whether it was the important one or not, would probably prevent the woman from crying out on account of the shock. The whole of the air passages were uninjured, so that if she was first forced on to the ground she might have called out. The bruises over the collarbone may have been caused by finger pressure. There were no marks suggestive of pressure against the windpipe.

Coroner: Did you detect any skill in the injuries?

Dr Phillips: Any knowledge of how effectually to deprive a person of life, and that speedily.

Coroner: Are the injuries to the abdomen similar to those you have seen in the other cases?

Dr Phillips: No, Sir. I may volunteer the statement that the injuries to the throat are not similar to those in the other cases. ...

... The knife that was used could not have been so large as the ordinary butcher's slaughter knife.

Coroner: Were the finger-nail marks on the body those of the woman herself?

Dr Phillips: My impression is that they were caused by another hand. These marks were caused after the throat was cut. ...

Coroner: ... The first point the jury have to consider is as to the identity of the deceased woman, and, fortunately, in regard to that there is no question. There is an interval of nearly five hours from when McCormack saw the deceased until she is seen between half-past eleven, and twelve by some women in Flower and Dean Street. This is the last that was seen of her. At a quarter-past twelve a constable had his supper under the very lamp under which the deceased was afterwards found, and at that time no one was near. Another constable was there at twenty minutes past twelve, and the place was then all right. The officer next entered the alley at twelve fifty, and it was between those times that the murder must have been done. When the body was discovered there was no one about, and nothing suspicious had been seen. Had there been any noise, there were plenty of opportunities for it to have been heard. There is great similarity between this and the other class of cases, which have happened in this neighbourhood, and if the same person has not committed this crime, it is clearly an imitation of the other cases. We have another similarity in the absence of motive. None of the evidence shows that the deceased was at enmity with any one. There is nothing to show why the woman is murdered or by whom. I think you will agree with me that so far as the police are concerned every care was taken after the death to discover and capture the assailant. All the ability and discretion the police have shown in their investigations have been unavailing, as in the other cases. The evidence tends to show that the deceased was attacked, laid on the ground and murdered. It is to be hoped that something will be done to prevent crimes of this sort and to make such crimes impossible. It must now be patent to the whole world that in Spitalfields there is a class of persons who, I think, cannot be found in such numbers, not only in any other part of this metropolis, but in any other metropolis; and the question arises, should this state of affairs continue to exist? I do not say it is for you to decide. The matter is one for a higher power than us to suggest a remedy. But it certainly appears to me there are two ways in which the matter ought to be attacked. In the first place, it ought to be attacked physically. Many of the houses in the neighbourhood are unfit for habitation. They want clearing away and fresh ones built. Those are physical alterations, which, I maintain, require to be carried out there. Beyond this there is the moral question. Here we get a population of the same character, and not varied, as in a moderately sized town or village. Here there is a population of 20,000 of the same character, not one of who is capable of elevating the other. Of course there is an opinion among the police that it is a proper thing that this seething mass should be kept together rather than be distributed all over the metropolis. Every effort ought to be made to elevate this class. I am constantly struck by the fact that all the efforts of charitable and religious bodies here are comparatively unavailing. It is true a great deal has been done of late years, especially to assist the moral development of the East End, but it is perfectly inadequate to meet the necessities of the case. If no other advantage comes from these mysterious murders, they will probably wake up the

Church and others to the fact that it is the duty of every parish in the West to have a mission and localise work in the East End, otherwise it will be impossible to stop these awful cases of crime. Here is a parish of 21,000 persons with only one church in it. There are not only cases of murder here, but also many of starvation. I hope at least these cases will open the eyes of those who are charitable to the necessity of doing their duty by trying to elevate the lower classes.

The jury, after a short deliberation, returned a verdict of 'Wilful murder against some person or persons unknown'. ...

So here we have another prostitute murdered eight months after Mary Kelly's body was found. This victim has all the signs of having been murdered by the same killer as the previous victims. She was killed by having her throat cut, and her body was mutilated, although not to the degree of her predecessors. There were marks to her neck that suggested she was throttled.

The murder scene was north of Whitechapel Road, near the previous murder locations, which reinforces the theory that the killer came from outside the area.

My ability to state conclusively that this murder was connected to the previous killings is not helped by the failure of Dr Bond and Dr Phillips to agree. However, in the light of my theory as to how and when the organs were removed from the earlier victims, I suggest Alice McKenzie was indeed a Ripper victim.

I am also puzzled as to why the Assistant Commissioner of the Metropolitan Police chose to state categorically that McKenzie's murder was not linked to the others. Did Anderson know the identity of the killer of the previous victims, and that the killer was for, whatever reason, no longer in a position to kill again? Or was it that he did not want to cause public hysteria? Some of these questions I hoped I would find answers to as my investigation gained momentum.

But first there is a final murder to consider, which occurred almost eight months later.

CHAPTER NINE

FRANCES COLES

Twenty-three-year-old Francis Coles was the last possible Ripper victim and perhaps the prettiest of them all. She was murdered in the early hours of 13 February 1891 under a railway arch in Royal Mint Street. Her throat was slashed only moments before a policeman arrived on the scene. There were no abdominal mutilations. She had injuries to the back of her head consistent with being thrown to the pavement and her throat had been cut while she was lying on the pavement. The policeman who discovered the body heard footsteps walking away, but police rules required that he stay with the body as she appeared to be still alive. Had he followed the footsteps, he may have caught the murderer.

Coles was last seen alive at 1.45am and found dying at 2.15am. At 1.45am, she had bumped into fellow prostitute Ellen Gallagher in Commercial Street, passing 'a violent man in a cheese cutter hat'. Apparently Gallagher remembered the man as a former client who had given her a black eye and warned Coles not to entertain him, but Coles ignored her friend's advice and solicited the man. She and the stranger headed toward the direction of the Minories. This was the last time she was seen alive. It appears that no follow-up enquiries were carried out by the police to trace or identify the man.

The medical reports of Dr Phillips, who performed the post-mortem, and Dr F.J. Oxley, the first doctor at the scene, revealed the following.

- The victim appeared, from a number of injuries to the back of the head, to have been thrown violently to the ground.
- Her throat was cut, most likely, according to both Dr Phillips and Dr F.J. Oxley, while she was lying on the pavement.
- Phillips believed the killer held her head back by the chin with his left hand, cutting the throat with his right.
- The knife passed the throat three times – first from left to right, then from right to left, and once more from left to right (Phillips). Oxley believed there were two wounds as there was only one incision in the skin but two openings in the larynx.
- The killer struck from the right side of the body (Phillips) or from the front (Oxley).
- The body was tilted at the moment the wound was inflicted in a manner so that the killer would avoid becoming bloodstained.
- The victim's clothes were in order and there was no abdominal mutilation.
- The killer exhibited no anatomical knowledge (Phillips).
- Part of the left ear had been torn off, as if as a result of an earring being ripped from the ear some time previously, but the injury was thoroughly healed.
- Tenpence was found hidden behind a lamppost or downpipe – presumably the victim's earnings from her final client.

Was Frances Coles a Ripper victim? Her throat was cut, but, unlike in the other Whitechapel slayings, a blunt knife was used. There seems to have been no evidence of strangulation. There was no mutilation of the abdomen and the clothes were not disarranged. The murder site, as in the case of Elizabeth Stride, was south of Whitechapel Road.

The Ripper may have ceased his onslaught for eight months and then resumed his slayings with Frances Coles. Or was she just another victim of the violent world of Whitechapel of the time? My initial impression is that her murder is perhaps not connected to any of the others, but during my investigation I may be able to uncover other evidence to prove or disprove this.

Having examined the murders in great detail and highlighted both the important differences and the similarities, I now had to look at what motives there could be for any of the murders; to examine any evidence pointing to a suspect or suspects; and to try to establish whether all or some of the murders were the work of one killer or different killers.

PART TWO
ON THE TRAIL OF THE RIPPER

CHAPTER TEN

MOTIVES

What could have been the motive for these savage murders? Whatever it was, I suggest that the same motive for this type of crime is still around today. At a cursory glance, the murders seem to be lacking motive. The victims, for a start, were prostitutes, belonging to the lowest and most poverty -struck areas of Victorian society. They lived on a day-to-day basis, many soliciting just to survive. The East End was a slum and, during that time, life was incredibly tough and ruthless.

Indeed, the Whitechapel murders have been widely considered to be the work of a serial killer and it is accepted that most serial killers do not have a motive in the usual sense. They do not murder out of jealousy, revenge or greed. They murder because they have an overpowering desire to do so. They get a thrill, often sexual, out of murder and mutilation.

The killer — assuming for the moment that just one was responsible — left no evidence of sexual assault other than the fact that some of the victims were found with their clothes pushed back above the waist. There is no record of seminal fluid having been found in any of the victims, although it must be said that the doctors seem not to have addressed this question in their examinations. But all the victims appear to have gone to the murder locations for some purpose. Could it have been for sex? All were prostitutes, after all. Yet, when found, hardly any of them had a penny to their name. I doubt a single one of them would have gone to the murder location with anyone unless she had been paid in advance or the person propositioning her was a man of wealth who had shown her he had more than enough money to pay her after any sexual act. If the killer had paid in advance, I am sure he would have taken his money back after the killing.

So what motive could the killer have had for committing these murders? Could he have had a hatred of women, maybe dating back to his childhood or adolescence? Perhaps he was abused by his mother and father, or even given away or abandoned. Could he have held his mother responsible for something that had happened to him in later years?

Was he motivated by the desire specifically to kill prostitutes? All his victims were prostitutes. Did he form a hatred of such women because he had caught a disease from one, and, if it was syphilis, was his condition perhaps so far advanced that it was driving him insane. Was the killer what we would describe today as a psychopath? Had he developed a deranged lust for killing? Did he, like the schizophrenic serial killer Peter Sutcliffe, the 'Yorkshire Ripper', hear voices telling him to rid the streets of prostitutes?

Some researchers today suggest the killings were ritualistic, because the murder sites form a pentagram. Over the years stories have circulated about items, rings, coins and other items being placed 'ritually' at the feet of Annie Chapman, but this was an invention of the press. Other theories regard the placing of the organs and the cuts made to the faces of some of the victims as part of a ritual of some kind. There are many possibilities, but, on the face of it, the murders do not seem to display any ritualistic pattern.

Was the motive connected with some form of Masonic initiation rite? This suggestion has been with us for many years. I will cover the reasons for its persistence later, when I discuss the suspects. However, this idea of Masonic involvement goes back to the Old Testament, to the murder of King Solomon's grand Masonic master, Hiram Abiff. The offenders were brought to justice and Solomon had their throats cut and their intestines cut out and thrown over their left shoulders. Unfortunately for those who wish to draw a parallel, both Chapman's and Eddowes's intestines were found on their right shoulders.

After all this time the question of motive remains unanswered. Many, both at the time and still today, have believed that the killer could have been a local resident who held a menial job that allowed him enough freedom to move about more or less as he pleased. But consider the days on which the killings took place. These were mainly weekends, which suggests a weekday routine of employment.

Whoever the killer was, he clearly had a hatred of women, and the crimes were sexual in nature inasmuch as he attacked reproductive organs. In the murders, the killer showed signs of what are known by practitioners of criminal profiling as organised and disorganised characteristics. Time and time again he escaped detection and capture. Also, he was apparently capable of gaining the trust of his victims. Both these abilities suggest an organised offender. On the other hand, the risks he took with his choice of some of the crime scenes and the state in which he left the victims both suggest a disorganised offender, although one who, in my view, was cool and calculated.

If, as I suggested earlier, the murders could have been committed by several different people, we could have one serial killer plus several separate killers not connected to one another. If that is the case, it is likely that there were separate motives for the different murders.

CHAPTER ELEVEN

EVIDENCE

In a time before forensic science, and even fingerprinting, the only way to prove someone committed a murder was to catch either him or her in the act, or get the suspect to confess, or alternatively have sufficient witnesses to prove the case.

Unhappily, the Whitechapel murders fall into this period. One interesting feature of this case is that not one but two police forces carried out investigations. The Metropolitan Police were responsible for crimes committed in all the boroughs of the capital except the City of London.

This single square mile in the heart of the capital had, as it still does, its own police force. Catherine Eddowes's murder occurred within the jurisdiction of the City of London Police and so brought them into the case. It is believed that the rank and file of the two forces got along and worked well together, but there is evidence that their senior officers did not. How much influence their failure to co-operate fully had on solving the case is not known. It would be wrong to criticise either force for failing to solve the mystery of Jack the Ripper, for catching serial killers is still a hard task, even with the advantages of today's science and technology. Beyond referring to post-mortem reports and taking statements from anybody who might have seen something or known something of relevance, there was little that either police force could do.

The attitude of the people at the time was that the police were incompetent and the only use for the Commissioner of the Metropolitan Police, Sir Charles Warren, and his force was policing crowds and keeping order, and certainly not detective work. Warren was especially criticised for not offering a reward in the hope that a confederate or accomplice would emerge and inform on the Ripper. In fact, Warren had no objection to the offer of a reward and it was his superior, Henry Matthews, the Home Secretary, who initially rejected this approach, although after the killing of Mary Kelly a pardon was announced for any accomplice of the murderer. This attempt to obtain direct evidence on the killer proved fruitless, however.

The City of London Police seem to have made a better job of their part of the investigation. Although they did not apprehend the killer, their officers made crime-scene drawings and took many photographs of Catherine Eddowes. They also took photographs of Mary Kelly, even though she was not murdered within their jurisdiction. She was the only Ripper victim who was ever photographed at the crime scene.

So, as far as any direct evidence is concerned, the police had none at the time of the murders, and none has come to light since. Given the passage of so much time, it is highly unlikely that there will ever be any.

Unlike their counterparts today, the police did not preserve the murder scene. It was the accepted practice, after a doctor had visited the site and certified the person dead, to remove the body on a handcart to a mortuary, where it was stripped and laid out ready for the post-mortem. After this, the victim's clothes were discarded. Already, following the removal of the body from the crime scene, any blood found there would have been washed away with buckets of water, destroying all traces of evidence.

Even circumstantial evidence in these murders is sparse, except for vague descriptions of persons seen with some of the victims before their deaths, these statements supposedly corroborated by timings that cannot be totally relied on. None of this testimony furnished a wholly accurate description of anyone who appears more than once throughout the enquiry into the series of murders.

I have no doubt that with the aid of modern investigative methods these murders would have been detected and the killer caught. So how have today's methods changed from those of Victorian times?

Before considering this question I should explain how a murder inquiry is set up and the gathering of evidence takes place. At the start of the inquiry the police's activity is split into two parts, but these run in conjunction.

One part begins with the finding of the body and includes the preservation of the murder scene and the gathering of forensic evidence. A police surgeon is called and pronounces life extinct. Meanwhile, the murder scene is preserved. It is crucial to protect a crime scene at the beginning of any investigation, to safeguard evidence. Therefore, the body is covered and the murder scene is usually cordoned off, along with the immediate area surrounding it. Scenes-of-crime investigators examine not only the scene where the body is found but also, later, a much larger area. Many clues can be obtained from their thorough examination. They examine the position of the body, items near the body or the condition of the ground around the scene for evidence such as footwear impressions and blood-flow patterns. If the crime scene is not preserved properly, valuable evidence may be destroyed or altered and fibres or DNA material may become contaminated. To prevent such contamination, scene-of-crime investigators wear special clothing.

I remember attending a lay-by beside a busy main road, where a body of a man had been discovered in the ditch. Everything in and around the body and the ditch was seized. One item I took possession of was a discarded recent till receipt from a mini-market some 120 miles away. On the face of it, this was insignificant, but it turned out to be one of the most crucial pieces of evidence in that murder case. The date and time shown on the receipt roughly matched the time when the victim was last seen. It transpired that the victim also came from the area where the shop was located. Enquiries were made at the shop, where the CCTV showed the victim in company with two other men, and these were identified from the CCTV images, arrested and later charged with murder. They had murdered the man in the lay-by and dumped his body, but the till receipt had been either thrown away or unintentionally dropped. This sort of find is what makes the search of a crime scene so important.

If a body is discovered at night, a thorough examination of the scene does not take place until daybreak, although a cursory examination may occur in the dark. When daylight comes, a photographer takes many photographs and videos the crime scene and the surrounding area.

In some murder inquiries, a forensic pathologist attends the scene and makes an initial examination of the body before it is moved to the mortuary, where he performs the post-mortem and seeks further evidence. If it is dark, the initial examination is left until daylight.

For removal to the mortuary, the body is placed in a body bag. A police officer accompanies the body on the journey and is met by the coroner's officer. Nowadays this post is civilianised, but usually a retired police officer is appointed. The coroner's officer takes charge of the body and is also present when the forensic pathologist carries out the post-mortem. This continuity ensures that no one touches or tampers with the body, and thus preserves the evidence. In the Whitechapel murders this was not done, leaving us with the unresolved question of where, when, how and by whom the organs were removed and taken away.

The body is then stripped and each item of clothing bagged separately and retained for later forensic examination. This examination may reveal fibres which can be forensically matched and screened for DNA, or there may be other forms of DNA that may have come from the killer. The bag containing the body is also preserved and forensically examined in case any valuable evidence has become dislodged or fallen off during removal of the body.

Before starting the post-mortem, the forensic pathologist makes a detailed examination of the body from top to bottom, which is recorded on video. As well as searching for marks on the body, he looks for fibres and hairs from the killer that may have been transferred to the victim. The victim's hair is also combed and the comb and the residue from the hair are individually bagged for more detailed forensic examination.

Fingernail scrapings are taken as these are very important, and they would have been particularly crucial in the Ripper murders. It appears that his victims may have been throttled or strangled before mutilation began, in which case they may well have attempted to break free and in doing so dug their nails into their attacker, leaving his DNA under their nails.

The pathologist then carries out a detailed examination of the body to establish the cause of death and whether a weapon was used. If so, what type of weapon and what size? He also seeks to establish an accurate time of death.

In addition, he takes swabs from the mouth and other orifices of the body. This is to ascertain if any DNA from another person is present. In the Whitechapel murders, this information too would have been invaluable. All the victims were prostitutes and it is unknown if any contact was made between the victims and the killer, by kissing, oral sex, or vaginal or anal penetration, before they were killed. A DNA result may have answered that question, although because the victims were prostitutes many different DNA profiles may have been found. Even so, because each of us has our own unique DNA profile, such information would have been of great value.

Another important DNA issue relating to the Whitechapel murders concerns the half of a kidney sent to George Lusk, president of the Whitechapel Vigilance Committee. The letter accompanying this, known as the 'From Hell' letter, purported to be from Jack the Ripper and stated that the half kidney was from the one the killer had removed from Catherine Eddowes's body. A DNA examination would have determined conclusively whether it had indeed come from this victim.

If a positive identification could have been made, the police could have focused more effort on the letter, for it would have been good evidence that the letter was from the Ripper himself. They would then have had more information to work on in analysing the handwriting, paper and ink. The same benefit would have applied to all the other letters supposedly sent by the Ripper.

If modern technology had been available in 1888, experts could have obtained fingerprints and DNA from the letter, the stamp and the box containing the kidney. Many a crime has been detected from DNA obtained from saliva on a stamp or on a gummed envelope that was licked to seal it. Forensic handwriting experts would also have been available to the police. Sadly, fingerprinting was not introduced in England until 1901.

Having covered the forensic issues and the initial police action in respect of the body, let us now look at the other part of the inquiry, which is in effect the main part for the police. As soon as a body is found, the police seek to identify the victim as a matter of urgency, and the murder inquiry begins in earnest. This line of enquiry is invaluable in obtaining evidence on the last movements of the victim etc.

In addition, police officers are dispatched at once to begin initial house-to-house enquiries near to where the body was found. It is vitally important to obtain as much evidence as soon as possible. A full house-to-house operation is carried out later. This involves tracing, interviewing and taking statements from everyone residing in nearby dwellings. Even if an interviewee tells police that they did not see or hear anything, a statement is still taken. Statements will later be read back to interviewees at the incident room, which is normally at the nearest police station. Today statements are keyed into a computer database and cross-referenced, but it was not so long ago that manual databases and index cards were still used to store them. Anything of importance derived from statements is then followed up.

To give an example relating to the Whitechapel murders, if a witness had stated that they had seen a horse-drawn cab in the locality around the time of one of the murders, police officers would (or should) have been told to find and interview all drivers of horse-drawn cabs who may have been operating in that area at that time. It may have been that the killer escaped by summoning such a vehicle.

Returning to today, if the murder scene or the immediate location was covered by CCTV, the officer in charge instructs officers to seize camera footage in the hope that the victim was caught onscreen in the company of the killer. CCTV footage may prove of no help here, but the police may have traced a witness or witnesses who claim to have seen the victim with a person they believe to be the killer. In this case the witness is asked to co-operate in making a sketch or a computer image. Over the years this technique has improved greatly, with artists paying greater attention to details such as hair length and shape, distance between the eyes, shape of the nose and chin, and so on. The more sketches they did, the more artists realised that many facial features can be broken down into 'sets' or 'types'. This led to the development of the Identikit technique, in which sheets of clear plastic, each imprinted with a separate facial feature, are superimposed on one another to create a composite image of what a suspect may look like. Nowadays, though, the police use computer imaging instead. This offers a larger variety of features to choose from and generally creates a far more accurate and lifelike image in a much shorter time.

It is important to bear in mind that no artist, no composite image and no computer can provide an accurate picture without a witness who can provide a good description of the suspect. Drawings of suspects would have been very useful in the Whitechapel murders, given the large number of men witnesses claimed to have seen with some of the victims before they were murdered. In fact, this technique was available to the police of the day, but it seems that it was not used in this case, despite the wealth of descriptions provided by witnesses.

In murder cases today the most valuable weapon the police have is DNA. Had it been around at the time of the Whitechapel murders it would have been of crucial importance, especially in relation to the blood that was found in large quantities at all the murder scenes. Maybe the killer cut himself during his savage attacks and left traces of his own blood. DNA would have identified which blood was whose.

DNA testing would, in the case of Catherine Eddowes, have been particularly important with regard to the bloodstained piece of apron. An examination of the blood on the apron would have shown whether it was hers. It would also have shown whether, as I suggest, the blood was from menstruation or another source. The apron was also wet, and DNA testing would have shown whether this was rain or the victim's urine. It would also have shown any unknown DNA – perhaps the killer's.

A forensic scientist would also have been able to state conclusively whether the piece of fabric did come from Eddowes's apron and whether it was torn or cut, by forensically matching the edges of the apron and the piece.

In the recent history of crime investigation, DNA testing has been the biggest breakthrough. Under British law, almost everyone arrested now has to give a DNA sample and their fingerprints. A DNA sample is taken by a simple mouth swab. This is then sent to a laboratory for analysis and a profile is made of each individual. The odds against two people having the same profile are many millions to one. The profile is then placed on a national database, making it easier to identify suspects from DNA found at crime scenes. The DNA and fingerprints are then continuously the subject of speculative searches relating to unsolved crimes.

However, DNA and fingerprints can only help the police if they have a suspect or a speculative search has identified a suspect. When a crime is committed by a person who has not come to their notice before, the police will not have that person's DNA or fingerprints. In this case, they must persist with old-fashioned methods of investigation in the hope that the suspect will come to their notice and that they are in a position to arrest, which will then allow them to take a DNA sample and fingerprints.

Britain's police have the powers to take a non-intimate DNA sample and fingerprints by force if necessary. A non-intimate sample is a mouth swab or a strand of hair, fingernail scrapings, a footprint or similar impression of any part of the body, except part of the hand. When a sample is taken by force, this involves either a mouth swab or a strand of hair. In the case of a person arrested for a serious offence the police also ask for an intimate sample, which may be a sample of blood, urine or any other tissue fluid, a semen sample, pubic hair, a dental impression and a swab from any other orifice of the body (except the mouth, for which a non-intimate request would be made). None of these can be taken by force and they are taken by a doctor.

In later years the FBI were asked to look at the murders with a view to providing a psychological profile of the murderer. This is what they came up with:

- White male, aged 28 to 36, living or working in the Whitechapel area.
- In childhood there was an absent or passive father figure.
- The killer probably had a profession in which he could legally experience his destructive tendencies.
- Jack the Ripper probably ceased his killing because he was either arrested for some other crime, or felt himself close to being discovered as the killer.
- The killer probably had some sort of physical defect, which was the source of a great deal of frustration or anger.

Being an old-fashioned police officer, I am not a great believer in the accuracy of profiling. The results it provides are very hit and miss, tend to generalise rather than be specific and at times can hinder an investigation by leading officers to change the line of enquiry to accommodate the profile.

The FBI profile is not convincing in terms of its description of the killer. We know from witnesses the approximate ages of men seen with some of the victims before their deaths. Assuming we accept this data, the likely ages of these men seen were already documented, so here the FBI profile reveals nothing that is not already known.

As to the suggestion that the killer probably lived in Whitechapel, the FBI had a 50/50 chance of being right, so again this is not a major revelation.

When evaluating the profile's suggestion that the killer had no father figure, we must bear in mind that in Victorian times many births were illegitimate, many children who had parents were fostered at birth because their parents could not afford to keep them, and some young children were simply abandoned on the street. So, again, the FBI profile offers nothing striking.

As to the killer having a job with destructive tendencies – a slaughterman, fishmonger or butcher come immediately to mind – it is well known that in the East End there were two major fish and meat markets as well as many backstreet slaughterhouses. I suspect this part of the profile derived from the idea of police officers at the time that the killer possibly had a job of this type.

As to why the killer stopped, I suspect that this theory was already common at the time of the murders, just as it is today. Nevertheless, I disagree with the suggestion that he stopped because he thought he was nearing capture. Serial killers do not suddenly stop for this reason. Once they have a hunger for killing they continue until capture or take their own life. So, once again there is nothing new in the profile to take the inquiry forward.

The East End was a very cosmopolitan area, as it still is. It was also a very violent area, with brutal crime a common occurrence, and knives were widely carried for use in criminal acts as well as for self-protection. Over the years it has been suggested that the cutting of the victims' throats was unique to these crimes and therefore linked them as having been committed by the same person. However, it is a fact that an aspect of the violent society of that day was that the accepted method of killing a person was to cut their throat. So, while the Whitechapel victims were all killed in this manner, it was not unique to these murders. This means of killing was far more common then than it is today, when very few murders that are committed with a knife are the result of the victim's throat being cut.

CHAPTER TWELVE

THE RIPPER LETTERS

During the autumn of terror of 1888 hundreds of letters were sent to the police and local press, all purportedly written by Jack the Ripper. At the time, most were deemed to be fakes written by either newspaper journalists trying to start a story or fools trying to incite more terror. I can only assume that the police would have examined each and every one of the letters in an attempt to ascertain if there was a link between any of them and the murders, or if the same person could have written some of them. I believe every one of them to be a hoax. Other experts believe some are genuine. I have reproduced a selection below.

The 'Dear Boss' Letter
This letter was received by the Central News Agency in London on 27 September 1888, after the murder of Annie Chapman. Three days later the 'double event' of the murders of Elizabeth Stride and Catherine Eddowes made the police reconsider whether the killer had indeed written the letter, especially once they learned that a portion of Eddowes's ear lobe had been found cut off from the body – a detail eerily reminiscent of a promise made in the 'Dear Boss' letter. At the time, they deemed the letter important enough

to reproduce it in newspapers and posters and handbills in the hope that someone would recognise the handwriting.

This is the first letter referring to the Whitechapel murders to be signed 'Jack the Ripper', and from now on the killer would be known universally by this name.

Dear Boss,
I keep on hearing the police have caught me but they wont fix me just yet. I have laughed when they look so clever and talk about being on the <u>right</u> track. That joke about Leather Apron gave me real fits. I am down on whores and I shant quit ripping them till I do get buckled. Grand work the last job was. I gave the lady no time to squeal. How can they catch me now. I love my work and want to start again. You will soon hear of me with my funny little games. I saved some of the proper <u>red</u> stuff in a ginger beer bottle over the last job to write with but it went thick like glue and I cant use it. Red ink is fit enough I hope <u>ha. ha.</u> The next job I do I shall clip the ladys ears off and send to the police officers just for jolly wouldn't you. Keep this letter back till I do a bit more work, then give it out straight. My knife's so nice and sharp I want to get to work right away if I get a chance. Good Luck.

Yours truly
Jack the Ripper
Dont mind me giving the trade name
PS Wasnt good enough to post this

After I looked closely at Eddowes's murder, it appeared to me that her ear lobe was cut off by the killer incidentally when cutting her throat and not deliberately severed, as implied by the letter. This, I am sure, was the conclusion that the original investigating officers also came to. If the killer had wanted to remove an ear or ears it would have been quite easy to remove it or them with the sharp knife that we know he possessed; and, besides, the letter referred to 'ears' not 'ear'.

The 'Saucy Jacky Postcard'

A postcard was received by the Central News Agency on 1 October 1888 which made direct reference to the murders of both Stride and Eddowes and the 'Dear Boss' letter. Believed to have been written by the same hand as that letter, it read:

I was not codding dear old Boss when I gave you the tip, you'll hear about Saucy Jacky's work tomorrow double event this time number one squealed a bit couldn't finish straight off. had not the time to get ears for police. thanks for keeping last letter back till I got to work again.

Jack the Ripper

The handwriting is similar to that of the 'Dear Boss' letter. Those who believe it to be genuine argue that the removal of Eddowes's ear lobe and the fact that the postcard mentions the double event before it was described by the press both testify to its authenticity. However, I suspect that a hoaxer could have gleaned details of both the previous letter and the murders in an early-morning paper of 1 October and written the letter before delivering it to the Central News Agency the same day.

In later years it was disclosed by a senior police officer that a newspaper reporter had been responsible for faking both the 'Dear Boss' letter' and the 'Saucy Jack' postcard. A reporter would have been able to obtain first-hand information on the murders and details of the post-mortems and would know that sending or delivering the hoax letters to the Central News Agency would ensure maximum exposure for them. Had the killer written the letter and postcard, would he have known of the existence and role of the Central News Agency? Perhaps not. In that case, had he wanted to inform the press he would surely have sent them direct to one or more newspapers, or direct to the police.

'From Hell' Letter

On 16 October George Lusk, the president of the Whitechapel Vigilance Committee, received a three-inch-square cardboard box in his post. Inside was half a human kidney preserved in wine, along with the following letter:

From hell.
Mr Lusk,
Sor

I send you half the Kidne I took from one woman and prasarved it for you tother piece I fried and ate it was very nise. I may send you the bloody knif that took it out if you only wate a whil longer
signed

Catch me when you can Mishter Lusk.

Dr Openshaw Letter

On 29 October 1888 this letter was sent to Dr Openshaw, who had performed a medical examination on the half kidney sent to George Lusk with the 'From Hell' letter. Dr Openshaw found the kidney to be very similar to the one removed from Catherine Eddowes, though his findings were inconclusive. The letter read:

Old boss you was rite it was the left kidny i was goin to hoperate agin close to your ospitle just as i was going to dror mi nife along of er bloomin throte them cusses of coppers spoilt the game but i guess i wil be on the jobn soon and will send you another bit of innerds
Jack the Ripper

O have you seen the devle
with his mikerscope and scalpul
a-lookin at a kidney
with a slide cocked up

1988 Letter

Dated 17 September 1888, this letter was only recently discovered in a sealed report envelope in the Public Record Office in London in 1988. Its authenticity is hotly debated, many believing it to be a recent hoax placed surreptitiously in the records.

Dear Boss
So now they say I am a Yid when will they lern Dear old Boss! You an me know the truth dont we. Lusk can look forever hell never find me but I am rite under his nose all the time. I watch them looking for me an it gives me fits ha ha I love my work an I shant stop until I get buckled and even then watch out for your old pal Jacky.

Catch me if you Can
Jack the Ripper
Sorry about the blood still messy from the last one. What a pretty necklace I gave her.

But did Jack the Ripper write any of the taunting letters received by the press and the police?

One of the interesting aspects of this case is the copious amount of correspondence received by the press, police and even private citizens from a sender or senders claiming to be 'Jack the Ripper.' In all, the press and police received over six hundred 'Ripper' letters. Several individuals, including two women, were arrested and charged with hoaxing. The 'Dear Boss' letter, since discredited, as we have seen, was published in every major newspaper in the early days of October 1888 and sparked a storm of hoax letters.

Many researchers consider the letter sent to George Lusk, which contained many spelling and grammatical errors and was not signed 'Jack the Ripper', more difficult to reject as a hoax. Some experts consider the Lusk letter to be from the killer. Others contend that it was a prank pulled by a medical student. Whether the half kidney that accompanied the letter in a small paper box was the one taken from Eddowes is impossible to tell. However, if, as I suggested earlier, Eddowes's kidney and uterus were not removed by the killer, this letter is definitely a hoax. As I also suggested, it may have been written by the same medical student who was involved in taking the organs from the body in the mortuary.

The jury is still out on whether any of the Ripper letters were written by the killer, although there is a consensus among modern researchers that the vast majority are hoaxes. In the case of the letters that contain accepted facts about the murders, most of this information could have been obtained either from the press or by someone attending the public inquests of the victims.

In murder cases through the ages there has always been someone prepared to admit the crime either by letter or face-to-face confession. Today this most often occurs via a telephone call or a taped message sent to the police. A good example is the Yorkshire Ripper murders, where the police received taped messages from a man calling himself 'Wearside Jack' and claiming to be the killer. For a time the police took this man seriously until they were able to eliminate him from the enquiry. The main reason for their being able to do this was that there were several taped messages, so after comparing them they were able to state categorically that the same person produced all the tapes.

Before leaving the subject of the Ripper letters, I would like to mention briefly some new documents that I came across in 2004. I was always of the belief that there are still case papers and documents relating to these murders which have not seen the light of day since Victorian times. During my researches, I was fortunate enough to come across several official documents, including a statement taken by Sir Charles Warren from a person who claimed to have information on the murders. To the best of my knowledge, these have never been made public. The discovery of these documents added weight to my suspicion that there are yet more in existence and still to be examined.

I have examined these original official documents, so I know they are genuine. I am not going to reveal how I came to do so, or divulge the full contents or the identity of the holder of the documents, to avoid unwelcome intrusion from Ripper enthusiasts. However, I have reproduced a small extract from one of the documents. This is from a statement given to Sir Charles Warren by a man named Charles De La Ree Bott and is dated 3 November 1888, six days before the murder of Mary Kelly. No address is given for Bott and it is unclear if this is his correct name. However, the man did exist, for he personally gave the statement to the police, and he may have had sufficient standing in society for the police initially to treat him seriously.

Bott states: 'Regarding the Whitechapel outrages they may have been committed by perhaps 20 persons with some connivance. There is no necessity for immediate action, they are stopped for the present unless they occur again for mere bravado.'

Charles de La Re'e Bott was described by Sir Charles Warren as 'An educated man who has studied hard, and appears to have eccentric ideas, though he is probably not a lunatic'.

I have researched the contents of the letter and Mr Bott himself and my belief is that he had no direct knowledge of who the killer was. This is borne out by the subsequent murder of Mary Kelly. Nevertheless, I am sure Mr Bott gave his statement in good faith.

CHAPTER THIRTEEN

A LONG LIST
OF SUSPECTS

Before considering any likely suspects I had to see if there was any direct evidence I could use after analysing the murders that would help me to identify the killer. There was none. All I had to go on were vague descriptions of men seen with some of the victims before their deaths and the MOs — the *modus operandi*, or method of killing — used in each murder. As I looked at each suspect, my aim was to see if any of them matched any of these descriptions, but, even if they did, I knew that this fact would be no more than weak circumstantial evidence.

The list of suspects for the title of Jack the Ripper now stands at around 140. Among the illustrious names put forward over the years are the famous children's writer Lewis Carroll and Dr Barnardo, who did so much good work for orphaned children. Why is there such a long list? Well, in addition to unsubstantiated theories in later years about likely suspects, it seems that at the time of the murders anyone who had a conviction for a stabbing offence became a suspect, as did anyone confessing to be Jack the Ripper after a night of heavy drinking or anyone coming into police custody for any similar type of murder. So the list grew and grew. For several years after the murders ceased, police continued to interview anyone arrested for any offence involving the use of a sharp knife against a female, in the hope of finding the Ripper.

Over the years the list of suspects has come down to the following: George Chapman, Montague Druitt, Aaron Kosminski, Prince Albert Victor, Francis Tumblety, Joseph Barnett, Walter Sickert, John Pizer, Michael Ostrog, James Maybrick and Thomas Cutbush.

I intended to reinvestigate all of these suspects in search of new evidence to connect one of them to the murders. In addition, I decided to re-examine the evidence that has already been investigated, hoping that this too would either suggest or discount the likelihood that a particular suspect was involved.

The difficulty I had was that very few of these suspects were ever arrested and interviewed at the time of the murders. Most were suggested years afterwards. The original investigating officers allegedly suspected some of them, but only years later. As to how these men came to be suspected and whether there is any substance to the suspicions, I hoped my investigation would prove fruitful. I was aware of the thorough enquiries carried out over the years by researchers, but all appeared to have pursued the same lines of enquiry. So, in my hunt for new evidence, I decided to try new lines of enquiry.

I wrote to the Prime Minister, Tony Blair, and the then Home Secretary, David Blunkett, asking if I could examine any correspondence in the archives which may have been overlooked between the Prime Minister at the time of the murders, Lord Salisbury, and the then Home Secretary, Henry Matthews, and Queen Victoria, to see if any new evidence or new clues could be obtained from any of these letters or official documents.

Tony Blair sent my letter to the Home Office, which forwarded it to the Public Record Office. This assisted by searching the archives, but the search failed to reveal any new correspondence between any of the above individuals about the murders. The Home Office did not reply but forwarded my letter to the Public Record

Office. From this, I later received a standard letter setting out details of documents and papers relating to the murders of which I was already aware and which have been widely available for years. I was left feeling frustrated.

I then wrote to the Queen for leave to examine letters and correspondence in the Royal Archives. Her Majesty was most helpful, instructing the Archives to forward me copies of several letters between Queen Victoria and Lord Salisbury. Unfortunately, these revealed nothing other than Queen Victoria's concern about the murders. In fact, they also revealed that in Victorian times the need for secrecy was as important as it is today. Whether the writer was Queen Victoria or Lord Salisbury, every letter was written in code and decoded on receipt. Had there been any sensitive material in any of the letters, I suspect that a final paragraph would have stated, 'After reading please destroy'. Already it seemed that my new lines of enquiry were likely to prove negative, but they had to be followed.

Then an official from the Royal Archives pointed me in the direction of the archives of Lord Salisbury at Hatfield House, Hertfordshire. I discovered that no previous researchers seemed to have taken this route, and I was very hopeful that there would be in existence letters and other documents between Lord Salisbury, Queen Victoria and Henry Matthews that would reveal fresh evidence or clues.

However, my first letter to Robin Harcourt Williams, the Senior Archivist at Hatfield House, drew a curt, one-paragraph reply stating that my application was refused. Never one to be deterred, I wrote personally to Lord Salisbury. I received an acknowledgement and, several weeks later, a second letter from Robin Harcourt Williams, who had been asked to reply on behalf of his lordship. The answer was still no.

I again contacted Robin Harcourt Williams, who, after a long telephone conversation, relented slightly. He told me that in fact he did not know what the archives contained and he had never been asked to look. But he agreed to do some research on Queen Victoria, Henry Matthews, Sir Charles Warren and James Monro. I then made arrangements to meet him in person at Hatfield House several weeks later.

I kept the appointment and met Robin Harcourt Williams at Hatfield House. On meeting Robin in person, I found him to be a most charming and helpful man. He had worked for the Salisbury family for over 30 years, and I was amazed by his knowledge of its history right back to 1600. Robin's initial refusal, he explained, was prompted by his feeling that any letters and documents contained in the archives were private and not for public viewing. I should point out that he was speaking of the archives in general rather than specifically of any documents on the Whitechapel murders.

Until this time, I had remained optimistic that Robin was going to produce a letter or a document that had remained filed away for over a century and would unlock the mystery. This was not to be. Robin told me that he had searched the archives and could find no letters or documents between any of the persons in question relating to the Whitechapel murders.

I accept that I have to take Robin at his word, and that perhaps he could have told me this when, in fact, he *had* found documents or letters containing valuable information about the murders that he had decided were best left in the archives. However, as an investigator, I find that my first impression of people I interview is very important. I have to say I do not think I was being misled. When Robin says he found nothing I firmly believe him. To add more weight to my belief, I had failed to provide Robin with the name of Sir Robert Anderson, but while I was at Hatfield House I mentioned this name and I was with him when he checked the archives in relation to Anderson but found nothing.

I knew now that it was back to basic, old-fashioned detective work. It was time to look at each suspect individually.

CHAPTER FOURTEEN

MONTAGUE JOHN DRUITT

At time of the Whitechapel murders Druitt, a barrister and a teacher, was 31. He was put forward in 1894 as a suspect, along with Thomas Cutbush, Michael Ostrog and Aaron Kosminski, and these three I discuss below. The names of the four suspects appeared in a so-called confidential memorandum written by Sir Melville Macnaghten and dated 23 February 1894, more than five years after the murders began. Macnaghten joined the Metropolitan Police as Assistant Chief Constable and was second in command of the Criminal Investigation Department at Scotland Yard in June 1889. There is no evidence of contemporary police suspicion of any of the four men at the time of the murders.

Although Macnaghten was not involved in the investigation of any of the murders, as a senior police officer in later years he would have been aware of ongoing and past enquiries into the murders. He would have been in a position to pass comment on persons who, several years after the murders ceased, had come to the notice of the police in relation to the murders, and would also have known the results of the subsequent enquiries. These would have been conducted by the handful of officers still seeking Jack the Ripper.

Macnaghten referred to Montague Druitt as follows in the memorandum:

> I have always held strong opinions regarding him, and the more I think the matter over, the stronger do these opinions become. The truth, however, will never be known, and did indeed, at one time lie at the bottom of the Thames, if my conjections be correct!
>
> Mr M.J. Druitt a doctor of about 41 years of age & of fairly good family, who disappeared at the time of the Miller's Court murder, and whose body was found floating in the Thames on 31st Dec [1888]: i.e. 7 weeks after the said murder. The body was said to have been in the water for a month, or more – on it was found a season ticket between Blackheath & London. From private information I have little doubt that his own family suspected this man of being the Whitechapel murderer; it was alleged that he was sexually insane.

I looked closely at the background to Macnaghten's statement that 'from private information I have little doubt but that his own family suspected him to have been the murderer', and it was obvious that he had no evidence at all. There are no clues as to the identity of the informant to whom he refers, but, from the way his statement is worded, it would seem as if it was a Druitt family member. Yet, if one or more of Druitt's relations had informed Macnaghten that they suspected he might have been the Ripper, would Macnaghten not rather have said he had evidence that Druitt's family believed him to be the killer?

I found many discrepancies in Macnaghten's notes on Druitt. He stated that Druitt lived with his family, but records show that he lived alone at 9 Eliot Place, Blackheath, south-east London. He stated that Druitt had committed suicide around 10 November 1888, three weeks before he is thought to have done so. (The date of Druitt's death is not confirmed, because when the body was examined no more than an approximate time for his suicide could be given as it was in a state of decomposition from being in the water for some time.) Macnaghten also stated that Druitt was about 41 at the time of his death, but, in fact, he was 31. Finally, he describes Druitt as a doctor, when he was a barrister and schoolmaster.

As to Druitt's appearance, he had a moustache, as did the man seen with victims if the Ripper, according to some witnesses. He was also of respectable appearance, always known to have been well dressed. One witness described the suspect as having the appearance of a sailor. Another described seeing a man of 'shabby genteel appearance'; others described the man as respectable.

However, my theory that the killer did not live in Whitechapel did not totally rule out Druitt as he was living in Blackheath during the murders. If he was the killer, he could have used that address as a 'base' for the murders. However, Blackheath is too far to walk from Whitechapel and would have required a journey by train or horse-drawn cab. Alternatively, Druitt could have used his barrister's chambers at King's Bench Walk, just west of the City, within walking distance of Whitechapel and in the direction the Ripper took after killing Eddowes.

In Druitt's defence, he was a keen cricketer and is known to have played in Dorset on 1 September, the day after Mary Ann Nichols's murder. Could he have had time to commit the murder and be down in Dorset for the start of play mid-morning? I suspect not.

On 8 September, the day of Annie Chapman's murder, Druitt played cricket in Blackheath at 11.30am. So could he have killed Chapman at 5.30am and had time to catch a train to Blackheath, remove his bloodstained clothes, wash, eat breakfast and be on the cricket field by 11.30am? It's possible but very unlikely.

There is another issue to consider: it is believed that Druitt was a homosexual and the reason for his dismissal from the boys' school where he taught was his engaging in homosexual acts with boys, the disgrace of which drove him to suicide. If we accept that he was homosexual, would a homosexual commit crimes against women in this brutal way? The answer is no.

The truth is that the only 'evidence' to suggest he was the killer came out in 1894 and it can be said that this is not evidence in the true sense. So why were the investigating officers not made aware of this at the time by the person who initially suspected Druitt? I would have thought that anyone with information leading to the apprehension of the killer would have been only too willing be a part of apprehending one of the most notorious killers that London had ever seen.

This leads me to believe that perhaps Macnaghten was basing his claims on hearsay rather than private information he himself had received. He did not join the police force until 1889 and did not write his memorandum until 1894. So could his reason for writing of his suspicions several years after the murders be the possibility of financial gain? Perhaps more evidence or documents are still to be found that will shed some light on Macnaghten's motives for suggesting Montague Druitt was Jack the Ripper. After all, apparently he stated that he had been in possession of other documentation about the murders which, for reasons he kept to himself, he destroyed.

So was Druitt the killer? Well, if it is accepted that the two murders after Mary Kelly's were not committed by the same killer/s, he cannot be discounted totally (as Coles and McKenzie were murdered after Druitt himself had died). However, if they were all by the same figure, he was not the killer of all or any of the women.

Druitt's suicide and the fact that the police closed the inquiry in early January 1889 make him a convenient scapegoat. I do not believe he was the killer of all or any of the women. I can find no evidence or any motives to support the theory that he was the Ripper. In fact, the only links with the Ripper are his likeness to the vague descriptions of the man seen with Ripper victims and the suggestion made by an ageing police officer several years later.

CHAPTER FIFTEEN

THOMAS CUTBUSH

Although Macnaghten put Thomas Cutbush forward as a Ripper suspect, he did state: 'No one ever saw the Whitechapel murderer; many homicidal maniacs were suspected, but no shadow of proof could be thrown on any one. I may mention the cases of 3 men, any one of whom would have been more likely than Cutbush to have committed this series of murders.'

So why did he mention Cutbush?

In 1891 Cutbush was arrested and charged with maliciously wounding two women in Kennington, south London. When arrested he was found to be in possession of a long knife that he had used in his attack on the women.

Cutbush is said to have studied medical books by day and wandered about at night, often returning home with his clothes covered with mud. However, little reliance could be placed on these statements, which were made by his mother or his aunt, both of whom appear to have been of a very excitable disposition. It was impossible to ascertain his movements on the nights of the Whitechapel murders and there was no evidence to suggest he was ever in Whitechapel. The knife found on him at the time of his arrest was bought in Houndsditch about a week before he was detained.

It was thought that Cutbush also spent a portion of his day making rough drawings of the bodies of women and of their mutilation. This supposition was based solely on the fact that two scribbled drawings of women in indecent poses were found torn up in his room. The head and body of one of the women had been cut from a fashion plate and legs were added to show a woman's naked thighs and pink stockings.

I regard the police's suspicion of Cutbush as clutching at straws. After the main Ripper inquiry was scaled down, a number of officers still worked on the case and, as I noted earlier, these would have looked closely at anyone committing similar crimes involving a knife. Cutbush was one of a number of people interviewed for this reason. Very little is known about him, which makes it difficult even to suggest he had any motive for the killings. At the time there was nothing more than I have mentioned here to suggest he was the killer, nor has anything else come to light since, and I have no reason to suspect otherwise now.

CHAPTER SIXTEEN

AARON KOSMINSKI

Macnaghten's Ripper suspect Aaron Kosminski was a Polish Jew who apparently had lived in Whitechapel since 1882. This was a man who was 'supposed' to have an extreme hatred of women, especially prostitutes. It has also been suggested that he had strong homicidal tendencies and a history of brutal crimes. If this were correct, it would have given him a motive. However, there is no documentary evidence to support any of these suggestions.

Kosminski would have been around 25 at the time of the murders. No witness describes seeing anyone of about this age in the murder locations or in the company of the victims before their deaths. It seems that Kosminski could speak only Yiddish, so this would have given him great difficulty in propositioning prostitutes, and, even if he did speak a little English, no witness who heard suspects talk mentioned any of them having a foreign accent.

Macnaghten mentions Kosminski by surname only, so it is not certain to whom he was referring. It is likely that there was more than one young man named Kosminski in an area that had become home to many Jews from eastern Europe. There is also doubt as to why, several years after the murders, Kosminski was put forward as a suspect, for he had no criminal convictions.

So what do we know of Aaron Kosminski? A family with that surname was known to reside near Goulston Street, where the graffito and bloodstained piece of apron were found, but it is not known whether it was Aaron's or another.

Kosminski supposedly had a history of carrying and using a knife and, being a barber, he used cut-throat razors in his work. However, we know that a knife, not a razor, was the murder weapon in all the Whitechapel murders. I believe that the suspicion about the knife and the fact of his habitual use of a cut-throat razor alone were enough to have made him a suspect, but the first was supposition and the second was true of any man in the same occupation, yet it would not necessarily have made him a killer. In fact, Kosminski was never a suspect at the time of the murders. It is known that there was an incident when he threatened his sister with a knife. This was before he was sent to the asylum and may well have been the deciding factor in the decision to send him there. However, the incident occurred two years after the murders ceased. There is no evidence to say he was living in Whitechapel at the time of the murders.

Macnaghten also suggested that the police had received information that Kosminski was the killer. If there was indeed any information, what it was, who supplied it and who received it is not known. This question has been the subject of many theories and much speculation over the years. As a result of this information, it is suggested, the police staged some form of identification procedure at a location which some say was a seaside home in Brighton and others say was a workhouse in London. It is known that Kosminski was in a workhouse at some point. The police took a witness to the location. The name of this witness is not known but it may have been one of the two who saw a man with Catherine Eddowes before her murder. Or could it have been a new witness who had given new information? Whoever this witness was, he appears to have been another Jew, who supposedly made a positive identification and then told the police he would not testify against a fellow Jew knowing that the outcome would likely be hanging.

In any event, if this ever took place, the evidence is questionable. The identification procedure the police adopted is today known as a 'direct confrontation'. I suggest that, even in that day and age, this evidence would have not been sufficient to charge Kosminski, let alone secure a conviction.

The identification was made almost two years after Eddowes's murder, a time gap that raises considerable doubt about the witness's accuracy. I also have to ask: what was the witness being asked to make an identification on? And why was only one witness used when several witnesses had given the police descriptions of men they had seen with some of the victims before their murders?

In any event, the witness may not have had a clear view of the suspect as the sighting took place at night, when it was almost totally dark, and to have had such a view he would have had to have been fairly close to the man. All in all, there are major doubts surrounding this identification.

None of the descriptions of the suspect given by witnesses appears to fit Kosminski in terms of age. Neither do they in terms of dress. To take a key example, several witnesses referred to the suspect wearing hats of various kinds, yet there is no evidence to show Kosminski ever wore a hat of any description.

If this identification did take place, it leaves some burning questions:

- Why did the police not officially document the identification at the time? This would have been a major breakthrough, but no police records are available to confirm that it took place.
- After the identification, why did the police not arrest Kosminski or at least interview him? There is nothing in police records to show that either was done or to

explain why neither was done. I would have expected the police to put this significant identification to Kosminski. They could have told him he had been positively identified – there was no need to tell him that the witness was not going to give evidence – just to see his reaction. This information alone may well have been enough to make him confess, should he have been Jack the Ripper.

- Why did the police take Kosminski to the supposed location for the identification procedure, if they ever did? This would surely have been against normal police procedures, even in those days. As a suspect, he should have been formally arrested.

Kosminski was supposedly committed to an infirmary for the insane in late 1890, although Macnaghten states that it was in March 1889. According to the records at the asylum, Kosminski was not considered a danger and was never placed in a straitjacket. Also, he only ever spoke Yiddish while there. He died of gangrene in 1919, still an asylum inmate.

Was Kosminski the killer? In the absence of anything direct to link him to the murders, there must be serious doubt. We know he lived in Whitechapel, but we know nothing of his whereabouts and movements at the time of the murders. Before being committed to the asylum he had been living on the streets, refusing handouts of food and instead eating from the gutter and drinking from public taps. Had he been living in the way suggested at the time of the killings and had he been the killer, I am sure that the police would have received information on or about him from the local community and would have built up a strong picture and background on him through the course of their investigation. In the absence of this information, we can assume that there was no reason to suspect him at the time.

As to the actions of the police at the time, they appear to have broken many rules. I suspect that they had much more of a free hand than officers have today. Nevertheless, if, as has been suggested, they were satisfied that Kosminski was Jack the Ripper but could not bring him to justice owing to his insanity, this surely would have been documented. After all, the murders were high-profile crimes and the issue of Kosminski would have been reported somewhere and Queen Victoria herself made aware. In addition, the police would have wanted to publicise the fact that the killer had been found and incarcerated, just to put the public at ease. Furthermore, the acclaim that the police would have received for identifying Jack the Ripper would have made the suppression of their findings very difficult.

Today, when the police charge a person with murder and there is a suggestion that he may be insane, provided he has initially been certified by a doctor as being fit to be interviewed and the evidence is sufficient to charge him, he is put before a court. However, the person may later be deemed unable to stand trial if further medical examination results in his being classed as 'Unfit to plead' owing to mental illness. In this case, an order is made under the Mental Health Act for an unspecified period of detention in a secure institution. This would have been an option open to the police in the case of Kosminski. As I have said, to do so would have put the public at ease and provided an opportunity to regain the people's confidence in the police. This, by all accounts, was still lacking two years later.

Kosminski has been of great interest to researchers over the years, mainly because hardly anything concrete is known of him, and no one has been able to eliminate him totally as a suspect. On the other hand, no evidence has been put forward to make him any more of a prime suspect than the others. Precisely because of this, researchers have continued to speculate and theorise and been able to keep alive the possibility that he was Jack the Ripper.

My own view is that the police looked at Kosminski in later years as a result of his threatening his sister with a knife, probably aware of the fact that he may well have lived in Whitechapel at the time of the murders. Whatever they did in connection with this suspect they did with good intent, but all to no avail. The reality is that all the facts surrounding Kosminski have been distorted over the years, and, after considering this, I can still find no motive and no evidence to suggest he was Jack the Ripper.

CHAPTER SEVENTEEN

GEORGE CHAPMAN

A Polish immigrant who had changed his name from Severin Klosowski, George Chapman was suggested in later years as a prime suspect by Inspector Frederick Abberline, one of the officers who had been involved in the investigation of the Ripper murders. Chapman was never arrested and interviewed during this inquiry and only became a suspect when arrested in connection with the poisoning of a number of women, among them his wife. This was in 1902, long after the Ripper inquiry had been scaled down.

It appears that Chapman's arrival in England coincided with the beginning of the murders in Whitechapel. There is also a coincidence in the fact that the murders ceased in London when he went to America. And then a similar murder occurred in America shortly after he landed there. The fact that he studied medicine and surgery in Russia before he settled in London is well established, and it is curious to note that it was suggested at the time that some of the Whitechapel murders were the work of an expert surgeon. The murders committed by Chapman in later years employed poison and displayed a more than elementary knowledge of medicine.

Chapman's wife's story of how he attempted to kill her with a long knife has been put forward as another reason for his being a suspect in the Ripper murders. However, we know that domestic arguments do occur between man and wife and it is fair to say that, in a crisis, threats to kill are uttered by both parties without anything going further than that. It is also fact that, in the heat of the moment, one or both parties may pick up some type of weapon, whether a household object or a kitchen knife. So I do not see in his wife's account a reason for making Chapman a suspect.

Other similarities between Chapman and the Ripper have been suggested. Chapman had a regular job and it is suggested that the Ripper also did, since the murders all occurred at weekends. But, at the time, Chapman was single and free of responsibility for a family, so he could have worked by day and been out at all hours of the night. In fact, his ex-wife stated that, when they were married, he was in the habit of staying out until the early hours. Furthermore, if his many affairs and relationships are anything to go by, Chapman had an outrageous sexual drive. While it seems that there was no sexual motive behind the Ripper's murders, he might be seen as a sexual serial killer in that he mutilated his victims' reproductive organs.

Inspector Abberline did admit there was a problem with Chapman's being the Ripper. One major discrepancy is that witnesses who stated that they saw a person they believed to be Jack the Ripper with the victims at one time or another put his age at about 35–40. None of them thought the man they saw was as young as Chapman in 1888, 23. Furthermore, Chapman was in the public eye in the East End, as he worked as a barber there, and so would probably have been easily recognised had he been in the vicinity of any of the murders

Finally I looked at the 'similar murder committed in America' referred to by Abberline and others as evidence that Chapman was the Ripper. This murder was that of an elderly prostitute named Carrie Brown and known as 'Old Shakespeare' – a nickname that derived from her penchant for quoting the author when drunk. She was murdered in a common lodging-house in Jersey City, New Jersey, on 24 April 1891, first strangled and then mutilated. I have seen photographs of her wounds and find it hard to agree that these are, as they have been described, savage mutilations. For this reason alone, there must be serious doubt that this killing is linked to the Ripper murders.

A housekeeper at the lodging-house saw the man with whom Brown entered and described him as aged about 32, five feet eight inches in height, of slim build, with a long, sharp nose and a heavy, light-coloured moustache. He was clad in a dark-brown cutaway coat and black trousers and wore an old black bowler hat with a heavily dented crown. He was described as a foreigner, possibly a German. Since it is well documented that thousands of European immigrants had flocked to America by that time, this description is not unique to Chapman. On the other hand, although far from perfect for police purposes, it does point loosely to him.

But was Chapman in New Jersey at the time of Carrie Brown's murder? A census register shows he was still in London on 5 April and there are no records from America to establish that he was there before 24 April. The only assumption that can be made is that it was the death of their son the previous month that prompted Chapman and his wife to move to America. But they must have left London after the census register of 5 April. This would have given Chapman 19 days to move out, settle into Jersey City and murder Brown. It would have been possible.

However, on 26 April, two days after Brown was killed, police arrested an Algerian Frenchman named Ameer Ben Ali in connection with the murder. Nicknamed 'Frenchy', Ben Ali was well known in the district. It appears he often stayed at the hotel and on the night of the murder was in a room across the hall from the victim's.

However, Ben Ali's was totally different in appearance from the man seen entering the lodging-house with Brown. The Algerian was dark-skinned and not Caucasian, unlike the man seen with Brown when she checked in.

The police case against Ben Ali was that, after the departure of the man who had entered the lodging-house with Brown, Ben Ali went to her room, where he killed her and stole her money. The police case against Ben Ali rested on a trail of blood found between Brown's room and his. He was tried, found guilty of murder and sentenced to life imprisonment. Later he was moved to a hospital for the criminally insane.

In 1902, Ben Ali's sentence was quashed as the original evidence was discredited and considered unsafe. This came about as a result of information presented by several journalists who believed he had been wrongly convicted. They suggested that the trail of blood that was the backbone of the police case could have been made by journalists and the coroner at the crime scene in walking back and forth between the two rooms, thereby contaminating the crime scene. This was enough to make the conviction unsafe.

Whoever killed Carrie Brown, there are several major differences between her murder and the Whitechapel murders which, in my view, rule her out as a Ripper victim:

- Brown was killed in a common lodging-house where many people were staying and moving about at all hours of the night. None of the Whitechapel victims was killed in this type of location.
- If the person seen entering the lodging-house was the killer, he was taking a big risk. He would have known that he had been seen entering the house. He would have known that he would have been likely to be captured should Brown have screamed out at any time or made an attempt to get away.
- Brown's throat was not cut, whereas those of all the Whitechapel victims were.

Where does this leave us with regard to the suggestion that Chapman was Carrie Brown's killer and also a Ripper suspect? We know Chapman had medical skills and was foreign-looking and had an accent similar to those described by witnesses in his US lodging house. He lived somewhere in the East End around the time of the murders. The first series of London murders ceased once he moved to America, where Brown was killed in similar fashion. Almost everything fits except for his MO.

A pressing question is whether a savage mutilator can transform himself into a calculating poisoner seven years later. Another unanswered question is, if Chapman was the Whitechapel killer, why did he suddenly stop? Had he fulfilled his grisly intentions? Did he fear capture? If neither, why did he not continue to commit similar crimes once there? And why did he not recommence killing when he returned to Britain? As I said earlier, serial killers do not stop killing without good reason.

Criminologists and behavioural experts differ on whether murderers maintain their *modus operandi*. Some have stated that they can change their MO as they gain experience. My experience of murderers leads me to disagree. So I ask, if Chapman was the killer, did he change from a savage brutal killer into a passive poisoner? I don't believe so.

Bear in mind also that Chapman was a womaniser who had a liking for young, attractive women. Would such a person have shown any interest in older, dishevelled, dirty prostitutes? I suggest not; not even for the purposes of murdering them.

Finally, I would have expected that, had the police suspected Chapman of being the Ripper, they would have interviewed him while he was awaiting execution. The visit may or may not have taken place. In any event, no meeting was recorded. If the police did question Chapman and he was the killer, he may well have unburdened his conscience before going to meet his maker. This we may never know.

So, was Chapman the killer? I suggest not. Like other suspects I have considered here, he came to notice in later years for killing a number of women, albeit by a different method from the Ripper's. The fact that there was a similar murder in America while Chapman was known to have been there may well have caused the police to take more than a passing interest in him. However, Inspector Abberline was a well-respected officer and I am sure that if he had real suspicions about Chapman the suspect would at least have been interviewed and this would have been documented. In the absence of any such record, I can only assume there was nothing to suggest he was Jack the Ripper.

Chapman was hanged at Wandsworth Prison on 7 April 1903, having been convicted of killing his wife and several other women by poisoning them.

CHAPTER EIGHTEEN

MICHAEL OSTROG

It has been suggested that Michael Ostrog, the last of Macnaghten's four suspects, came under scrutiny by the Metropolitan Police at the time of the Whitechapel murders. It is also said that his whereabouts could never be satisfactorily accounted for. Ostrog was a petty criminal and confidence trickster who used numerous aliases, including Dr Grant, and also claimed that he was a former surgeon in the Russian Navy. He spent much of his time in police custody for various instances of fraud and theft. Certainly, he was a persistent offender, but was he a killer?

Ostrog became a high-profile suspect when it was stated in the *Police Gazette*, around the time of the Whitechapel murders, that 'special attention is called to this dangerous man'. This publication, long sent regularly to all police stations, both sets out details of persons sought by specific police officers in connection with specific crimes and highlights certain criminals who are suspected of being engaged in criminal activity.

It is likely that Ostrog's appearance in the *Police Gazette* was due to his petty criminal activities and the description 'dangerous' was a mistake. If he had been suspected of being the killer or wanted for questioning as a suspect, this would have been stated in the piece. In any event, considering the number of times he was arrested for petty crimes, the police would have had ample opportunity to question him about the murders. It appears that this was never done.

Macnaghten wrote of him: 'Michael Ostrog, a mad Russian doctor and a convict and unquestionably a homicidal maniac. This man was said to have been habitually cruel to women, and for a long time was known to have carried about with him surgical knives and other instruments; his antecedents were of the very worst and his whereabouts at the time of the Whitechapel murders could never be satisfactorily accounted for. He is still alive.' I wonder where Macnaghten obtained his information, for the character of the man he describes is totally different from that of Ostrog. Although he had numerous convictions for theft and fraud, Ostrog had no history of violence, either in general or specifically towards women, nor is there any record of his using or carrying a knife.

As to Ostrog's being the Ripper, I can find no motive for the murders and I suggest he did not kill any of the women. Three of the four suspects discussed so far were put forward as a direct result of the Macnaghten memorandum, which was not a document from the time of the murders. I have already highlighted important discrepancies between the memorandum and other available evidence, and suggested reasons why the document came to light a number of years after the killings. My research leads me to believe that the document is based purely on hearsay. And, in the absence of any further evidence to substantiate its contents or any direct evidence to connect any of the four suspects with the Whitechapel murders, my conclusion is that it is unreliable in identifying any of these men as potentially responsible for the Whitechapel murders.

CHAPTER NINETEEN

JOHN PIZER

I will mention John Pizer for the reason that he was one of the very few Ripper suspects arrested at the time of the murders. His arrest followed the murder of Annie Chapman on 8 September 1888.

A Jew living in Whitechapel, Pizer was known as 'Leather Apron' because he worked in the leather trade, work that involved the use of long-bladed knives. He also owned a leather apron similar to that found at the scene of Chapman's murder. He was supposedly seen arguing with Chapman before she was killed. Pizer not only had a stabbing conviction, but also displayed a well-known dislike for prostitutes. The reason for this hostility is not known, but it could be seen as a motive for murder.

However, a lengthy interrogation failed to shake Pizer's solid alibi in relation to the Chapman murder. Later, he sued the authorities and received a compensation payment from the libel courts for unlawful arrest.

CHAPTER TWENTY

FRANCIS TUMBLETY

The vast majority of Ripper experts of recent years believe the American Francis Tumblety to be the prime suspect for the killings. Tumblety did not emerge as a real suspect until 1993, when a letter belonging to a crime writer was unearthed that mentioned Tumblety.

This letter also cast doubt on the authenticity of the letters previously attributed to the Ripper. The 'Littlechild Letter' was written in 1913 by an ageing police officer, Chief Inspector Littlechild, who was the head of Britain's Special Branch and at the time of the Whitechapel murders was investigating terrorist activities. His letter, written to George R. Sims, of 12 Clarence Terrace, Regent's Park, London, has been edited to focus on its reference to the murders:

> 8, The Chase,
> Clapham Common S.W.
> 23rd September 1913
>
> Dear Sir,
> ... Knowing the great interest you take in all matters

criminal, and abnormal, I am just going to inflict one more letter on you on the 'Ripper' subject. Letters as a rule are only a nuisance when they call for a reply but this does not need one. I will try and be brief.

I never heard of a Dr D. in connection with the Whitechapel murders but amongst the suspects, and to my mind a very likely one, was a Dr T. (which sounds much like D.) He was an American quack named Tumblety and was at one time a frequent visitor to London and on these occasions constantly brought under the notice of police, there being a large dossier concerning him at Scotland Yard. Although a 'Sycopathia [sic] Sexualis' subject he was not known as a 'Sadist' (which the murderer unquestionably was) but his feelings toward women were remarkable and bitter in the extreme, a fact on record. Tumblety was arrested at the time of the murders in connection with unnatural offences and charged at Marlborough Street, remanded on bail, jumped his bail, and got away to Boulogne. He shortly left Boulogne and was never heard of afterwards. It was believed he committed suicide but certain it is that from this time the 'Ripper' murders came to an end.

With regard to the term 'Jack the Ripper' it was generally believed at the Yard that Tom Bullen of the Central News was the originator, but it is probable Moore, who was his chief, was the inventor. It was a smart piece of journalistic work. No journalist of my time got such privileges from Scotland Yard as Bullen. ...

... I knew Major Griffiths for many years. He probably got his information from Anderson who only 'thought he knew'.

Faithfully yours,
J. G. Littlechild

Having studied this letter, I find nothing other than the writer's suspicions, which recall Macnaghten's assumptions, in the absence of solid evidence, about his own suspects. Anderson, referred to at the end of the letter, is Sir Robert Anderson, who was Assistant Commissioner, in charge of CID, in 1888. In later years, Sir Robert also stated on record that the police knew the identity of the Ripper. Although he did not name the person, he intimated that he had been caged in a lunatic asylum. This suggests the killer could have been Kosminski. However, I cannot believe – regardless of whether the murderer could have been prosecuted or, having been declared insane, could not – that in a major case such as the Whitechapel murders the police would have failed to reassure the public that the murderer could kill no more. However, since no such step was taken, I must assume that Anderson's views were no more than suspicion and that we may never know on what basis he formed them.

So what did my enquiries into Francis Tumblety reveal? He was born in America and at the time of the murders was 56 and posing as a doctor. Eccentric but shrewd, he was financially stable. He had a tendency towards violence.

Tumblety had behind him a failed marriage to a woman who turned out to be a prostitute, and, as far as a motive for murder is concerned, this experience may have given him a hatred of such women. Afterwards he became a practising homosexual, turning his attentions to younger men. He is known to have had a collection of female body parts in a cabinet at his home in America many years before coming to Britain. It is not known how he acquired this collection, but nothing is documented that suggests it was by killing and mutilating women. From the facts of this collection and his practice as a doctor, bogus though this was, the inference has been drawn that Tumblety may have had some anatomical knowledge. However, if my theory of how organs came to be removed from Ripper victims is correct, this suggestion must be dismissed.

Tumblety was in London at the time of the murders. It has been suggested that he may have been lodging in the East End, as it is known the police were watching a lodging-house there for an American suspected of being involved in terrorist activities. If this is so, he may have had some knowledge of the area, but there is no evidence to corroborate the suggestion that he was in the East End.

It is alleged that a bloodstained garment was found in a lodging-house at 22 Batty Street after the Stride and Eddowes murders on 30 September 1888. A 'mysterious' American man had quickly disappeared after arriving back at the lodging-house at 2am on the night of the double murder. However, there has never been confirmation of either the discovery of the bloodstained garment or the American's movements on the night of the murders, and it would appear that this story was another invention of the press.

From my personal experience and knowledge of police work, if Chief Inspector Littlechild's officers from Special Branch were watching a suspect they would certainly have identified who that person was and would be closely watching him day and night. However, they may have had this information but not shared it with other branches of the police service, as still happens today. If the suspect was Tumblety, I am sure he would have been put forward at that time as a suspect. The only explanation for this not happening is that Special Branch felt terrorism was far more serious than murder and deliberately suppressed any information they had that suggested he was the murderer. However, I seriously doubt that this was the case.

Many years before coming to England, Tumblety had been arrested in America in connection with the assassination of Abraham Lincoln, although there was no evidence of his involvement. Therefore, it was obvious he was not averse to becoming involved in political issues, and it would be wrong to totally dismiss the terrorist theory.

In November 1888, Tumblety was arrested in London for

offences of gross indecency involving male persons. He subsequently obtained bail and fled the country on 24 November, making his way back to America via France. Scotland Yard and the American police were in contact many times concerning his flight from France to New York. A detective inspector was supposedly sent to New York at the time, perhaps to pursue Tumblety or to liaise with the American Police, although for what purpose we do not know. Some say it was in connection with the killing. However, I feel inclined to believe it was about terrorism.

Tumblety seemingly evaded capture in New York City once again. However, according to an unconfirmed account, the New York Police traced him to a lodging-house at 79th East 10th Street. Supposedly, they kept watch on him but could not arrest him as there was no evidence of his being involved in the Whitechapel murders and the offence of jumping bail was not one that gave the British Police extradition powers. Tumblety is said to have remained at this address until December and then disappeared yet again. He was not heard of again until 1893, when he turned up at his sister's house.

I firmly believe Tumblety's status of prime suspect is undeserved. His homosexuality would rule him out as a suspect, for homosexual serial killers are concerned solely with male victims and would be uninterested in female prostitutes.

How many victims were there? If there were more than five and Alice McKenzie (killed on 17 July 1889) and Francis Coles (13 February 1891) are included, Tumblety is ruled out, because he fled England in November 1888 and never returned.

In truth, there is no more direct evidence to suggest he was Jack the Ripper than there is for any of the suspects I have looked at so far. After all, if he was a prime suspect wanted for questioning, and if it is true that his whereabouts were known up until December 1888, he could have been arrested and interviewed at some stage before his death. Given that this did not happen, we may assume that in the eyes of the authorities at the time he was not suspected of the Whitechapel murders.

Tumblety died in America in 1903. The property listed for him at the time of death included two imitation gold rings. It was suggested in the press that these were the rings that were ripped from the fingers of Annie Chapman. I suspect this was another story hatched by the newspapers to boost sales.

CHAPTER TWENTY-ONE

JOSEPH BARNETT

At the time of the Whitechapel murders 30-year-old Joseph Barnett was the boyfriend of Mary Kelly and had been living with her at 13 Miller's Court, where she was found murdered. However, at the time of Kelly's murder, he was not living at that address, as they had fallen out and he had moved into nearby lodgings. Nevertheless, it is documented that they were still seeing each other regularly.

Barnett was interviewed about Kelly's murder but gave an alibi that appears to have been accepted by the police at the time. His explanation was that he was playing cards with others at his lodging-house until 12.30am and then went to bed and did not go out again. Lacking any evidence to disprove it, the police had no choice but to accept Barnett's alibi.

However, my instincts tell me that it would be wrong to rule out totally the possibility that Barnett killed Mary Kelly and made it look like she was another victim of Jack the Ripper. Some researchers have gone as far as to say that Barnett could have been Jack the Ripper.

But what motive could he have had? Leaving aside the other murders, the main one that springs to mind in relation to Mary

Kelly is jealousy. They had been carrying on a normal relationship and Kelly, although she had worked as a prostitute, did not do so while they were together.

Barnett was employed in the fish market, but, when he lost his job and was unable to support both of them, Kelly told him she was going to return to prostitution. He was strongly against this. I would by no means discount the possibility that Barnett murdered Kelly out of jealousy as a result of the demise of their relationship and made the killing look as if it was another committed by the Ripper.

However, if my theory that the organs of the previous victims were removed after the bodies were taken to the mortuary, and not at the murder scene by the killer, is accurate, Kelly could have been killed by the person who killed Nichols, Chapman and Eddowes and, possibly, Tabram, McKenzie and Coles.

If my theory is not correct, Kelly was killed by another, possibly Barnett. The thinking behind this is quite simple. Looking back to the medical reports from both the murder scene and the post-mortem, there is no suggestion that any of the body parts that were removed from Kelly were removed by anyone with anatomical skills. These mutilated body parts were found in her room.

So, did Barnett kill Kelly and was he also Jack the Ripper? There are a number of similarities between the two men, but was Barnett the killer? His physical description tallies very well with a number of witness descriptions of men seen with Ripper victims, particularly in terms of height (five feet seven), age (30), build (medium), complexion (fair) and the presence of a moustache.

His link with Mary Kelly could explain why the killings ceased after her murder. However, this is not the case if the Ripper committed either of the two later murders.

Police found ginger-beer bottles in 13 Miller's Court on 9 November. In the 'Dear Boss' letter the author says that he 'saved some of the proper <u>red</u> stuff in a ginger beer bottle over the last job to write with'. However, ginger beer was a popular drink of the day.

There is also the mystery of Kelly's locked door. It was locked when police arrived, which indicates that the killer either had a key or locked the door behind him when he left and took the key with him. We know the key was missing, as the police had to break the door down, although later Barnett stated that, as far as he was aware, the key had gone missing previously. The fact that the door was locked could be explained either by Barnett's still being in possession of a key or by his knowledge of the layout of the room, including the fact that, by reaching through the broken window, one could open the door even if the key was on the inside. However, the same could apply to the killer. It is not known whether Barnett was still in possession of a key to the room despite what he told the police about the key being missing.

It is readily accepted that Kelly took her killer to her room voluntarily after meeting him on the street. But this may not have been the case. What if the killer was prowling the streets, as we know he did? What if he looked through the window, saw Kelly lying asleep on the bed wearing only her underclothes and let himself in by reaching through the window and unlocking the door, then killed her as she slept, as has also been suggested?

In my opinion, Barnett was not Jack the Ripper. However, I cannot totally rule him out as Kelly's killer. But, if he did kill her and it was a crime of passion, would he have mutilated the body of someone he loved to that extent, just to make it look like the work of the Ripper? After all, he could have simply killed her as he had an alibi that would have stood or fallen whether he had killed and mutilated her or only killed her.

If Barnett did not kill Kelly, I am left firmly believing that the same person killed her, Eddowes, Nichols, Chapman and possibly the later victim McKenzie and Tabram. Stride and the other later victim, Coles, could have been killed by separate killers.

Before leaving the Kelly murder, I have an observation to make about the witness George Hutchinson, who told the police he had seen Kelly with a man near to her house and gave them a 'detailed' description. The description did not fit Barnett. Nevertheless, his statement is interesting. Hutchinson seems to have been the last person to see Kelly alive. Inspector Abberline interviewed him, and quite rightly so in my opinion, as the description he had given of the man he saw with Kelly was too accurate to be plausible. He described the man as having a dark complexion and a heavy, dark moustache, turned up at the corners, dark eyes and bushy eyebrows. He was 'Jewish looking'. He wore a soft felt hat pulled down over his eyes, a long, dark coat trimmed with astrakhan and a white collar with a black necktie fixed with a horseshoe pin. He wore dark spats over light, button-over boots. On his waistcoat there was a massive gold chain with a large seal with a red stone hanging from it.

The problem with Hutchinson's account is that at that time and in that location it would have been very dark. He stated that he was standing under a streetlight, but we do not know how far away he was from the man. To take note of so much detail, he would have had to be very close to him.

Hutchinson described seeing a red stone hanging from a large gold chain. All dark colours look the same in half-light, so how could he have been certain it was red? He described the man as wearing a horseshoe pin, but this too would not have been easy to notice unless he was very close to him. Hutchinson said the man's eyes were dark and his eyebrows bushy. As the man and Kelly passed him, the man lowered his head, he said, yet he was still able to describe the colour of his eyes and the form of his eyebrows. It would have been difficult to be sure of either in those conditions. All of these statements would have made me too want to question Hutchinson in greater detail.

After Hutchinson was interviewed, the police were happy to accept his account as correct. Or were they? This was the most savage murder to date and the police had nothing to work on except his statement. Public outrage was growing at the unsolved crimes, but the police would have been able to save face to some extent by saying the description given by Hutchinson was the nearest they had come so far to identifying Jack the Ripper, although I suspect that they thought he could in fact be the Ripper. If the police had dismissed his statement and the press had found out, there would have been more adverse criticism of their work on the case. For this reason, I suspect, they chose outwardly to accept Hutchinson's description but continued to investigate him discreetly.

But, if Hutchinson was the Ripper, why did he come forward with a statement? He had not been seen by anyone else at the murder location, so it would have been sensible for him to keep quiet. Was he really there at that time? Or was he just an attention-seeker who made up this story in an attempt to obtain money from the press? After all, he did not come forward until several days after the murder. He would have known by now that the police had no other witnesses and so his credibility would not be questioned.

Or was he at the location as Mary Kelly's pimp, watching over her? This is highly unlikely, I think. If so, he would have been much closer to her room, would have kept a closer eye on her and would have seen much more than he described. Also, it is well known that prostitutes don't remain long with a client unless they are being paid handsomely. They like to get back on the streets, where they can earn more money. If Hutchinson had been using her, I believe he would have taken steps to get her back on the streets by going and knocking her door.

Was there another reason why he was watching the man and Kelly? Was he intending to rob him when he left Kelly's room? After all, he also stated that after Kelly and the man went off towards her room he hung around for some 45 minutes, until 3am, before leaving. He also stated that at that time he had no money. If his description of the man was correct, the man was plainly wealthy. This makes the motive of robbery a possibility.

All in all, a mystery surrounds George Hutchinson. Very little is known about him and his whereabouts at the time of the other murders are unknown. A number of researchers suggest he was the Ripper. I disagree, as did the police at the time.

CHAPTER TWENTY-TWO

PRINCE ALBERT VICTOR

Royal scandals have fascinated the public of every monarchy, and almost a hundred years after the Whitechapel murders took place Britain had one that revolved around Prince Albert Victor, Duke of Clarence, grandson of Queen Victoria and an heir to the throne. It was suggested that the Prince was either directly involved in the murders or knew who was. Others who have been suggested as being involved in some way include Sir William Gull, the Queen's physician, and John Netley, a royal coachman.

The theory about a conspiracy involving the royal family first surfaced in 1973 in BBC TV's *Jack the Ripper*. The programme's investigators had supposedly solved the Ripper mystery at last, citing a conspiracy and a cover-up at the highest levels of society. The story goes that, while researching the programme, they were told to contact a man named Joseph Sickert, who claimed to know about a secret marriage between Prince Albert and a poor Catholic girl named Alice Mary Crook. Sickert related a strange story involving Prince Albert, Lord Salisbury, Sir Robert Anderson, Sir William Gull and even Queen Victoria herself.

Joseph Sickert was the son of the famous painter Walter Sickert, who told him the story in his later years. The younger Sickert later retracted his account after great pressure was put on him by an unidentified figure or figures. Earlier he had said that his father lived in the East End during the time of the murders and was a close friend of the royal family. The Prime Minister, Lord Salisbury, asked Walter Sickert to take Prince Albert Victor under his wing and look after him. Joseph Sickert's father eventually introduced the Prince to a poor girl named Annie Crook, who worked in a shop in Cleveland Street, in London's West End. The Prince became infatuated with Annie and soon got her pregnant. They set up home together in the East End and were living quite happily with their daughter, Alice, until the Queen discovered her grandson's indiscretion and demanded that the relationship end. Annie was not only a commoner but also a Catholic, and Queen Victoria feared that the prospect of a Catholic heir to the throne would spark a revolution. She ordered Lord Salisbury to resolve the matter quickly and discreetly. He, in turn, allegedly went to Sir William Gull. The couple were traced and Prince Albert Victor was taken away and Annie was taken to one of Gull's hospitals, where he performed experiments on her designed to erase her memory and drive her insane. Their child, however, escaped the raid unharmed with her nanny, Mary Kelly.

Kelly had been a co-worker of Annie's, as well as a model for Sickert, and she became the child's nanny soon after its birth. Knowing that baby Alice was in danger, Kelly hid her with nuns and fled back to the East End. Eventually she told the story to her friends and fellow prostitutes Polly Nichols, Liz Stride and Annie Chapman and the four decided to blackmail the government, as they needed money to pay local protection gangs. When Lord Salisbury learned of the threat of blackmail, he called on Sir William Gull again.

Gull devised an elaborate scheme, based on Masonic ritual, to silence the women. Enlisting the help of royal coachman John Netley, he created Jack the Ripper. Sir Robert Anderson helped cover up the crimes and acted as lookout during the murders, which were carried out by Gull in the royal carriage.

The killing of Eddowes, Joseph Sickert was told by his father, was a mistake. She often used the name of Mary Kelly and it was a case of mistaken identity. Once the truth was known, the real Mary Kelly was found and silenced. The conspiracy closed in upon itself and for some reason Montague Druitt was chosen as a scapegoat to take the blame for the murders and, Joseph Sickert hinted, was himself murdered for it. Alice grew up and later, by an odd series of twists and turns, married Walter Sickert and gave birth to Joseph.

Records show that there was an Annie Crook who worked in a shop in Cleveland Street and had an illegitimate daughter named Alice. However, there is no evidence that Crook knew Kelly.

My enquiries led me to conclude, for various reasons, that this story is pure fiction and that Prince Albert Victor cannot seriously be considered to be a Ripper suspect. Alice Margaret Crook was born on 18 April 1885, which means that her conception must have occurred between 18 July and 11 August 1884. At that time the Prince was 400 miles away in Heidelberg with his German tutor. He arrived there in June and returned to England on 18 August. These facts are confirmed by documents in the Royal Archives at Windsor Castle.

As to the idea of the Prince and Crook having wed, the Royal Marriages Act was still operative and, under this, any marriage between them could have been set aside as illegal, because the Prince was under 25 at the time and had married without the Queen's consent.

I wrote to Her Majesty the Queen informing her that it was my intention to exonerate Prince Albert Victor of being a Ripper suspect for all these years. Subsequently, I was sent documents from the Royal Archives that gave him cast-iron alibis for the murders.

The documents revealed the following facts. In a letter dated 8

August 1888, the Prince of Wales wrote that Prince Albert Victor was laid up in York with gout. At that time, Prince Albert Victor was stationed there with his regiment, the 10th Lancers, and so could not have been involved in the murder of Martha Tabram on 7 August.

Between 31 August and 7 September, the Prince was staying with Viscount Downe at Danby Lodge, in Grosmont, Yorkshire. The murder of Mary Ann Nichols occurred on 31 August.

Between 7 and 10 September, he was at the Cavalry Barracks in York. Annie Chapman was murdered on 8 September.

Between 27 and 30 September, he was at Abergeldie, Scotland, where Queen Victoria recorded in her journal that he lunched with her on the 30th. Stride and Eddowes were murdered between 1 and 2am on that day.

Between 2 and 12 November, he was at Sandringham. Mary Jane Kelly was murdered on 9 November.

On 17 July 1889, when Alice McKenzie was murdered, the Prince wrote in a letter to his brother dated 21 July that he was again in York.

On 13 February 1891, when Frances Coles was murdered, it is documented that he lunched at Marlborough House en route from Osborne House, on the Isle of Wight, to York.

In any event, can we really believe that any member of the royal family, and especially an heir to the throne, would be allowed to do as he pleased to the extent of setting up home in the East End of London with a commoner and living as a normal person?

I also examined the suggestion that Sir William Gull, the Queen's physician, was involved in the murders and that they were committed in the royal carriage. This I can easily discount. The reports from the doctors who examined the victims at the murder scenes all clearly state that they were killed where they were found. If they had been killed in a carriage, their bodies could have been taken to and left in any isolated spot, rather than in places where someone was likely to see them being dumped. In fact, it would have been impossible to drive a carriage to some of the locations where the bodies were found.

Another important fact is that at the time of the murders Sir William Gull was 71 and had suffered a stroke. His physical condition would have rendered him incapable of murdering anyone, let alone mutilating the corpse savagely. He died of a further stroke in 1890.

Is there any other form of evidence to support Joseph Sickert's story? The answer is no. What motive did he have for coming forward with this story? The answer is none, other than perhaps financial gain from the press and television. For the problem with the Whitechapel murders and the huge interest they continue to generate is that someone will always appear out of the woodwork with another suspect or another theory. All of these seem to offer nothing conclusive and no means of corroboration. But, because people all over the world remain fascinated by these horrendous crimes, the media will pounce on any story that promises to finally identify Jack the Ripper.

CHAPTER TWENTY-THREE

JAMES MAYBRICK

In the early 1990s, a diary surfaced in Liverpool that was allegedly written by Jack the Ripper. Since then there have been as many believers as non-believers in the authenticity of the book.

So how did the diary appear after all this time? Its owner was a Liverpudlian, Michael Barrett, who stated that a friend gave him the diary in May 1991 and that this friend died a few months later without having revealed how he came by it. Nothing beyond these sparse facts is known, so extreme caution is called for when trying to establish its authenticity and its contents.

The diary contained confessions ostensibly made by a businessman from Liverpool by the name of James Maybrick, who claimed to be the Whitechapel murderer. Maybrick was a real person, a cotton merchant who visited London frequently on business, but there are insufficient details of his daily movements to indicate where he might have been on the dates of the murders.

On the face of it, the diary had all the signs of being genuine, with pages torn out and passages scribbled out. Yet, when it first came to light, instead of laying to rest for ever one of the greatest criminal cases of the previous century, it did the opposite, leading some self-styled Ripper experts to say it was genuine and others to dismiss it as a forgery.

Experts in the fields of paper and ink who examined the diary stated that the diary was written on paper of the Victorian era and that the ink also could have been of that period. However, when the handwriting of the diary was compared with that of James Maybrick's will, they did not match. Some who wanted to believe that the diary was authentic tried to sidestep this problem by suggesting that the will was a forgery.

In any case, Maybrick's age is wrong for him to have been the killer. At the time of the first murder, he was 50, according to the diary, but none of the witnesses who claimed to have seen a man with a Ripper victim described a man as old as this.

Many people suspected the diary was a modern forgery. Then, in 1995, Michael Barrett issued an affidavit in which he confessed to having forged it with the help of his wife. Later he retracted some of his confessions, but, over the subsequent years, restated them in further affidavits. He claimed that he had been forced by verbal threats and physical assault, which he reported to the police, to retract his original confession. Extracts from the affidavit of 5 January 1995, in which he admitted to forging the diary and explained how it was done, are transcribed below, and I firmly believe this statement to be true.

I MICHAEL BARRETT, make oath and state as follows:—
That I am an Author by occupation and a former Scrap Metal Merchant. I reside alone at XXXXXXXXXXXX....

Since December 1993 I have been trying, through the press, the Publishers, the Author of the Book, Mrs Harrison, and my Agent Doreen Montgomery to expose the fraud of 'The Diary of Jack the Ripper' ('the diary').

Nobody will believe me and in fact some very

influential people in the Publishing and Film world have been doing everything to discredit me and in fact they have gone so far as to introduce a new and complete story of the original facts of the Diary and how it came to light.

The facts of this matter are outlined as follows:–

I Michael Barrett was the author of the original diary of 'Jack the Ripper' and my wife, Anne Barrett, hand wrote it from my typed notes and on occasions at my dictation, the details of which I will explain in due course.

The idea of the Diary came from discussion between Tony Devereux, Anne Barrett my wife and myself, there came I time when I believed such a hoax was a distinct possibility. We looked closely at the background of James Maybrick and I read everything to do with the Jack the Ripper matter. I felt Maybrick was an ideal candidate for Jack the Ripper. Most important of all, he could not defend himself. He was not 'Jack the Ripper' of that I am certain, but, times, places, visits to London and all that fitted. It was too easy.

I told my wife Anne Barrett, I said, 'Anne I'll write a best seller here, we can't fail'.

Once I realised we could do it. We had to find the necessary materials, paper, pens and ink. I gave this serious consideration.

Roughly round about January, February 1990 Anne Barrett and I finally decided to go ahead and write the Diary of Jack the Ripper. In fact Anne purchased a Diary, a red leather backed Diary for £25.00p, she made the purchase through a firm in the 1986 Writers Year Book, I cannot remember their name, she paid for the Diary by cheque in the amount of £25 which was drawn on her Lloyds Bank Account, Water Street Branch, Liverpool. When this Diary arrived in the post I decided it was of no use, it was very small. My wife is now in possession of this Diary in fact she asked for it specifically recently when I saw her at her home address XXXXXXXXXXXXXX. ...

I feel sure it was the end of January 1990 when I went to the Auctioneer, Outhwaité & Litherland, XXXXXXXXXXXXXXXXXXXXXXXXX.

It was about 11.30am in the morning when I attended the Auctioneers. I found a photograph Album which contained approximately, approximately 125 pages of photographs. They were old photographs and they were all to do with the 1914/1918 1st World War. This Album was part of lot No. 126 which was for auction with a 'brass compass', it looked to me like a 'seaman's Compass', it was round faced with a square encasement, all of which was brass, it was marked on the face, North South, East and West in heavy lettering. I particularly noticed that the compass had no 'fingers'. ...

When I got the Album and Compass home, I examined it closely, inside the front cover I noticed a makers stamp mark, dated 1908 or 1909 to remove this without trace I soaked the whole of the front cover in Linseed Oil, once the oil was absorbed by the front cover, which took about 2 days to dry out. I even used the heat from the gas oven to assist in the drying out.

I then removed the makers seal which was ready to fall off. I then took a 'Stanley Knife' and removed all the photographs, and quite a few pages.

I then made a mark 'kidney' shaped, just below centre inside the cover with the Knife.

This last 64 pages inside the Album which Anne and I decided would be the Diary. Anne and I went to town in Liverpool and in Bold Street I bought three pens, that would hold fountain nibs, the little brass nibs. I bought 22 brass nibs at about 7p to 12p, a variety of small brass nibs, all from the 'Medice' art gallery.

This all happened late January 1990 and on the same day that Anne and I bought the nibs we then decided to purchase the ink elsewhere. ...

Anne Barrett and I visited the Bluecoat Chambers Art shop and we purchased a small bottle of Diamine Manuscript ink. I cannot remember the exact price of the Ink. I think it was less than a pound.

... We decided to have a practice run and we used A4 paper for this, and at first we tried it in my handwriting, but we realised and I must emphasise this, my handwriting was too distinctive so it had to be in Anne's handwriting, after the practice run which took us approximately two days, we decided to go for hell or bust. ...

Several days prior to our purchase of materials I had started to roughly outline the Diary on my word processor.

Anne and I started to write the Diary in all it took us 11 days. I worked on the story and then I dictated it to Anne who wrote it down in the Photograph Album and thus we produced the Diary of Jack the Ripper. Much to my regret there was a witness to this, my young daughter Caroline.

During this period when we were writing the Diary, Tony Devereux was house-bound, very ill and in fact after we completed the Diary we left it for a while with Tony being severely ill and in fact he died late May early June 1990.

During the writing of the diary of Jack the Ripper, when I was dictating to Anne, mistakes occurred from time to time for example, Page 6 of the diary, 2nd paragraph, line 9 starts with an ink blot, this blot covers a mistake when I told Anne to write down James instead of thomas. The mistake was covered by the Ink Blot.

Page 226 of the Book, page 20, centre page inverted commas, quote 'TURN ROUND THREE TIMES, AND CATCH WHOM YOU MAY'. This was from Punch Magazine, 3rd week in September 1888. The journalist was P.W. WENN. ...

When I disposed of the photographs from the Album by giving them to William Graham, I kept one back. This photograph was of a Grave, with a Donkey standing nearby. I had actually written the 'Jack the Ripper Diary' first on my word processor, which I purchased in 1985, from Dixons in Church Street, Liverpool City Centre. The Diary was on two hard back discs when I had finished it. The Discs, the one Photograph, the compass, all pens and the remainder of the ink was taken by my sister Lynn Richardson to her home address, XXXXXX XXXXXXXXX. When I asked her at a later date for the property she informed me that after an article had appeared in the Daily Post, by Harold Brough, she had destroyed everything, in order to protect me.

When I eventually did the deal with [the publisher] Robert Smith he took possession of the Diary and it went right out of my control. There is little doubt in my mind that I have been hoodwinked or if you like conned myself. My inexperience in the Publishing game has been my downfall, whilst all around me are making money, it seems that I am left out of matters, and my Solicitors are now engaged in litigation. I have even had bills to cover expenses incurred by the author of the book, Shirley Harrison. ...

I have now decided to make this affidavit to make the situation clear with regard to the Forgery of the Jack the

Ripper Diary, which Anne Barrett and I did in case anything happens to me. I would hate to leave at this stage the name of Mr Maybrick as a tarnished serial killer when as far as I know, he was not a killer.

I am the author of the Manuscript written by my wife Anne Barrett at my dictation which is known as The Jack the Ripper Diary. ...

Yours Truly – Michael Barrett.

Sworn at Liverpool in the
(Signed)
County of Merseyside, this
5th day of January 1995.   Before me: (Signed)

A Solicitor Empowered to Administer Oaths

D.P. HARDY & CO.,
Imperial Chambers,
XXXXXXXXXXXXXX
XXXXXXXXXXXXXX.

It would have been of great interest if the whole issue of the diary had been the subject of a criminal investigation. The police would have had the diary examined by professional experts who could have determined whether it is a forgery. Handwriting samples would have been obtained from those allegedly involved in the creation of the diary, in order to test its authenticity. Even so, as often happens in such situations, others would have tried to refute the findings of the professionals, whatever conclusion they had reached, and we may still have been left in doubt as to the truth.

James Maybrick died in 1889 from arsenic poisoning. His wife was accused of murdering him.

Was Maybrick Jack the Ripper? The answer is no. Did Maybrick write the diary? Again the answer is no. For me, Michael Barrett's affidavit quoted above provides wholly convincing detail of how the alleged diary came to be forged.

CHAPTER TWENTY-FOUR

WALTER SICKERT

German-born Walter Richard Sickert, who settled in London and became a famous artist in his later years, was the father of Joseph Sickert (see Chapter Twenty-Two) and another suspect to emerge more than a hundred years after the Whitechapel murders.

Walter Sickert would have been 28 at the time of the murders. He was closely examined as a suspect in 1993, when the US crime novelist Patricia Cornwell decided to examine him seriously for a book called *Portrait of a Killer: Jack the Ripper, Case Closed*. She saw him a real suspect, though in my opinion this was a questionable conclusion, notwithstanding the integrity of her work.

Cornwell was prompted by the fact that Sickert had been said by his son, in a BBC television programme 20 years earlier, to have been associated with Prince Albert Victor and high-ranking government officials at the time of the murders.

According to Cornwell, in his early years in London Sickert frequented the slums of the East End, where, she stated, he had a number of secret rented studios. This has never been proved, but it is known that he rented studios in Camden Town, north London. Sickert's models for his paintings were supposedly poor, unattractive female prostitutes. One such painting that fuelled

Cornwell's suspicions was *The Camden Town Murder*. There is some similarity between this work and the murder scene of Mary Kelly as photographed by the police. However, this painting and others Sickert painted in the same vein were not painted until many years after the murders and the photograph of the Kelly murder scene would have been readily available by then, as it still is today.

Cornwell's main suspicions, however, arose from her study of the Ripper letters. In many of the letters sent to the police and the press, the sender stated that he hated prostitutes and was ridding the world of them. Cornwell suggested that Sickert also had good reason to hate prostitutes, as his grandmother had been a prostitute working in a dance hall, and her daughter, Sickert's mother, was illegitimate. In Victorian times it was an accepted belief that, if a woman was immoral or a prostitute, she suffered from a genetic defect that could be passed down the bloodline.

Sickert, Cornwell stated, was born with a genetic defect of his penis that required surgery in his adolescence, her suggestion being that this would have prevented him having sexual intercourse and fathering children. She believed therefore that she had strong circumstantial evidence linking Sickert to the Whitechapel murders. In fact, she went so far as to say she suspected he was the Ripper himself. But she knew she would need direct evidence to prove this.

She thought that if she could obtain DNA from letters purporting to be from the Ripper, she could compare them with letters known to have been written by Sickert. It was at this stage, I suggest, that her theory was doomed to fail, for many experts have stated on record that all of the letters were hoaxes. I am sure she must have considered this fact, but, undeterred, she came to London with a team of forensic experts. Here she was given permission to examine the letters now contained in the Public Record Office. However, she discovered that the letters had been heat-sealed under plastic to preserve them, a process that degrades primary DNA. None of the letters had any trace of any DNA, primary or secondary. She then came into possession of a letter that, strangely enough, had not been handed over to the archives and had not been heat-sealed, so was suitable for DNA examination.

An initial test found that the letter had no trace of primary DNA. But it did have something no one had apparently seen before on a Ripper letter or, if they had, they had considered it unimportant. This was a watermark from Perry & Sons, an exclusive stationery manufacturer of the day. In the Sickert archives, Cornwell found that the artist had used the same stationery at the time of the Ripper crimes in 1888. An examination of other archive letters revealed four different watermarks on Ripper letters, which were also found on stationery used by Sickert and his wife during the time of the murders

In an attempt to acquire Sickert's DNA, Cornwell acquired some of his paintings and tore them apart, examining the frames and canvas for fingerprints or traces of blood, but found nothing. It was the same story with his painting table.

After the first test failed to find DNA on the unsealed letter, Cornwell's team decided to conduct a test for secondary, or mitochondrial, DNA. This test did find traces of secondary DNA on the letter. It also found secondary DNA on Sickert's letters, but the DNA was a blend of DNA from many different people. There was a match between the secondary DNA on the Ripper letter and the secondary DNA on the Sickert letters. Cornwell's hopes were somewhat dashed when her DNA expert pointed out that it was probably a mixture of different DNA, which matched a DNA sequence from the Ripper letter. At that time, Cornwell believed that the Sickert and the Ripper mitochondrial DNA did come from the same person. This view was not supported by her experts.

So is there any evidence to refute Cornwell's theory that Sickert was the Ripper? Well, there are uncorroborated reports that Sickert was not even in the country at the time of some of the murders. He is said to have been painting in France between August and October 1888, although Cornwell argues that he was a man of mystery and not even his close friends knew where he was at any one time, but she has produced no positive proof of this. Her theory that Sickert was unable to have sexual intercourse and to father children is not correct, as he had a son, Joseph.

Despite what Cornwell believed, the DNA results she obtained do not conclude that Walter Sickert was the author of the Ripper letters. The findings are that the person whose mitochondrial DNA was found on Sickert's correspondence could not be eliminated from the percentage of Britain's population who could have provided an exact mitochondrial DNA match. Sickert's DNA no longer exists as he was cremated after his death, so this cannot be compared with the DNA found on his correspondence.

I looked at the method and results of the mitochondrial DNA testing used in Cornwell's investigation. Mitochondrial DNA test is widely used by many forensics laboratories for identification and, although it is a secondary test, it is considered as valid a method as primary, or nuclear, DNA testing. The important difference, however, is that it is much less specific and less accurate. Unlike primary DNA, secondary DNA is not unique. The discovery of a mitochondrial DNA match between two samples does not mean that one person left both, but that people from a certain percentage of the population could have left both.

To make it easier to understand, if you compare mitochondrial DNA testing to blood grouping, which police and scientists relied on before DNA came to the fore, if blood was found at the scene of a crime and identified as coming from a specific blood group, this evidence would be only circumstantial as it would be accepted that perhaps 20 per cent of the world's population would have the same blood group. So, a mitochondrial DNA sequence found in Person A may also be found in Persons B and C, regardless of whether or not they are related by blood.

According to Cornwell, her experts calculated that only 1 per cent of the population of Britain at that time could have left the DNA found on the Ripper letter, and that the person whose DNA was found on Sickert's letters was one of that 1 per cent. Other DNA experts disagree and state that the percentage could be anywhere between 0.1 and 10 per cent of the population. Following the census of 1901, it was estimated that there were nearly 40 million people in Britain. This means that, if the mitochondrial DNA on the letter is Sickert's and her experts' figure of 1 per cent is correct, Sickert was one of approximately 400,000 people whose mitochondrial DNA shared those same sequences. If the other experts are correct, he could have been one of four million.

Cornwell's findings are not conclusive evidence and she has failed to produce any evidence that would stand up in a modern court. All she has done is show that Walter Sickert cannot be eliminated from suspicion of having written, or hoaxed, one or more Ripper letters, along with up to four million other residents of Britain at that time who also could have been responsible.

Looking at the watermarks found on both the Ripper and the Sickert letters – A. Pirie & Sons, Joynston Superfine and Monkton's Superfine – Cornwell claimed she could match the watermark to Sickert and Sickert alone, because it matches the lot number that the paper was cut from. Basically, she believed that she had convincing evidence that Sickert wrote at least three or four Ripper letters, although she went as far as to say 90 per cent of the Ripper letters were written by him.

Cornwell also brought with her to England a forensic handwriting expert and, given that she has not produced any evidence from this expert's examination of all the letters in the archives, we can only assume that her suspicions of the percentage of letters written by Sickert are now unfounded. Cornwell has answered this objection by suggesting that Sickert used to disguise his handwriting, but she has produced no evidence to corroborate this. In any event, if Sickert was the killer, and the writer of a number of Ripper letters, why would he disguise his handwriting by writing in different ways? In my experience, some killers do disguise their handwriting but, in order to make sure that the police are aware who the sender is, they stick to one style of disguised handwriting. In any event, if this had been the case here, a good forensic handwriting expert would have been able to match some characteristics from the letters he examined, but, as nothing was forthcoming, I can only assume no letters written in a disguised hand were found.

On the question of the watermarks, there were only around 90 paper mills operating in Britain in the late 1880s. Pirie was one of the largest. Furthermore, while the Joynston and Monkton brands may not have been as popular as Pirie, paper from these two manufacturers is likely to have been used during that era for documents and letters written by a large percentage of the population who could read and write.

So, what do I deduce from Cornwell's research and findings? She set out to prove or disprove some interesting theories and was the first person to use modern forensic science in an attempt to solve the crimes, and for this I admire her.

Many researchers, including me, have wondered whether it was possible to extract useable DNA from any of the documents left behind in the archives. We now know that this is possible, although equally we know that in the absence of samples for comparison any results would be worthless, as turned out to be the case with Cornwell's examinations.

Cornwell's final conclusion was that Sickert could not be totally ruled out as being responsible for writing at least one of the Ripper letters. However, most Ripper experts believe that all of these were hoaxes, so in their view she fails to prove that Sickert was Jack the Ripper or was ever connected with others in committing the murders.

Nor can I find any evidence to convince me that Walter Sickert was involved in any of the murders.

CHAPTER TWENTY-FIVE

WHO WAS JACK THE RIPPER?

I have asked myself many times who the killer was. Was he a tinker, tailor, soldier, sailor, rich man, poor man, beggar man or thief? It is probably true to say that, over the years, representatives of all of these walks of life and many occupations besides have been suspected. I've always believed that, should the truth ever come out, the killer would be revealed as someone who did not fall under suspicion at the time and has not been mentioned by any researcher to date. After investigating the prime suspects and satisfying myself that none of them was Jack the Ripper, this conviction was even stronger.

The experienced investigator sometimes has to go with gut feelings and hunches, and this approach certainly paid many dividends throughout my career as a detective. For a long time I've suspected that Jack the Ripper may have been a merchant seaman. I could find nothing to suggest that the police had pursued this line of enquiry at the time. This was strange and suggested to me that they were perhaps very blinkered in their approach to solving the murders.

After the double murders on 30 September, they should have seen that a pattern was beginning to form. In short, since the docks were so close to the murder locations, they should have looked at the possibility that the killer was a merchant seaman. Between 30

September and 7 November, they had ample opportunity to explore this line of enquiry, and, had they done so, after Mary Kelly's murder they would have been in a position to take positive action in this direction.

To add weight to my suspicion, I came across an unconfirmed newspaper report of a string of murders of prostitutes in Managua, the capital of Nicaragua. These murders supposedly took place within a ten-day period in January 1889. Managua does not have a port for vessels, but the nearby city of Granada does. In Victorian times, smaller merchant vessels from the Caribbean would have been able to sail to Granada up the San Juan River. As can be seen from an article that appeared in *The Times* of 18 February 1889, these killings were identical to the Ripper murders. The newspaper quoted the New York *Sun* of 6 February, which had published a dispatch from Managua dated 24 January:

> Either 'Jack the Ripper' of Whitechapel has emigrated from the scene of his ghastly murders or he has found one or more imitators in this part of Central America. The people have been greatly aroused by six of the most atrocious murders ever committed within the limits of this city. The murderer or murderers have vanished as quickly as 'Jack the Ripper', and no traces have been left for identification. All of the victims were women, and of the character of those who met their fate at the hands of the London murderer. Like those women of Whitechapel, they were women who had sunk to the lowest degradations of their calling. They have been found murdered just as mysteriously, and the evidences point to almost identical methods. Two were found butchered out of all recognition. Even their faces were most horribly slashed, and in the cases of all the others their persons were frightfully disfigured. There is no doubt that a sharp

instrument violently but dexterously used was the weapon that sent the poor creatures out of the world. Like 'Jack the Ripper's' victims, they have been found in out-of-the-way places, three of them in the suburbs of the town and the others in dark alleys and corners. Two of the victims were found with gaudy jewellery, and from this it is argued that the mysterious murderer has not committed the crimes for robbery. In the cases of the other four a few coins were found on the persons, representing no doubt the prospective consideration for the murderer or murderers. All of the victims were in the last stages of shabbiness and besottedness. In fact in almost every detail the crimes and the characteristics are identical with the Whitechapel horrors. ...

As my enquiry intensified, I took a step back to recap the facts that had led me to suspect Jack the Ripper was a merchant seaman. These are:

London's docks were not far from Whitechapel. In any town or city where there are docks there are prostitutes, and sailors and merchant seaman trawl the local streets and alehouses, eager to buy their services after spending many weeks at sea.

Witnesses described the suspect seen with Ripper victims as having 'the appearance of a sailor' or being 'of shabby appearance'. Merchant seamen did not wear naval uniform but whatever clothes they preferred. This could account for the fact that the killer was described by witnesses as wearing slightly different clothing at the various murder locations.

If the killer was a merchant seaman, after each killing he would have found it very easy to get back to the docks unchecked and unnoticed. At weekends, when the murders occurred, there would have been even fewer people than usual around the docks whose suspicions he might have aroused.

He may well have had his own small cabin on a boat and so would have been able to return unnoticed and to clean himself, if bloodstained, without attracting attention. In addition, he would have been able to hide a large knife in his cabin or in his belongings without it being found. This he would have had to do, as most merchant ships had a rule that no weapons were to be kept by crewmembers.

As a lone seaman, he would have had no family with him and he may even have been unmarried. He would have had very few close friends and effectively no one to answer to. For these reasons, he would have had no problem in staying out until the early hours. On a small merchant vessel, the crew would have been small in number, which would have made it easy for him to keep himself to himself without arousing suspicion.

If the murderer was a merchant seaman, this may explain in large part why no information about the killer's identity came out of Whitechapel throughout the murders, despite the major police presence in the area and the huge outcry by the press and public. The police believed the killer to live in Whitechapel and, it appears, never considered the possibility that he was a seaman who was living either on board a ship or in seamen's short-term lodgings nearby.

The dates of the Whitechapel murders could fit in with the voyages of a seaman in respect of both the gaps between the murders over the initial four-month period of killings and the gaps between the later murders of Alice McKenzie and Frances Coles.

I knew this part of the investigation was going to be very complicated. For murder squad officers, with today's substantial resources and manpower, it would be an enormous undertaking, but for one person with no resources it was a frightening prospect. However, undeterred and smiling in the face of adversity, I decided to see what I could uncover.

The scale of my task soon became clear. At the time of the

murders in Whitechapel, there were two docks within walking distance of Whitechapel. These were London Docks and St Katharine's Dock. On any one day there were approximately 40 vessels berthed in these two docks. Each vessel had a crew of probably 25, so there were about 1,000 merchant seaman at any one time in that area alone. There were also other docks further east and just south of the Thames:

East and West India Docks: 3 miles
Royal Victoria and Royal Albert Docks: 5 miles
Surrey Commercial Docks: 3 miles
Tilbury Dock: 23 miles
Millwall Dock: 6 miles
Canal Dock: 3 miles.

Including these gives a total of more than 200 merchant vessels and 5,000 merchant seamen in London on any one day, with new ships coming and going each day.

The Merchant Shipping Act of 1835 required masters or skippers of all ships to file crew lists with the Register Office of Merchant Seamen. This office's indexes of seamen provide a method of tracing the careers of merchant seamen. However, I found out that only the period 1835–57 was covered.

It soon became clear that there were going to be further limitations. First, if a seaman were born before 1780 or after 1843, I was told, the chances of finding his name in these records would be poor. Second, rules were meant to be broken. Some masters did not file the documents, as they were required to do. Some seamen objected strongly to the system and used false names. The handwriting on the documents was often almost illegible and the spelling was often phonetic. All this meant that, should a likely suspect emerge, these registers or other maritime documents would need careful searching, including thorough checking of all possible variations in spelling of names. I knew it would be time-consuming and tiring to search through the material. I knew also that several different series of registers were compiled during the period, all varying slightly in format and in the amount of information they contained, but that a search of these could result in a full service record for a given seaman, including the destinations of his voyages, a physical description of the man and a small amount of biographical detail.

Clearly, it was going to be a daunting task to check all the vessels in all of London's docks and obtain crew lists for every one of them. So I decided at first to narrow my enquiry and look at the two docks nearest to Whitechapel, as it would have been much easier for a merchant seaman to walk the short distance to that area from these docks than to get there from any of the others. I also reasoned that if he were looking for prostitutes to kill, there probably would have been just as many in the areas where the other docks were situated, in which case there would have been no need for him to travel so far. Unless, of course, he had a specific reason for choosing Whitechapel.

So, my first line of enquiry was to try to establish the details of any boats docked in London Docks and St Katharine's Dock on the dates of the murders, to see if any of them were berthed on all the murder dates between August and November 1888. After combing through the records I discovered that between the murders of Martha Tabram on 7 August and Mary Kelly on 8 November three merchant vessels were berthed in the two docks on all the dates. Two of the boats I was able to discount as they were shown as not being operational and had been in the docks for some time without crew.

Extensive enquiries into the third boat revealed that she was a British-registered vessel named *Sylph*, owned by Henry Thomas Bridges of Bristol and in London Dock. The boat's tonnage was 599 and therefore it would have had a small crew of about 20. Captain Notley was shown as being the captain.

Maritime records show that this boat sailed back and forth from the Caribbean. But the important point is that it arrived in Britain on 13 July 1888 (before the Tabram murder) from Barbados and sailed from Britain back to Barbados on 22 November (after the Kelly murder). So, although this was not direct evidence for what I was looking for, it was certainly strong circumstantial evidence to add weight to my theory. At the very least, it puts the crew of that boat in the immediate location of the crimes and at the material times.

The *Sylph* was berthed for a long time, which was unusual for merchant vessels, which normally would unload their cargo and reload within a shorter period. I am also aware that the crews of merchant vessels signed on with a ship for one voyage at a time, at the end of which they could leave and look for another vessel or wait and sign on again with the same vessel.

My enquiries revealed that the *Sylph* had been en route to London when she became disabled through mechanical failure and had to be towed into dock in London. The repairs she needed obviously took longer than expected. At this stage, I could only speculate as to what happened to the crew. Could they have been allowed to stay on board, since the boat would be sailing back to the Caribbean as soon as the repairs were completed? Or did they disperse and take lodgings nearby? Or did they simply sign on with other vessels? At that time, I could find no official records to establish the facts. But, if they had lodged somewhere, it would probably have been near the boat, making it easy for the killer to move back and forth between Whitechapel and their lodgings.

However, if Alice McKenzie was a Ripper victim, this particular theory may be weakened, as this same boat was not in London at the time of her murder on 17 July 1889.

I discovered that, of the crew lists and logs for merchant vessels that had been kept and survived the mass clearout of Britain's

Public Record Office in the 1960s, 70 per cent were held at the Marine Institute of the Memorial University, Newfoundland, Canada. The remaining lists were held at the National Archives in Kew, the National Maritime Museum in Greenwich and local public record offices across Britain.

However, my initial searches at all of these offices failed to locate the crew lists or the logs for the *Sylph* for the voyage to London ending on 12 July 1888 or the voyage from London commencing on 28 November 1888, or indeed any lists from 1887–8.

So near yet so far. Jack the Ripper seemed destined to go on eluding detection. Without the crew lists for those two voyages of the *Sylph*, I would not be able to prove my suspicion that the killer was a merchant seaman and could have been on that boat. However, sometimes during investigations you have to recheck the results of enquiries, and a further visit to Kew revealed one of the missing crew lists for the *Sylph*. This related to the voyage from London in November, after Mary Kelly's murder, and showed that six crewmen had listed their previous boat as the *Sylph*. I now had six potential merchant seaman suspects who had either stayed with the boat or were in the immediate vicinity on all the dates of the murders:

Name	Age	Position
H. Notley	61	Captain
R. Field	31	First mate
P. Rosman	50	Carpenter
A. Jones	26	Steward
E. Byl	60	Cook
J. Johannson	21	Able seaman

If it is accepted that the murders between August and November were the work of the same killer, in theory, the killer could have been one of these men, as the *Sylph* was in London during that period, although age most likely rules out the three eldest. The possibility that any of these six men were on other boats docked in London at the time of Alice McKenzie's murder cannot be proved or disproved. In any case, a question mark hangs over whether she was, in fact, a Ripper victim.

On the question of the reported murders in Nicaragua, I sent out numerous letters and emails in an effort to confirm whether these actually took place or the story was invented by the press. I managed to enlist the help of a member of staff of the British Embassy just outside Managua, Bruce Gallow, who obtained for me names of several officials in the government and police who could possibly help me. Letters and emails were sent to them to try to obtain information on the murders.

Whether these took place or not, I established that all the crew of the *Sylph* could be eliminated from my enquiries as the ship's log showed that it was nowhere near Nicaragua at the time. I received no reply from Managua; nor had I expected to. Long politically unstable, Nicaragua has priorities above looking into matters that occurred there over a hundred years ago. I have to keep an open mind but the fact that the only mention of the alleged murders was in a newspaper leads me to suspect that they did not occur after all. Alternatively, somehow they could have become mixed up with the murders in Britain.

Having obtained some corroboration of my initial line of enquiry, I felt sure there was more to uncover. So I decided to expand my investigation and look at 'all' London's docks in much greater detail. Here a lovely lady by the name of Ruth Wareham from the Marine Institute in Newfoundland proved invaluable. She provided me with maritime records and information in connection with this part of my enquiry and shaped its final outcome.

My enquiry revealed that, in the Royal Victoria Dock on all the murder dates from August to November and on 17 July 1889, two much larger merchant vessels were docked. The first was the British-registered *Silvertown*, which arrived from Spithead, off

Portsmouth. There were no crew lists for this period or for 1889, but no doubt the *Silvertown*'s crew would have been British. It appears that between August and November she did not move from that dock and I am sure that, as with the *Sylph*, a token crew would have been kept on board, probably no more than ten. Who they were, we may never know.

The second boat was another British-registered vessel, the *Diogenes*, which had arrived from Southampton. This boat was docked in London on all the murder dates in 1888, but not in July 1889. Like the *Silvertown*, she did not leave the dock between those dates, and I suggest that she too kept a token crew on board, possibly ten strong, although again there were no crew lists for this boat.

Further enquiries showed that there were two further large merchant vessels in the same docks. The *Kangaroo* and the *Calabria* were both also there on the 1888 murder dates. Both vessels either came from Egypt or were bound for Egypt; the records are not clear on this point. Nor could I find crew lists for either vessel. But, again, I suggest that a small number of crew members would have been retained. So, out of hundreds of boats in all of the London docks, I was able to narrow my list down to four, all in the Royal Victoria Dock. And from those four boats there would have been approximately 40 merchant seamen who were likely to have been in London on the murder dates, any one of whom could have been Jack the Ripper. Had the crew lists been available, some of these men would have been eliminated from suspicion because they were considerably older than the man described by witnesses.

A more detailed examination of the capital's dock records revealed a regular movement of small German merchant vessels in and out of London Docks and St Katharine's Dock. The records also showed that, on the dates of all the murders up to and including that of Frances Coles on 13 February 1891, there were German merchant vessels in one or other of these docks. However, at the time it appeared that none of these were docked here on all of the murder dates.

These German vessels that used either of the two docks travelled back and forth between London and either Hamburg or Bremen and each would have had a crew of around 20 men. Below I have set out the cases where these boats' stays in London correspond with the murder dates, and in doing so I suggest that the Ripper could have been on one of them on one, some or all of these dates.

7 August 1888	*Reiher* (Bremen)	*Silvia* (Hamburg)
31 August	*Reiher* (Bremen)	*Vesta* (Hamburg)
8 September	*Nerissa* (Hamburg)	*Sperber* (Bremen)
30 September	*Sperber* (Bremen)	*Olivia* (Hamburg)
7 November	*Reiher* (Bremen)	*Falke* (Bremen)
		Nerissa (Hamburg)
17 July 1889	*Reiher* (Bremen)	*Olivia* (Hamburg)
		Schwann (Bremen)
13 Feb 1891	*Falke* (Bremen)	*Adler* (Bremen)

The movements of these boats from Bremen or Hamburg suggest that, had the killer arrived in London on one or more of them, he would have had the time and the opportunity to commit some or all of the murders.

But first I had to locate the crew lists for these vessels and their voyages, to establish which seamen, if any, were here on all of the murder dates. This was going to be another difficult task. My enquiries revealed that no records of German vessels or the crew lists were kept in this country. So, once again, the enquiry became global as I checked sources as far afield as Nicaragua and Jamaica. The *Nerissa*, *Vesta* and *Olivia* turned out to have belonged to Adolph Kirsten of Hamburg, but no crew lists for these boats for the relevant times were still in existence.

The *Reiher*, *Sperber*, *Albatross*, *Falke* and *Adler* were all steamships belonging to the Norddeutscher Lloyd Line and all were registered in Bremen. Crew lists for these vessels were still in existence in

Bremen, and I obtained copies but found some of them incomplete. Unlike crew lists for British vessels, which showed a crewman's name, age, place of birth and previous boat, the lists from Bremen showed only the name, previous boat and occupation on the present boat.

These crew lists showed that the majority of the crew of these vessels were German and that the majority were present when the vessels were in London on all the murder dates. Interestingly, some of the lists showed that a small number of British seamen were taken on as crew.

However, because the lists did not give the ages or other personal details of the crew, I was not able to eliminate any of them from suspicion. Had I been able to obtain this information, a considerable number of the crew could have been eliminated from suspicion because of age alone. In addition, as the majority of the crewmen were German, I could not establish their grasp of English. This is something that a police inquiry could have done at the time. Some of the crew, if they were unable to speak the language, would have been eliminated as suspects.

The German connection seemed to be even stronger when I came across a press report of an undetected murder of a female that occurred in October 1889 in Flensburg, which at the time was a German Baltic port used by merchant vessels from Bremen and Hamburg. The female victim appears to have been a prostitute, and this killing had all the hallmarks of the Ripper murders.

There are additional factors that I see as lending further weight to my suggestion that Jack the Ripper could have been a merchant seaman.

First, the question of age. Unfortunately, I do not have full details of the various crewmembers of these German vessels, or of crewmembers of the vessels that used the docks previously investigated. However, it is safe to assume that some seamen from all of the vessels would have met the age criteria suggested by witness testimony.

Second, description. A merchant seaman of the time would have dressed mainly in work clothes or clothes that were shabby, and his dress would probably have led to his being taken for a seaman. The witnesses describe a man who looked like a sailor and was of shabby appearance.

Third, motive. A merchant seaman would probably have not been married and is therefore likely to have used the services of prostitutes. He may well have visited Whitechapel before for this purpose and perhaps contracted a sexually transmitted disease from a prostitute. If so, he may have returned to the area to seek his revenge on her personally, or to take out his anger on prostitutes in general. This motive could also explain why there was no direct evidence to suggest that sex had taken place between the victims and their killer.

Fourth, opportunity. A merchant seaman whose vessels repeatedly used London's docks, particularly those closest to Whitechapel, would probably have known the area very well. I have further suggested that the killer was in London, as a crewman on a German-registered vessel, on all the murder dates.

Fifth, the FBI profile. Although, as I said earlier, I have my doubts about the value of profiling, there are certain elements of the FBI's profile that could suggest a merchant seaman. Let's consider these again.

'In childhood there was an absent or passive father figure.' Many seamen came from poor families. Boys as young as 12 joined the merchant navy. A lot of sailors never knew their fathers.

'The killer probably had a profession in which he could legally experience his destructive tendencies.' Merchant seamen have always had to be rough and tough to survive in the often harsh environment of the sea. In addition, the majority of merchant seamen in those days were men looking to escape the clutches of the law, some of whom would have been violent and some perhaps murderers.

'Jack the Ripper probably ceased his killing because he was either arrested for some other crime, or felt himself close to being discovered as the killer.' Up until noe we don't know what became of Jack the Ripper. If he was a seaman, perhaps in his travels he was arrested and sent to the colonies, as happened then, or perhaps he committed a crime in some faraway country and was sentenced to a long term of imprisonment. Either fate would have prevented him from killing again. As for the killer's fearing that he was nearing detection and for this reason ceased his killing, I said earlier that I discount this because it is not the way serial killers think. To digress from the FBI's assessment, it may have been that he contracted a sexually transmitted disease which, without treatment, killed him. Whoever he was, I suspect that he did not die of old age.

'The killer probably had some sort of physical defect, which was the source of a great deal of frustration or anger.' As I don't have a specific suspect, I cannot speculate on his physical or mental condition.

I accept that up until now I have not been able to solve the Whitechapel murders. However, given all the circumstantial evidence I have uncovered to corroborate my suspicion that Jack the Ripper may have been a merchant seaman – evidence I consider much stronger than any of the evidence there is against the other suspects I investigated in this book – I feel I have put forward a plausible case.

Had I been conducting this part of the enquiry back in 1888, I would most certainly have questioned at great length all the seamen from the vessels mentioned, in an attempt to trace their movements on the dates of the murders. Had the police at the time conducted their enquiries correctly, they too could have found out the same information as I did. In fact, even more information would have been available to them than there was to me about the vessels' movements and the names and other details of crewmembers. It would have been an easy police operation to task a squad of officers to wait for the German boats I have listed to return to London and then board and start enquiries before the crew were allowed ashore. In addition, a search of crewmembers' belongings may have revealed a long, sharp knife in the possession of one of them. Such a discovery would have narrowed down the list of likely suspects to a very small number, who could then have been questioned in much greater detail. And, who knows, perhaps the investigation would have culminated in the capture of the Ripper. However, as we know, the world is full of ifs and buts and if onlys.

CHAPTER TWENTY-SIX

THE FUTURE

Would Jack the Ripper ever be positively identified? Over the past ten years, new facts have emerged about the case and new information has been gathered by criminological scientists. During this time there has been more serious research conducted on the mystery of the Ripper than at any other time since the case was officially closed. Many researchers still speculate on why this decision was taken within two months of Mary Kelly's murder and the case was never reopened, not even when two more, similar murders came to light later on.

Plainly, the police had their reasons. I suggest one reason could have been the huge cost of having so many officers working on the murders. All the extra manpower would have had to be paid for out of police funds, which would have been stretched to the limits. Indeed, this same problem arises today, with local forces having to secure extra funding from the government for protracted murder cases.

When there were no more killings within that two-month period following Kelly's murder, it may have been decided to scale down the inquiry, leaving only a handful of officers to continue with it. This is still normal practice nowadays, and there is a logic to it.

I must say that up until now it was debatable whether the case would ever be solved. If, as some researchers suggest, the police did solve it but for some reason kept the killer's identity a secret, I believe the odds are good that the answer would be rediscovered. Unfortunately, I do not believe that the police did solve the case. It is clear they had suspicions but no one has ever been convicted on mere suspicion, and, whatever these suspicions were, they were not fully documented at the time.

When the later murders occurred in 1889 and 1891, the police, I imagine, did not relish the thought of chasing shadows again, after carrying out their initial enquiries into the murders. I think they did not want to cause fear and panic once again, so they chose not to publicly link the later murders to Jack the Ripper, despite the obvious similarities that I have highlighted.

As I stated earlier, I firmly believe that there are case papers and other documents relating to the murders still in existence somewhere. What they contain, only time will tell; if they ever come to light at all. Tantalisingly, it could be that missing material is gathering dust in a loft or cupboard of a distant relative of one of the main investigators.

The challenge to find answers is now far greater as today's researchers must find new evidence rather than unearth what has been lost, as I set out to do at the start of my investigation. As to the extent of the papers that have been lost or destroyed, we cannot tell. Supposedly, most of the City of London Police files were lost in the Blitz during the Second World War. What remains of the Metropolitan Police files is available to the public but the files are sparse and reveal nothing that has not been widely known for many years. Some claim that the files were purposely destroyed to keep the murderer's identity a secret. Others suggest that important case papers were stolen from the files and are now in the hands of a collector. I know that the Metropolitan Police believe this is what happened, and I was asked by them if I knew anyone who had a collection of case papers. Even if this theory is correct, I suspect that the material may not contain the identity of the killer. Even if it does, whoever has it would surely have wanted to reveal the Ripper's identity after all these years, particularly since, owing to the passage of time, they would not be liable to criminal prosecution for being in possession of old police documents obtained by criminal means.

When Inspector Abberline, one of the main Ripper investigators, was interviewed at home in 1903, the journalist noted that official files surrounded the retired Scotland Yard inspector. Police officers in those days were not averse to taking files home, so it may well be that case files from serving police officers of the day are still in existence. This could be one reason why the main Scotland Yard files contain very little information.

The truth about the 'missing' documents may be far more pedestrian and unromantic. Over the years when original documents could be physically examined in the Public Record Office, it was easy for documents to be removed from the files as souvenirs. As a result, the remaining documents were put on microfilm. In Victorian times, when filing space was required, clerks would often simply dump old files by the armful.

Did senior police officers know the identity of the killer? I think not, as in all murder cases the main investigation is done by rank-and-file officers. Any leads or major revelations would have emanated from these officers, making it more difficult for senior officers to cover up, and, in any event, had this happened I am sure this fact would have been made public at some stage since then. Someone would have talked: everyone has a price.

Besides, as I noted earlier, Inspector Abberline stated in later years that at the time of the murders he had no suspicions. In later years, he mentioned his suspect George Chapman, but provided nothing concrete to support his suspicion. Other senior police officers, years after the case was closed, had their own favoured suspects, but they, like Abberline, did not offer evidence. My belief is that throughout the series of murders all police officers remained completely in the dark as to the identity of the killer.

Was there a cover-up at the highest level of government? This is highly unlikely. The only way it could have happened is if the killer was an important figure in society and his identity had been made known only to a select few and subsequent measures had been taken to ensure that he did not kill again. In this case, the Home Secretary, Henry Matthews, the Commissioner of the Metropolitan Police, Sir Charles Warren, and the Prime Minister, Lord Salisbury, would have been the only ones in a position to be party to a cover-up.

The letters I have examined from Queen Victoria suggest that she wrote several times to Lord Salisbury of her concern about the murders. So, if there was a cover-up, it stopped short of involving the Queen, but the protagonists played a dangerous game.

Of course, if a cover-up did occur it could explain why my enquiries revealed that the Public Record Office holds no correspondence between any of these figures on the Whitechapel murders. However, I don't believe there was a cover-up. The dearth of correspondence could be because, as I have suggested, there were no suspects, no clues and no evidence at the time of the murders. And, if the police were in the dark, the Home Secretary and the Prime Minister would have been even more in the dark. This idea is borne out by the new documents I unearthed that relate to November 1888, after the majority of the murders had been committed.

Having examined closely all aspects of these murders, I could find no evidence to suggest that any of the main suspects that I investigated was Jack the Ripper. After all these years, I think the time has come to let the dust settle forever on these suspects and to allow them to rest in peace. Yet I fear this will not happen, for there are still many people throughout the world who are obsessed with Jack the Ripper. I am sure they will continue to look at all these same suspects for many years to come, refusing to accept reality. Nevertheless, I am convinced they would do better to channel their efforts into seeking out new suspects, as I have done.

In conclusion, I believe I can claim to have cast serious doubt on some of the accepted facts that have been a part of the Ripper mystery for many years. Beyond this, I have introduced a new type of suspect through a new line of enquiry and, in so doing, have added a new chapter to one of the most intriguing cases ever seen in the history of murder investigation.

Like others, I would continue to search for that elusive piece of evidence that will write the final chapter to the Ripper story. As far as investigation by the police is concerned, the case is closed. I have been officially told this, and that it will never be reopened. For me, this simply brings to mind that famous saying, 'Never say never', which proved to be a wise maxim.

CHAPTER TWENTY-SEVEN

CASE CLOSED

For several years during the course of my investigation, I wondered if it would ever be possible to use 21st-century technology to solve the Whitechapel murders and identity Jack the Ripper. Back in 1888, of course, DNA testing and fingerprinting had not been invented, and any exhibits originally retained by the police have now been lost for ever, along with a mountain of valuable documents. So, up until now, I have just had to wonder.

However, I was aware of new technology which might be invaluable in taking my investigation even further than the traditional methods could have done. To date, no one had considered the possibility that this technology might finally identify Jack the Ripper. I'm talking about a computer program aptly named HOLMES, which is short for Home Office Large Major Enquiry System. This helps law-enforcement organisations to manage the complex process of investigating serious crimes. By enabling the police to improve their effectiveness and productivity in crime investigations, it helps them to solve crimes more quickly and improve detection rates. HOLMES is currently used by all UK police forces in the investigation of all murders, serious crimes and major incidents, and is an invaluable tool. Since 1986, it has been an integral part of the incident room in all major police inquiries.

So what led to the emergence of HOLMES? Long before computers were used in murder incident rooms, everything was done on paper. The incident room would be manned by a number of officers working under an incident-room officer, usually a detective inspector. A senior investigating officer, normally a detective chief superintendent, would lead the overall inquiry. Rank-and-file officers would assist in the incident room. The same staff structure is still used today.

Each of the officers in the incident room would be allocated specific tasks. One such job would be reading every statement taken by officers working on the outside inquiry teams. In each statement, incident-room officers would highlight relevant details such as descriptions and names of persons and details of motor vehicles. In fact, if the statement reader was experienced, nothing would go unrecorded. The statement would then be handed to an indexer, whose task was to enter manually all the highlighted details into a card-index system. Next, the statement would go to an action officer, who would read it and decide if further action was needed. For example, if a witness in a murder investigation stated that at the date and time of the murder he or she was at home with their spouse, a statement from the spouse would be needed to corroborate this assertion. This new action would take the form of a numbered written statement and the task of obtaining it would be allocated to an officer engaged in outside enquiries. A copy of the original statement would also accompany this document. Once the additional statement had been obtained, it would be sent to the incident room and be card-indexed.

Although this procedure had proved reasonably successful for many years, it had its limitations in the shape of human error in the indexing, the reading and the subsequent evaluation of the evidence by the senior investigating officer.

The card-index system's flaws and the consequent need for a

more efficient method were underlined by the case of the 'Yorkshire Ripper', Peter Sutcliffe, who was convicted of murdering 13 women between 1976 and 1981. All of these murders were committed within the jurisdiction of the same police force, which set up a separate incident room at the location of each murder. As the number of killings grew, along with an increase in the volume of statements coming into each incident room, the staff working in every one of the rooms were under severe pressure.

At the height of the investigation, the rooms were all operating independently, with no direct link between their respective card indexes. As a result, it was hit-and-miss whether any direct information was exchanged, and valuable evidence was overlooked which would have led the police to the killer much sooner. Sadly, Sutcliffe went on to kill other women before he was finally caught and imprisoned. In the light of both this and the fact that computers were rapidly becoming more accessible and widely used, the UK's police service wanted to reassess its strategies for dealing with major inquiries.

I had worked with HOLMES previously and was well aware of its capabilities. Now, as I investigated the Ripper murders, there were two burning questions. First, could HOLMES help me? The answer was definitely yes. The second question was: could I gain access to HOLMES? The program, developed by Unisys, is used by all of the country's police forces under strict licence and is available only to law-enforcement and government agencies. Nevertheless, with everything to gain and nothing to lose, I made a direct approach to Unisys's UK office in Uxbridge. To my surprise, initially they were very enthusiastic about my proposal and the thought of HOLMES being used to further my investigation. However, following many lengthy discussions, and after they had given me permission to use the system, they did a U-turn and withdrew their consent.

I felt it was a crying shame that the world had been deprived of the possibility that modern-day technology might help to solve a series of gruesome murders that has fascinated and horrified people all over the globe for more than a century. However, what followed both made the use of HOLMES academic and saved me a lot of time and money.

Losing the chance to use HOLMES was a bitter pill to swallow and for a while I did not even bother thinking about Jack the Ripper. But the mystery was like a magnet drawing me back and I kept thinking I may have overlooked something vital. So, once again, I took out all the case papers and documentation I had gathered and went back to the old-fashioned investigative method of manually checking and rechecking as I evaluated the results of my investigation to date.

Before long, I had several major breakthroughs. The first related to the German merchant ships previously mentioned. My initial inquiry showed that one which was of particular interest, the *Reiher*, was not shown as being docked in London on 8 September 1888, the date of Annie Chapman's murder. But one of my new lines of enquiry revealed that the *Reiher* left Bremen on 5 September bound for London and was involved in a collision on the Thames and immobilised; it was never actually officially recorded as being berthed in the docks but appears to have been anchored somewhere along the river. So it could have been possible for the crew to go ashore while waiting for the ship to be repaired.

The *Reiher* then returned to Bremen, where it was taken out of service for a short time for further repairs. Meanwhile a vessel from the same line named the *Sperber* sailed from Bremen shortly afterwards and was berthed in London on 30 September, the date of the 'double event' when Elizabeth Stride and Catherine Eddowes were murdered. The *Sperber* then returned to Bremen. In the meantime, the *Reiher* had been repaired and continued sailing back and forth between the two ports. It was in London on 8 November, the date of Mary Kelly's murder, and on 17 July 1889, when Frances Coles was killed. This new information, I suggest, adds further weight to the theory that Jack the Ripper could have been a German merchant seaman and quite possibly could have been on board the *Reiher*.

Still working on that belief, and in the knowledge that there had been murders in other parts of the world – for example, Nicaragua and Flensburg in Germany – the dates of which suggested that the same killer could have been responsible for all of these murders, taking into account the fact that none of the murders overlapped, all had similar characteristics and all fitted into a pattern which could be consistent with their having been committed by a traveller, possibly a merchant seaman, I continued with the investigation. My efforts were soon to be rewarded handsomely.

I expanded my initial lines of enquiry to see if any other Ripper-like murders had occurred outside of the parameter of the dates I had already looked at in respect of other countries. I discovered murders of women in Germany, committed after the previously mentioned murder in Flensburg in October 1889 and after the cessation of the original series of murders in Whitechapel. All were very similar to the Whitechapel series. I also uncovered similar murders in the USA, again after the Whitechapel murders. These were in addition to the murder of Carrie Brown in New Jersey in 1891, which I had already investigated.

These murders are set out below in chronological order. They all have a very similar MO and fit into a significant time pattern, and all remain undetected save for one, which would become very significant and subsequently lead to the identification of Jack the Ripper. For continuity and to highlight the similarities and timescale and the link between the Whitechapel murders, and those in Germany and the USA, I have also included details of the Carrie Brown murder. The details of the murders are given in most cases as reported in newspapers of the day. There are no known police files still in existence that refer to them.

• 11 April 1890 Hurley, Wisconsin, USA. Murder of Laura Whittlesay, AKA Lottie Morgan. Wisconsin's *Northern Star* reported: 'Hurley was last night the scene of a murder that equals in horror any of the Whitechapel crimes. Early this morning the body of Laura Whittlesay, alias Lottie Morgan, a woman of the demi monde, was found in the rear of Ives' saloon, the toughest place in town. Over the right eye was a deep, long cut which caused her death. An axe was discovered with bloodstains upon it in a shed near by. This was undoubtedly the weapon used by the murderer. A revolver identified as belonging to the victim was found near her head. None of the chambers were empty. Several valuable diamond rings and other jewellery and over $20 in cash were found on the body showing conclusively that the deed was prompted by other motives than robbery. The Morgan woman was last seen about eleven o'clock in John Sullivan's saloon, from whence she started up an alley towards her rooms. The murderer was probably lying in wait for her and struck her and left her as she fell. The only explanation offered at all plausible is that she was killed by a jealous lover of whom she had quite a number. The police say there is no clue to the perpetrator of the ghastly crime. Lottie Morgan was a favourite actress here in the balmy days of Hurley variety theatres but has since fallen to the lowest depths.'

A Bessemer, Michigan, newspaper reported on the day of the murder:

'Lottie Morgan, who was about twenty-seven years old and belonged to the demi monde, was found murdered behind a saloon in Hurley this morning, Her head was split open, cut off and awfully mutilated with an axe. The police are working on a clue. This is a Jack the Ripper case.'

This crime remains undetected.

• 28 April 1890, Benthen, Germany. A German newspaper reported: 'Another frightful atrocity, similar to those committed by

Jack the Ripper, was reported from Benthen, a German town on the Polish frontier. The body of a woman was found behind the Military hospital in that town. The abdomen had been cut open from the navel down, and the rest of the body subjected to savage mutilations, including the face, which was subjected to the same mutilations as those inflicted on Mary Kelly's face. The victim was identified as the wife of a local tailor.'

This crime remains undetected.

• 4 December 1890, Berne, Switzerland. It was reported: 'This city has been startled by a crime similar in many respects to those committed by Jack the Ripper in Whitechapel District in London. As some men were passing through a forest in the vicinity of this city today they discovered the body of a young peasant girl who had been murdered and mutilated in a most shocking manner. There is no clue to the murderer.'

This crime remains undetected.

• 24 April 1891, Jersey City, USA. Murder of Carrie Brown. It was reported: 'Carrie Brown, an elderly prostitute, checked into the East River Hotel New Jersey, on the southeast corner of Catherine Slip and Water Streets, with a man between 10:30 and 11:00 on the night of April 23rd. Her lifeless body was discovered lying on the bed the next morning, naked from the armpits down, according to the night clerk who found her. Her body was mutilated, she had wounds to her lower abdomen, her vaginal area and she had been strangled with a piece of cloth. The doctor who performed the autopsy, named Jenkins, is said to have thought that the killer had attempted to completely gut his victim.'

As I have previously mentioned, a man was later charged and sentenced for this murder but was freed on appeal after being found totally innocent. This leaves the murder undetected.

• 25 October 1891, Berlin, Germany. *The Times* of London reported the following day: 'The population of Berlin has today been thrown into a ferment by the report of a murder which in many of its details resembles the crimes of Jack the Ripper. It appears that a woman named Nitsche was accosted last night in the Holzmarkt Gasse, a small street in the northern part of the city, by an individual who accompanied her to a cellar dwelling in the same street kept by a married couple named Poetsch. The house was not the dwelling of the woman in question, but was only made use of by her from time to time. Almost as soon as the woman entered the room in the house she was attacked by the man accompanying her. The murderer, it would appear, first severed his victim's throat, and afterwards cut open the body from the throat downwards. Just at this moment a second woman, named Mueller, who also made use of the room, arrived, and attempted to open the door. As soon as she did so, the murderer forced his way past her, pushed aside Poetsch, who had been aroused from sleep by the victim's scream, and gained the street. A man who accompanied the woman Mueller gave chase, but failed to catch him. As soon as the police arrived an examination of the apartment was made, but with little result. The victim was lying on the ground fully dressed, and from the ferocity with which the deed had been accomplished it would almost seem as if the murderer was a person of unsound mind.

'Two knives were also found belonging to Frau Poetsch, the proprietress of the house, which had undoubtedly been made use of by the murderer. The police are, however, of opinion that these weapons were only used to make the second wound, and that the first, the one on the throat, was inflicted by a dagger-like knife which the murderer must have had in his possession, and which he took with him. The fact that the man accosted a number of other women of the same class before meeting with the woman Nitsche excludes the idea of the deed being one of personal revenge. The low class to which the woman belonged also puts the idea of robbery out of the question. This morning Baron von Richtofen, President of Police, issued a notice offering a reward for the apprehension of the assassin, who is described as being about 20 years of age, of middle height, and slightly built, with blonde hair and moustache.'

This crime remains undetected.

• 31 January 1892, New Jersey, USA. Murder of Elizabeth Senior. The victim was a 73-year-old woman named Elizabeth Senior who was found murdered in her own home, close to the Carrie Brown murder scene in 1891. Mrs Senior's throat had been cut and she had been stabbed repeatedly. The killer apparently washed the blood from his hands before ransacking the house.

This crime remains undetected.

• 3 April 1892. Berlin, Germany. It was reported: 'This city was agitated today by the announcement of a supposed ¡Jack the Ripperî murder. The body of a prostitute was found strangled on the staircase of a house near the police bureau in Kaiser Wilhelmstrasse. The murderer had apparently been disturbed while at his work and compelled to escape before he had time to mangle the woman.'

This crime remains undetected.

• 31 August 1894, New York. Murder of Juliana Hoffman. This murder was the most interesting. It occurred close to those of Carrie Brown and Elizabeth Senior, but the most significant point is that the perpetrator was apprehended while attempting to flee the scene moments after committing the murder. He was found with traces of blood on his hands. The murder weapon, a long knife with a six-inch, highly sharpened blade, was found near by and when examined by a doctor revealed traces of what was believed to be the victim's blood. When a later search of the suspect's room was conducted, police found a cloth bag, which they suggested was the bag in which the knife had been kept. Also found in the room was a whetstone for sharpening knives.

The arrested man was later convicted and sentenced to death for this murder. After losing his appeal, he was executed in the electric chair in Sing Sing Prison on 27 April 1896. The killer's name was Carl Feigenbaum. He was known to have used various aliases in his travels around the USA, including 'Anton Zahn', and indeed it was suggested that this may have been his real name. Another alias he was believed to have used was 'Carl Zahn'.

On closely examining this particular case and the information I subsequently discovered on Feigenbaum, and all the facts I had gathered through my protracted inquiry into the Whitechapel murders, I came to suspect that this man could be the elusive Jack the Ripper.

The details of Juliana Hoffman's murder and the subsequent trial of Carl Feigenbaum are set out below. They are taken from official court transcripts and from the judgment of the appeal court judge, all of which I subsequently obtained.

First is the appeal court judge's judgment, delivered after Feigenbaum's trial and conviction, which gives details of the murder and the defendant's original defence: 'On the night of Friday, August 31, 1894, in a house on Sixth Street in the city of New York, the deceased, Juliana Hoffman, a widow fifty-six years of age, was in the house with her son Michael, a boy sixteen years old, in two rooms on the first floor over a store of a building on Sixth Street, near Avenue A, in the city of New York. Carl Feigenbaum, a German, who came to this country in 1891, a gardener by occupation, having no family here, and, prior to the homicide, had drifted about in the city of New York and vicinity, occasionally getting employment, but having no steady work, and was poor and often without means. He had lodgings from time to time at various places, sometimes paying in part therefor, and in other cases staying for a few days at a place and leaving without paying the sum agreed. On Wednesday, August 29, 1894, he applied to the deceased for a room, and arranged with her that he should occupy the back room of the two rooms of her apartment for a sleeping room, he to pay therefor one dollar a week, and Mrs. Hoffman was to furnish him breakfast, for which he was to pay her eight cents for each meal. He occupied the back room on Wednesday and Thursday nights, and on Friday evening, about ten o'clock, went to his room, which opened out of the front room, leaving the deceased and her son therein. During Friday evening, while the three were together in the front room, the deceased took from a closet in that room, which was left unlocked, a small pocket book and left the house to purchase some bread for her and her son's supper, and on her return placed the pocket book in the closet again. After the defendant had returned to his room the deceased and her son went to bed, the mother sleeping on a lounge on one side of the room near one of the two front windows, the son sleeping on a couch at the foot of, and at right angles to, the lounge. The son was the only person who was an eyewitness to anything which occurred between the defendant and the deceased prior to the homicide. He was awakened about midnight, or a little after, by a scream from his mother. He then saw the defendant standing by the side of the lounge, with a knife in his hand, facing the deceased, who had partly raised herself up on the lounge. The son kicked at him and got out of bed, and the defendant then turned towards him with the upraised knife. The son fled to the front window furthest from the lounge, got out backward and stood upon the cornice of the building and cried ìmurder, police.î He testifies that he put his head into the room and saw the defendant strike his mother with the knife in the neck. His cries alarmed the neighbourhood, and a policeman and other persons ran towards the house. The defendant was then seen coming out of an alley at the side of the house on Sixth Street, having on a shirt or undershirt and trousers, but having no hat or shoes on and soon commenced to run, but was pursued and overtaken by the officers and brought back to the house and into the room, the scene of the homicide. The deceased was found lying on the floor near the lounge, bleeding from an incised wound in the neck, apparently unconscious, and she died shortly after. A witness who lived in a house overlooking the alley, hearing the alarm given by the son, went to the window of her room looking upon the rear of the house occupied by the deceased, and saw the defendant on the roof of an outbuilding adjacent to the bedroom which the defendant had occupied, from which he clambered down into the alley before spoken of. On searching the alley a short time after the defendant's arrest a knife was found, with which, as was shown, the wound in the neck of the deceased might have been inflicted, with bloodstains upon the blade. There was evidence also that there were bloodstains on the hands of the defendant when he was brought into the room after his arrest. In the room occupied by the defendant was found a whetstone, such as was used in sharpening tools, and a blue cloth cover, which was suitable for the covering of the knife found in the alleyway. Neither of these articles had belonged to the deceased or her son. The door of the closet in the front room was found open and the pocket book was lying open on the shelf. There was little or no money in it the evening before, after it was replaced by the deceased on her return from the baker's, but this was not known to the defendant. There was another large pocket book in a trunk in the room, which contained six dollars, which had not been disturbed. The sole defence was a denial of the identity of the defendant with the person who stabbed the deceased. The defendant was sworn as a witness in his own behalf and his story was that a man named Weibel with whom he had become acquainted, and who knew that he had a room in the house of the deceased, attracted his attention by a whistle after the defendant had gone to bed and he thereupon went down and let him into the house, and that both then got into the one bed, and that the witness was awakened by a scream from the deceased, and finding that Weibel had left the room, he got up, and supposing that Weibel had attempted to escape by the alley, he went out on the roof and into the alley to find him, and in this way he accounts for his being in the alley and going into the street. The improbable story of the defendant, as to which there was no corroboration, as might be supposed, was not credited by the jury. It is unnecessary to go into further detail of the evidence. There can be no reasonable doubt that the defendant was guilty of the crime charged and except for the grave character of the case, we should have deemed it quite superfluous to call attention by an opinion to the facts, which justified the Conviction.

'The question of motive is comparatively unimportant where the other evidence points unmistakably to the guilt of a defendant. In the present case there could not under the circumstances be any evidence from a living witness (other than the defendant) of what had transpired between the defendant and the deceased before the son was awakened by the screams of his mother. Whether the defendant went into the room to steal the pocket book and was discovered by the deceased, and this led to the tragedy, is mere matter of conjecture. It is sufficient to say that the guilt of the defendant was satisfactorily proven. The case was ably tried before an experienced and able judge. The few exceptions taken raise no serious question and none have been relied upon by the counsel for the defendant. The charge was clear, careful and impartial, and it becomes our duty to affirm the conviction.'

The doctor who examined the body stated that the wound inflicted on Mrs Hoffman had been caused by plunging the knife deep into the neck and drawing it deeply across it almost six inches, severing the jugular vein and almost severing the head. This method used by Feigenbaum suggests to me that he had killed before and knew exactly what he was doing. The same method of killing was used in the Whitechapel murders.

Here I would like to highlight certain medical aspects of this case, to show what tests doctors of the period used to identify blood, but also to underline how far forensic science has developed since then. Below appear extracts from the examination in chief and the cross-examination of the doctor and coroner who was involved in this investigation. Dr Cyrus Edson, a witness called on behalf of the prosecution, was questioned by Vernon M Davies, the Assistant District Attorney, and testified under oath as follows:

Q. Dr Edson, are you a physician and surgeon?

A. Yes, sir.

Q. Also a chemist?

A. Yes, sir.

Q. How long have you been engaged in the practice of medicine?

A. About 15 years.

Q. And chemistry?

A. About the same length of time.

Q. Have you made a special study at all of bloodstains?

A. Yes, sir.

Q. Did you receive a knife from me some time ago for the purpose of examining it to see whether the stains on it were bloodstains or not?

A. Yes, sir, on the 6th October I received it.

Q. And did you make an examination of that knife and stains upon it?

A. Yes, sir.

Q. And will you now describe to the jury the condition of the knife as you remember it?

A. The blade contained brown stains from the edge smeared about one inch from the point and to about half an inch from the edge on the blade. Towards its back there are some stains along the junction of the blade

with the handle and on the middle part of the handle
close to the blade.

Q. Now did you examine those stains and the blade with
a glass when you received it?

A. I did, sir. I subjected them to the microscope and
discovered that the stains contained blood corpuscles
which I measured and found that they corresponded to
the blood corpuscles found in human blood.

A. From the examination you made, are you able to
state what the stains were, whether or not it was human
blood?

A. I can only say that they are consistent with the stains
made by human blood.

Q. And from your examination of those stains have you
formed an opinion as to whether they were stains made
by human blood?

A. In my opinion I have, sir, but I hardly think I'll be
justified in swearing such an opinion.

Dr Edson was then questioned by the trial judge:

Q. Did you ascertain also through the examination of the
corpuscles that they corresponded in size with the
corpuscles found in human blood?

A. Yes, sir.

Q. And there are certain animals whose blood contains
the same corpuscles as the blood of a human being, are
there not?

A. There are certain animals the corpuscles of which are
about exactly the same size as those found in human blood.

Q. Yes, well, you can't give an opinion as to those
corpuscles being the corpuscles found in human blood,
you can't state positively?

A. No, sir, that is correct.

Q. Science has not been able yet to distinguish?

A. No, sir.

Q. With any degree of positiveness?

A. No, sir.

Q. So that in your opinion after the examination that you subjected those bloodstains to and the measurement made of the corpuscles according to your opinion it is human blood.

A. Yes, sir.

Q. But beyond that you do not say.

A. No, sir, that is correct.

Dr Edson was then questioned by the defence counsel, the judge and jury members:

Q. Now, doctor, I'll ask you another question, which is perhaps unnecessary because of the examination that the learned judge has just given you. If you were told that the stains on the knife were made by the blood of a pig, for example, that would be entirely consistent with the fact?

A. No, sir, that would not be; there are animals that would be consistent and not the pig in my opinion.

Q. There are only some animals?

A. I can name them if you choose.

Q. There are only some animals whose blood has corpuscles corresponding with the corpuscles in the human blood?

A. Yes, sir.

Q. Are those animals common to this part of the country? What are the animals?

A. The animals are the monkey, the kangaroo, the dog,

which is common to this climate, the guinea pig, the rabbit and the mouse.

Q. And as between those animals and human beings it is almost impossible to distinguish as to the corpuscles?

A. I think it is impossible to distinguish.

Q. Now, doctor, in your professional opinion, there is no doubt whatever about the stains on the knife being bloodstains, is there?

A. Not the slightest.

Q. And your examination was mechanical and not chemical?

A. Entirely with the microscope, yes, sir.

Q. I suppose you had to moisten them?

A. Yes, sir, I had to.

Q. To moisten the stains?

A. Yes, sir.

Q. And then you...?

A. I scraped the stains off so as to get little crumbs of it and then moisten the crumbs.

Q. Moistened them so as to bring out those corpuscles?

A. Yes, sir, that is correct.

Q. And then submitted it to an examination under the microscope?

A. Yes, sir, that is correct, measuring the corpuscles accurately.

Q. And that is the way that examination is made now?

A. Yes, sir, that is the accepted way, the best way.

After reading this material I dug deeper into everything connected to this murder and Carl Feigenbaum. The result was that further significant facts emerged which singly at that time amounted to little but which collectively later strengthened my suspicion that Feigenbaum was Jack the Ripper.

At his trial, Feigenbaum was represented by two attorneys acting as state-appointed public defenders. One was William Sanford Lawton, who was a partner in the New York City law firm of Foote and Lawton. After Feigenbaum's execution, Lawton broke his code of confidentiality to reveal details of conversations he had with the prisoner while he was waiting to be tried and later while he was awaiting execution. What he revealed would be crucial as far as the final pieces of my investigation were concerned.

During the two years between Feigenbaum's arrest and his execution, Lawton saw him on many occasions and built up a rapport with him to the extent that he seems to have been the only person Feigenbaum trusted. It is not unusual in murder cases for a prisoner to confide in his lawyer. However, any conversations between them at that time would have been the subject of confidentiality and Lawton would not have been permitted to reveal them to the police or the public without Feigenbaum's permission. Furthermore, if Feigenbaum had committed other murders and confessed them to Lawton during this period of confidentiality, he certainly would not have wanted them to be made public or even to give the authorities any idea that he had committed other murders.

Feigenbaum was brought to trial for the murder of Juliana Hoffman and, despite entering a plea of not guilty, was convicted. He protested his innocence after being found guilty, after the failure of his appeal and right up until his execution.

Following Feigenbaum's conviction and the rejection of his appeal by the appeal court, Lawton submitted a further appeal, this time asking the Sanity Commission for clemency on the grounds that Feigenbaum was insane. Had he, at this stage, admitted any other horrendous murders committed before Juliana Hoffman's, it might have lent more weight to this appeal. A similar result may have been achieved if, at his initial trial, he had entered a plea of insanity. However, after he was medically examined by the Sanity Commission, he was deemed to be sane and the appeal was rejected.

So what made Lawton break his client's confidentiality? Before revealing what Feigenbaum had told him, the lawyer explained that he was doing so because 'I felt it to be my duty to science and the law'. So what did Lawton reveal about Carl Feigenbaum? He said, 'I believe that Carl Feigenbaum, whom you have just seen put to death in the electric chair, can easily be connected with the Jack the Ripper murders in Whitechapel, London.'

For years, Lawton stated, Feigenbaum had been the victim of a malady, a disease which periodically preyed upon him and which forced him in spite of himself to satisfy the incarnate love he had for a woman by murdering and mutilating her. 'I was so startled that for the moment I did not know what to do. Then the Jack the Ripper butcheries occurred to me, and I began to search Feigenbaum's record. One night I stayed talking with him for over two hours and, during this time, he told me, "I have for years suffered from a singular disease which induces an all-absorbing passion, this passion manifests itself in a desire to kill and mutilate every woman who falls in my way. At such times I am unable to control myself."'

The lawyer went on to say, 'I began to search Feigenbaum's record. I learned that he was in Wisconsin at the time the country was startled by the news of the murder and mutilation of several women there [Hurley, Wisconsin, 11 April 1890]. When I saw him again I mentioned the Whitechapel murders to which he replied, "The lord was responsible for my acts, and that to him only could I confess." I was so startled that for the moment I did not know what to do. I then looked up the dates of the Whitechapel murders and selected two. When I saw Feigenbaum again and was talking with him, I said, "Carl, were you in London from this date to that one?" naming those selected. "Yes," he answered, and relapsed into silence. I then communicated with London and discovered that Feigenbaum was also there when other women fell victim to the knife of some mysterious assassin.'

The lawyer then stated, 'I later questioned him closely and found that he could converse with intelligence on surgery and dissection. When I asked if he knew anything about these subjects, he would feign an ignorance that was unnatural. The man was a devil. His motive for crime was his frightful desire for mutilation. I will stake my professional reputation that if the police will trace this man's movements carefully for the last few years their investigations will lead them to London and to Whitechapel. He had been all over Europe and much of this country. He seemed on first acquaintance to be simple-minded, almost imbecile, yet the man was crafty beyond measure. He had means of his own, as was proved by a will he made before his death, yet he always professed extreme poverty.'

Assistant District Attorney Vernon M Davis, who prosecuted Feigenbaum, said, 'If it were proved that Feigenbaum was ìJack the Ripperî, it would not greatly surprise me, because I always considered him a cunning fellow, surrounded by a great deal of mystery, and his life history was never found out. The case was an odd one, and the People had to furnish a motive for the murder. This was the money which was kept in Mrs Hoffman's closet or trunk.'

I sympathise with Lawton over the position in which he found himself in relation to the issue of confidentiality. I myself now work as a defence advocate and attend police stations daily to advise persons in custody. Over the years I have represented murderers, rapists and robbers. I always make a point of asking the client if he is guilty of the offence for which he has been arrested, and if he has committed any similar offences which may come to light through the police inquiry while he is in custody. There are clients who, when I ask this question, openly confide and tell all. There are other clients who just sit and smile. When this happens, my years of experience tell me that they are hiding other offences. More persistent offenders play the system. They may have committed other offences but they also know that, unless they make a full and frank admission to the police, there is every likelihood that there will never be any evidence to convict them. Of course, thanks to modern technology, offences do sometimes come to light several years after they were committed. In Victorian times, of course, police did not have such assistance.

So what was I able to find out about the mysterious Carl Feigenbaum? At his trial he stated that he came from Karlsruhe in Germany. However, during the trial a prosecution witness told the court that Feigenbaum had stated that he came from a town called Capitolheim. The court stenographer may have recorded this detail wrongly, as I can find no other reference to a town or city of that name in Germany. Feigenbaum told the court that he arrived in the USA in February 1890. This may be another lie, however, as there would be later evidence I discovered to suggest that he may have been travelling back and forth between Germany and the USA but did not take up residence until possibly 1891 or even later, as was mentioned during the trial. He had told another witness that he was married but gave no details of his wife or where she was or what had happened to her. However, when spoken to by a police officer after his arrest, he stated that he was single.

Another prosecution witness testified that Feigenbaum had stated that he was married and had children. Feigenbaum told the court that he had two sisters and a brother who were in Germany. But later during his trial he stated that he also had a brother called John who was supposedly living in Brooklyn, New York. Feigenbaum gave no specific details as to how he himself arrived in the USA or where he had been or what his early work was. I could not find his name or any name he is known to have used on any official immigration records that I checked. I firmly believe that he did not arrive as an official immigrant.

Feigenbaum stated that shortly after arriving in the USA he had been in Orange County, but it is unclear which one he meant, because there is an Orange County in California and another is a district of greater New York. During his trial he was asked if he had been to the following towns in the USA: Port Austin in Michigan, Sioux Falls in South Dakota and South Falls in Oregon. Astoria was also mentioned, but it is not known which of the three US towns of this name was being referred to: the one in Illinois, the one in Oregon or the one that is, again, a suburb of greater New York. It never became clear what the relevance of these questions was, but there must have been evidence to suggest that he had been to these places, probably from papers and documents found by the police which were subsequently connected to him and which I will discuss later. The prosecution may have been aware of other murders or non-fatal attacks on women in those towns and were trying to link him to them. Even so, these questions raised in court do appear to corroborate Lawton's statement that Feigenbaum travelled the country. But, because they were not directly connected to the trial, they were never properly expanded upon. Nevertheless, they would turn out to be important to my investigation, because some of those towns mentioned in court are located in the Midwest and, as previously documented, in a Midwest town called Hurley, there was an undetected Ripper-like murder; this further corroborates Lawton's statement that he knew Feigenbaum to have been in those locations at the time of the murder and that, in his view, he could have been the person responsible.

Feigenbaum gave his occupation as a flower gardener and indicated that he had followed this trade in Germany. At his trial the prosecution were able to portray him as a lone drifter during the months leading up to his arrest, producing evidence that he moved from lodging house to lodging house, staying for only a few days before moving on, sometimes owing money for rent. Coincidentally, women ran all these lodging houses.

Police enquiries at one of the lodging houses revealed a small box, containing papers and letters, which, it was suggested, he had left behind. Some of the papers were letters and documents in the names of men who had resided at lodging houses where

Feigenbaum had stayed. It is very likely that Feigenbaum had stolen these papers and, if so, I assume that it was in order to appropriate the owners' identities. However, what would turn out to be significant in my investigation were letters addressed to a man by the name of Anton Zahn. These would later add weight to my belief that Feigenbaum could be Jack the Ripper and could have been working as a German merchant seaman visiting London at the time of the Whitechapel murders.

At first, Feigenbaum denied both that the box was his and that his name was Anton Zahn but admitted that he had been using this name to stay at the lodging houses mentioned in court. He stated that Anton Zahn was someone he had befriended. Anton Zahn, he said, was a merchant seaman, working as a fireman, on a Bremen-registered vessel named either the *Ems* or the *Eider*, and Feigenbaum had been collecting his mail from the local post office in that name and had opened it. He stated that he did not know of this man's current whereabouts and that his reason for opening the letters was to reply to Anton Zahn's sister in Germany.

Coincidentally, my enquiries revealed that the ships Feigenbaum mentioned were in fact two steamers operated by the Norddeutscher Line of Bremen. These two vessels operated a passenger service between Bremen, Southampton and New York and were from the merchant line that operated the merchant vessels which sailed between Bremen and London at the time of the Whitechapel murders. I knew I had to reopen my previous line of enquiry with regard to the merchant-seaman theory. First, I needed to look into the two boats mentioned by Feigenbaum and their movements and whereabouts at the time of all the murders. Then I had to see if any crew lists for these boats were still in existence. In doing so, I hoped to gain information that would positively link Feigenbaum to either or both vessels by showing a crewman in the name of Carl Feigenbaum, Anton Zahn or Carl Zahn. If I could show that he had been a merchant seaman on either vessel, I hoped to be able to further prove that Feigenbaum was in London at the time of the murders. To do so would further corroborate the statements made by his lawyer William Lawton.

My first line of enquiry into the two ships proved very interesting. Feigenbaum had stated that Anton Zahn was a fireman on either the *Eider* or the *Ems*. By his own admissions, he was referring to a period of time shortly before his arrest. However, it is a fact that the *Eider* ran aground off the Isle of Wight on January 1892, over two years before his arrest. So Feigenbaum must have had some knowledge of, and direct contact with, that boat before January 1892. I did manage to obtain the crew lists for these two vessels for the period 1888–94. On examining these lists, which in places were scarcely legible, making it hard to decipher names and signatures of crewmembers, I found that the crew list for the *Eider* showed that an A Zahn was a fireman on the boat in October 1890 and a C Zahn was a crewman in November 1890. I could find nothing in the crew lists for the *Ems* relating to the name and aliases as known. If these crewmen listed as being on the *Eider* were Feigenbaum, and I believe they were, this indicates that he himself had been a merchant seaman and shows a direct link to the same merchant line whose vessels sailed in and out of the docks nearest to Whitechapel at the time of the Ripper murders in 1888.

In the crew lists for 1888–94, I found no other references to Anton Zahn, Carl Zahn or Carl Feigenbaum. So, if Feigenbaum had been a merchant seaman during these years, he was not shown under the names I had for him on the transatlantic route from Bremen to New York between August and November 1888. Had the lists shown he was, he could be eliminated as being Jack the Ripper. So where was he? Well, as I have suggested previously, he could have still been working as a merchant seaman, travelling back and forth between Bremen and London and other European ports.

As a professional investigator, it would be wrong for me to discount the possibility that, while working as a merchant seaman and after making his way to London, he took up residency for a time, perhaps with relatives or friends, in the Whitechapel area during the period of the murders. However, my instincts tell me that he worked continuously as a merchant seaman. In any event, Lawton had stated that he had discovered that Feigenbaum was in London at the time of the murders, but we don't know what enquiries he carried out to confirm Feigenbaum's movements. For the mystery remains, when Lawton made his statement to the press, why did no reporter ask him what enquiries he carried out and what were the results? I find it hard to believe that, although he was interviewed by several newspapers about this matter, no one bothered to ask those two important questions.

The other important issue connected with Feigenbaum's mention of the *Eider* and the *Ems* is that he stated that they were from the Bremen Line. My research revealed that indeed there was at one time a Bremen Line operating a fleet of merchant and passenger ships out of Bremen. However, it was taken over by the Norddeutscher Line in 1857. So I suggest that Feigenbaum may have spent the greater part of his life as a merchant seaman before becoming too old to subject himself to the heavy manual labour demanded of a fireman on a steamship.

At the time of his arrest, Feigenbaum was 54. It is a fact that young boys as young as 12 left home and joined the merchant service. When the Bremen Line was taken over, he would have been 17 and could have been at sea for several years.

My enquiries allowed me to eliminate the *Eider* and the *Ems* with regard to the Whitechapel murders. As I have mentioned, these ships were operating between Bremen, Southampton and New York and the maritime records show that neither vessel was in Southampton at the time of the murders. In any event, when the ships arrived in Southampton en route to New York, and on the return journey, they would remain in Southampton for just a few hours, to drop off and pick up passengers and mail.

Under cross-examination during his trial Feigenbaum admitted that he did in fact have a sister in Germany, called Magdalena Strohband. Strangely, the letters referred to previously and addressed to Anton Zahn were from a female called Magdalena. Feigenbaum finally admitted that the letters were from his sister to himself, leaving the court in no doubt that he and Anton Zahn were the same person.

The most important part of this new evidence related to the merchant-seaman issue raised by Feigenbaum and led me to believe that he must have had some past connection with the German merchant navy, and in particular these ships, and could have been at some time a merchant seaman on one or both of them. It is too much of a coincidence for a man who portrays himself as a gardener to know the names of two transatlantic steamships. He may well have known one, perhaps the ship that took him to the USA, but two stretches credulity. He could have been sailing back and forth between the USA and Germany on these two vessels using different aliases – during his trial, it became apparent that he was a compulsive liar.

If Feigenbaum was Jack the Ripper, I, like Ripper enthusiasts around the world, would to love to know what he looked like. No police photos have survived. I did, however, manage to obtain a copy of the admission sheet that he was asked to complete on arriving at Sing Sing Prison soon after his arrest. The following details come from that admission record, which is the only surviving prison document relating to him. This is the only known description of Carl Feigenbaum:

Born – Germany
Age – 54
Married [It is unclear whether the prison officer dealing with the form wrote this on it expecting 'yes' or 'no' in response, or whether Feigenbaum himself indicated that

he was married.]
Occupation – Florist
Height – 5.4ins
Weight – 126lbs
Religion – Catholic
Complexion – medium
Read – Yes
Write – Yes
Smoke – Yes
Shoe size – 8
Hat size – 6–7
Hair – Dark Brown thin on top of head
Eyes – Grey, Small deep set
Forehead – High and heavily arched
Nose – Large, Red with pimples
Teeth – Poor nearly all gone on left side
Tattoos – Anchor in Indian ink on right hand at base of thumb
Habits – MAD!

The last line is significant, as it suggests that Feigenbaum either believed he was mad or was cunning enough to think ahead to the possibility of raising a defence of insanity.

With the help of a UK company called Aspley Identifying Solutions and using 21st-century imaging techniques, I produced an E-fit picture of what I believed Feigenbaum would have looked like at the time of the Whitechapel murders. As can be seen, he would have been a very nondescript person who would not stand out in a crowd and there appeared to be nothing that would make him easily recognisable. His height of 5 feet 4 inches and the fact that he could have been doing heavy manual work on a merchant ship suggest that he would have been of stocky build and very strong.

While awaiting execution, Feigenbaum supposedly made a will

which indicated that he had money in a German bank in New York, which he left to his sister in Germany. He gave her name as Magdalene Strohband, but there seems to be nothing more known of her. The will apparently contained no information about a wife or any other family.

I have been unable to uncover further information on the will or Feigenbaum's sister. I would have expected the will to have been probated in the Westchester County Surrogate Court in New York State, which was the nearest probate office to Sing Sing. However, the court has no records of this will. Nor does the New York County Surrogate Court have any details. I came across a newspaper article from Cincinnati, Ohio, which gave details of Feigenbaum's execution and stated that his will would be probated there, but there is no record of its having been probated there either. My only other suggestion is that he gave the will to William Lawton, who had it probated elsewhere. However, because there is no central registry in the USA, tracking it down was impossible. The same applies to trying to trace his sister, whose surname he gave as Strohband. During his trial, he stated that this was her married name but that she had been widowed and reverted to the surname Zahn. However, if the details he gave about his sister were false and her real name was indeed Strohband, his surname could have been the same, so that Strohband may have been yet another name that he used.

I made extensive enquiries in an attempt to trace Lawton's original case papers. These could have been invaluable, as they may have shown what enquiries Feigenbaum's lawyer had made into his client's movements and what they had revealed, as well as perhaps giving me more of an insight into Feigenbaum himself, who was described by everyone as a man of mystery.

Sadly, this line of enquiry was also doomed to fail. In a cruel twist to the story, I discovered that William Sanford Lawton committed suicide on 13 February 1897 by shooting himself in the head in

Lincoln Park, Chicago. He had been in the city a week and was on his way to visit his mother in California. There was no known reason for his suicide and no note was left. However, I wondered if, as a result of breaking client confidentiality, he incurred the wrath of the Bar Council or the New York Lawyers' Council and had been, or still was at that time, the subject of disciplinary proceedings. If so, perhaps the fear of disbarment had played on his mind to the extent that he became unstable.

I previously stated in my profile of Jack the Ripper that I believed that the killer was between 40 and 50 at the time of the murders and that he may have been a loner. Lawton stated that Feigenbaum had a desire to kill and mutilate women. Feigenbaum was also described as being cunning, notably by Assistant District Attorney Davis at his trial for the murder of Juliana Hoffman. When arrested shortly after the murder in close proximity to the murder scene, Feigenbaum quickly came up with a plausible story which shows the ability of a man to think quickly on his feet. Similarly, leaping out of the window and on to a flat roof and then jumping to ground level showed the physical agility he still possessed at the age of 54. During the trial, it was also suggested that, after jumping out of the window and before making his escape, he stopped long enough to wash both his hands and the knife under a fire hydrant in a rear yard. This would explain the fact that only very small amounts of blood were found on his hands and the knife.

Looking back at the Whitechapel murders, no one was ever seen with blood on their hands or clothing after any of the murders, and there were many water troughs where the killer could have washed his hands and his knife before disappearing into the night.

Furthermore, despite inflicting such a ferocious wound on Juliana Hoffman, Feigenbaum managed to prevent his clothes becoming bloodstained, as no blood was found on his clothing after his arrest. The way in which he killed her suggests that he was right-handed and cut her throat from behind or to the right side, moving the knife from left to right and severing the jugular vein. This supposition is borne out by the fact that there were no signs of blood splattering, which was because none of the main arteries, which are located mainly on the left side of the neck, was cut. Likewise, in the Whitechapel murders there was very little evidence of blood splattering. The Whitechapel killer was also right-handed and the victims were killed in almost identical fashion to that used to kill Juliana Hoffman.

It is also noteworthy that Feigenbaum remained calm when interrupted by Mrs Hoffman's son. One might expect him to have tried his escape as soon as possible, or perhaps just have stabbed her in panic – he could even have attempted to kill the son to prevent him from being identified. But it appears that he continued his attack on his victim and was very precise in the way in which he killed her, and then, as he left the scene, even had the forethought to close the window behind him. He maintained this calmness even after his arrest, when he was taken back to the flat and made to stand in front of the victim because it was believed that she may have still been alive and the police were hoping to obtain from her a dying declaration and a positive identification of the attacker. But she was already dead.

At this point a police officer said to Feigenbaum, 'You see what you have done?'

Feigenbaum replied, 'God should punish me if I did that.'

The officer then said, 'Why did you do it?' and Feigenbaum replied, 'I didn't do it.'

Feigenbaum's cool cunning recalls Jack the Ripper's guile in getting away undetected from the scenes of the Whitechapel murders.

In fact, Feigenbaum was never properly interviewed about the murder of Juliana Hoffman. It seems that it was accepted practice to ask the suspect questions at any stage from arrest to subsequent charge and to note any relevant answers for use as evidence, but not to conduct a formal interview.

Now in possession of positive information, I wanted to look more closely at the murders in the USA and Germany mentioned above, to see if there were any similarities to the Whitechapel murders and any links to Feigenbaum. Unfortunately, owing to the passage of time, there were no official police records of any of the murders. The American police records were kept for 75 years and then destroyed, as were the relevant prison records.

Looking first at the murder in Wisconsin on 11 April 1890, there were a number of positive links to both Whitechapel and Feigenbaum. The first is that the victim in this murder was a prostitute. The second is that William Lawton stated that he knew Feigenbaum to have been in Wisconsin at the time, and at his trial the defendant was asked about the areas he had been to in the USA. Wisconsin is one of the states that border these areas and was a state where many German immigrants settled after arriving in the country.

The third positive link is the fact that the motive for this murder was not robbery and nor was this the motive for the Whitechapel murders. The fourth positive link is that no one was ever arrested for the murder and it remains to this day unsolved, like the Whitechapel murders. Finally, turning to the merchant-seaman theory, the *Eider* arrived in New York from Bremen on 9 April and if Feigenbaum was on that vessel he would have had ample time to get from New York to Wisconsin.

The negative point of the murder is the weapon used: an axe. If Feigenbaum was in this location, firstly we don't know how long he had been there or what he was doing there. He may have known the location well because he frequented it or worked casually there, or alternatively perhaps he was simply passing through. Lawton's description of Feigenbaum suggests that his client was a homicidal psychopath. Feigenbaum stated that he had a burning desire to kill and mutilate women which he could not control. Could it have been that, on this occasion, perhaps fuelled by drink and/or desire and unable to suppress the urge to kill, he took advantage of the situation and used whatever weapon was available to him in order to fulfil his desire? Or was he working as a gardener or handyman in that location and had access to a shed containing the axe? Or was this murder simply not connected to those of Whitechapel and other murders that followed? The victim in this murder either knew the killer or was caught off-guard, for she possessed a revolver which she never got the chance to use in self-defence. I would suggest that she was caught off-guard by the use of an axe.

The murder in Benthen in Germany occurred on 28 April 1890, less than three weeks after the Wisconsin murder. The question is, could Feigenbaum have committed both or only one, or was he responsible for neither? Both murders are believed to have been committed by Jack the Ripper. However, if Feigenbaum had carried out these two murders, he would have had to leave the USA and return to Germany by sea and then make his way back across the Atlantic by the same means.

This would have been possible, as steamships took between nine and eleven days to travel from New York to Germany. Of course, if the killer was working at the time as a merchant seaman on a passenger vessel sailing back and forth between the USA and Germany, it would certainly have been possible for him to have committed both murders. And, as we have seen, there were steamships and merchant vessels operating from the same merchant line previously mentioned in connection with the Whitechapel murders. The distance between Bremen and Benthen is 165 miles, and the distance between Benthen and the major German seaport of Hamburg is only 95 miles. My enquiries showed that one of the previously mentioned vessels, the *Eider*, sailed from New York to Bremen on 14 April. So Feigenbaum could have returned to Germany and committed the Benthen murder.

I have mentioned the murder of the peasant girl near Berne in Switzerland on or about 4 December for several reasons. The most obvious one is that it was looked on as a Ripper-type murder. The second is that it appears to have been undetected, like all the other murders discussed that occurred before Feigenbaum was arrested.

As for the possibility of linking Feigenbaum to the murder, Lawton stated that he knew Feigenbaum had travelled around Europe in the past but gave no specific dates. Feigenbaum's whereabouts in December 1890 are not readily known. Although I suggest that he could have been working on the *Eider* during the previous month and could have left the ship when it returned to Bremen and gone off on his travels again, there is no record of him, under any of the names we know he used, having any working links to the German merchant navy after November 1890.

My reason for earlier mentioning the murder of Carrie Brown, on the night of 23–24 April 1891, is that she was considered to be a possible victim of Jack the Ripper and was believed to have been murdered by one of the Ripper suspects, George Chapman, whom I investigated and concluded was not Jack the Ripper. But could Carrie Brown have been a Ripper victim? When we look at her murder in the same way as we did the Wisconsin murder, there are again positive points and negative points as far as links with Feigenbaum, Whitechapel and Jack the Ripper are concerned.

The positive points are that Carrie Brown was also a prostitute, she was mutilated and a knife was used. She was also strangled, as were some of the Whitechapel victims. Brown was killed in a room, as were one of the Whitechapel victims, Mary Kelly, and two of the other USA victims. Significantly, the key of the hotel room was missing. The key of Mary Kelly's room was also missing, presumed taken away by the killer.

As far as Feigenbaum is concerned, we know he was in the USA at the time of Carrie Brown's murder and that he was in the area where she died. In addition, there is the fact that he committed a similar murder in the same area in 1894. So there is every reason to suggest that he could have been there at the time of Brown's murder. The murder weapon, a knife, was recovered under the bed at the scene.

The man allegedly seen entering the building with her was described as aged about 32, five feet eight inches in height, of slim build, with a long, sharp nose and a heavy, light-coloured moustache. He was clad in a dark-brown cutaway coat and black trousers and wore an old black bowler hat with a heavily dented crown. He was described as a foreigner, possibly a German. The description given by the witness is, in any event, questionable, as the police at the time did not believe it was accurate. It does not fit Feigenbaum by reason of the man's age and the moustache.

The other possibility is that the man who was seen going into the building with Brown and who obviously paid for the room may well have been nothing more than a client who, having done his business with her, then left, leaving her with the room for the night. I cannot discount the fact that later that night she may well have gone back on the streets, picked up her killer and taken him back to the room. After all, she knew the room had already been paid for and presumably still had the room key.

The murder in Berlin on 26 October 1891 is another for which Jack the Ripper was said by some to be responsible. I find the newspaper report somewhat ambiguous, as it is unclear whether the man who was chased was the man who had initially entered with the woman, or whether there were two men: one the killer and the other completely innocent, who came across the body and did not want to be looked upon as the murderer. In any event, there is no description given.

However, the report does highlight a second murder committed in Germany which has many similarities to the Whitechapel murders. The victim was found murdered in a red-light district and it is unclear whether she was a prostitute. Furthermore, we now have in Carl Feigenbaum a German suspect who, by reason of his travels, could have been in Germany at that time. The distance between Bremen and Berlin is 240 miles, and between Hamburg and Berlin 177 miles. The *Eider* again comes into the equation. This ship arrived in New York from Bremen on 6 October and, taking into account a four- or five-day turnaround and the return voyage, it could have been possible for Feigenbaum to have committed this murder.

The murder of Elizabeth Senior on 31 January 1892 suggests more questions than answers. It was the first murder I had investigated where first indications appear to show a motive: robbery. However, as regards the murder of which Feigenbaum was convicted, I suggest this should not be accepted as fact. In the case of Elizabeth Senior, where the victim's throat was cut and she was stabbed repeatedly, was the murder the result of a robbery which went wrong? Was the offender disturbed and forced to kill her? If so, the murder is identical to that of Juliana Hoffman, for which Feigenbaum was found guilty. Was Feigenbaum the killer of Elizabeth Senior and, after killing her, did he steal property as an afterthought? This question would resurface later.

Police enquiries led them to suspect a German man who was using the name of August Lyntz. He had apparently been working locally and was allegedly seen in the area where the murder took place. After the murder, his details were circulated and sometime later he was arrested and spoken to but was released without being charged. Lyntz either had an alibi or there was no evidence to connect him.

Was Feigenbaum the killer? The only positive points that can be drawn are that the killer used a knife to cut Senior's throat and stab her repeatedly. Feigenbaum was known to frequent that location and was responsible for committing a murder in that same area in 1894. This murder is almost identical to the Hoffman murder, for which he was arrested. In addition, the killer is alleged to have washed his hands after committing the murder at the scene. Feigenbaum did the same after killing Mrs Hoffman. As far as any connection to a ship is concerned, there is no link with any of the previously mentioned vessels. And, as stated earlier, by the time this murder was committed, the *Eider* had been scrapped.

However, I believe that at the time of the murder Feigenbaum may have been drifting around towns and cities in the USA.

Finally, we must consider the murder of Juliana Hoffman and her killer Carl Feigenbaum. Naturally, this is the most important murder of the whole investigation. As we have seen, it was thought that the motive for the murder may have been an attempt to steal money from the cupboard. But, after considering the circumstances, I believe this may not have been the case. It was suggested that Feigenbaum knew where Mrs Hoffman kept her money and he tried to steal it while she was asleep, and that when she woke up and saw him he stabbed her in the throat and then cut it with such ferocity that her head was almost severed.

If Feigenbaum had been intending merely to steal, why was he carrying a knife? Holding this would have made it harder for him to search for the money. If he had wanted to steal and knew where Mrs Hoffman kept her money, why did he simply not wait for her to leave the house and then take it? After all, the cupboard where the purse was kept was never locked. I suspect that he intended both, which is consistent with the Elizabeth Senior murder, for it is documented that Feigenbaum had very little income and always seemed to be short of money.

It was suggested that the knife used by Feigenbaum had traces of old dried blood. Now, it is an accepted fact that serial killers as a rule will keep and use the same weapon again and again. No knives were found at the scene of any of the Whitechapel murders, nor at any of the murders in the USA (except at the Carrie Brown murder scene) or Germany. During the search of Feigenbaum's room following the Hoffman murder, a cloth bag was found which, it was believed, housed the knife, together with a whetstone for the purposes of sharpening the blade. So, obviously, he had this knife with him for some time and kept it hidden. At his trial, no witness was able to testify to ever seeing him with the knife.

I have highlighted the similarities linking the murders in the USA and Germany, and they suggest that Feigenbaum could have been responsible for some or even all of them. But was he Jack the Ripper and responsible for the Whitechapel murders?

There are also dissimilarities between the Whitechapel murders and the US and German murders. One is the modus operandi. The Whitechapel victims were all prostitutes. Two of the American victims, however, were not prostitutes and were not murdered on the street. So the question is, can a serial killer change his MO? In some cases, the answer is yes. I believe this is one such case. Whitechapel at the time of the murders was a poor, crime-ridden area with a high number of prostitutes of all levels plying their trade by day and night. The narrow, cobbled streets and alleyways were often fog-bound and dimly light by gaslights which often failed. These conditions would have provided perfect cover for Feigenbaum to stalk and fulfil his grisly desire to murder and mutilate by befriending prostitutes so desperate to earn money just to survive that they would go anywhere and do almost anything, making them easy prey.

Why Feigenbaum decided to put down roots in the USA is not known. But it is certain that, when he first arrived there, he would have encountered a new way of life. There were obviously areas where prostitutes solicited but these would have been very different from Whitechapel. He had told Lawton that he had tried to suppress his urges and the time gaps between the murders suggest that he had. But, inevitably, the desire and the urge overcame him, and psychotic killers must submit to their desires. We know that two of the American victims were prostitutes but the later two were not and we know that Feigenbaum killed one of these. This shows quite clearly that a killer can change his MO.

As I continued with my investigation, new facts emerged, which, taken together, made a very strong case that Carl Feigenbaum was Jack the Ripper. The first in what I believe to be a catalogue of horrendous murders committed by Feigenbaum was that of Martha

Tabram in Whitechapel on 7 August 1888. No other recorded murder in the UK from before this date was suggested to be the work of Jack the Ripper. And before this date there were no other Ripper-like undetected murders in Europe or elsewhere. So, if Feigenbaum was a transcontinental serial killer, where was he before August 1888? If he had these urges to kill, why had they not manifested themselves before? Or perhaps they had.

What if, in his native Germany, he had attempted such atrocities before but had not succeeded in killing his victim and as a result had been apprehended and either imprisoned or incarcerated in an asylum? Assuming this could have happened, he may have then been released after serving a sentence. Or he could even have been granted an emperor's pardon, for in those days it was the custom for a German emperor on ascending the throne to grant pardons to prisoners. It is known that a large number of these prisoners, when released, took up work as merchant seamen. Coincidentally, in June 1888, Prince Wilhelm II became emperor of Germany, and so Feigenbaum could have been released by his pardon. There were no Ripper-like murders before this date and unfortunately no police or prison records survive to prove or disprove that he was pardoned or imprisoned for a similar offence.

However, if he was pardoned in this way, after his release he could have taken up work as a merchant seaman or simply become an itinerant, in any event at some point making his way to London. Another possibility is that before August 1888 he was a soldier or a sailor and, after leaving either service, joined the merchant navy or lived an itinerant existence. The way the victims' throats were cut suggests to me that they were killed by someone who knew how to kill a person swiftly without the victim being able to cry out. A military man would have this expertise.

Between August and November 1888, the Whitechapel murders occurred, all of which I now believe to have been committed by Feigenbaum, with the exception of Elizabeth Stride's. My investigation revealed that, in addition to several ships shown as being docked in London on all the murder dates, one particular German merchant vessel was in the docks nearest to Whitechapel on all but one of the dates between August and November and on another Whitechapel murder date in 1889. This was the Reiher from Bremen. On the date when the Reiher was absent, another vessel, the Sperber, belonging to the same line and also from Bremen, was there.

Examination of the incomplete crew lists for the two vessels showed no crewman by the name of Feigenbaum, Zahn or Strohband. However, there were several German crewmen with the Christian name of Carl spelled with a 'C', and the crew lists for the Reiher for November 1888 did show a Carl with a surname that looked very much like 'Feigenbaum'. It could well have read 'Feigenbaum', but because the writing is poor it is difficult to be sure. However, we know that Feigenbaum used many aliases, so we have no way of telling if he was using aliases in 1888 and at that time (between August and November), and if so what they were. So it is quite conceivable that he could have been travelling back and forth between Germany and London using an alias. Or that, having arrived here on a ship, he left it and stayed for the duration of the murders, before leaving London after the murder of Mary Kelly, the last Whitechapel victim in the 1888 series, on 8 November.

Lawton stated that he had, from his own enquiries, ascertained that Feigenbaum was in Whitechapel during the time of the murders. As I said earlier, what is not known is what those enquiries were.

Here I will mention briefly the unconfirmed murders in Nicaragua and other murders discussed in earlier chapters.

• January 1889, Managua, Nicaragua. I have continued to try to confirm whether or not these murders actually occurred. Further enquiries have revealed that any official documents there may have been were partially burned or totally destroyed in an earthquake that devastated Managua in 1931 and any that remained were totally destroyed in a second powerful earthquake in 1972.

I made contact with an editor of a local newspaper in Managua, Arquimedes Gonzales, who has for four years been trying to uncover evidence related to these murders. His enquiries have also proved negative, so it is very unlikely that any further material on the murders will come to light.

If these murders did occur and if Feigenbaum was working as a merchant seaman then, he could have travelled to Managua on a merchant ship and committed these crimes in the manner that newspaper reports of the time suggested they had been carried out, namely by using the same methods as Jack the Ripper.

• 17 July 1889, Whitechapel, London. Alice McKenzie was murdered. She was discovered lying on the pavement, her head angled towards the kerb and her feet towards the wall. Blood flowed from two stab wounds in the left side of her neck and her skirts had been lifted, revealing blood smeared across her abdomen, which had been mutilated. The German ship the Reiher, from Bremen, was again docked near Whitechapel. Feigenbaum could have been on that vessel as a merchant seaman or could have remained in London living as an itinerant.

• October 1889, Flensburg, Germany. In a murder similar to that of Alice McKenzie, with all the hallmarks of Jack the Ripper, the body of a woman was found with the throat slashed, limbs dismembered and abdomen cut open. The victim was a prostitute and the area in which the crime was committed was a disreputable one. The killer was never caught. As Flensburg was a seaport, Feigenbaum could have been there at that time as a crewman of a ship.

• 28 April 1890, Benthen, Germany. Another atrocity similar to those committed by Jack the Ripper was reported from this town on the border with Poland. A woman's body was found behind the military hospital. The abdomen had been cut open from the navel down, and the rest of the body savagely mutilated, including the face, which showed the same mutilations as those inflicted on Mary Kelly's face. The victim was identified as the wife of a local tailor. This crime remains unsolved. Feigenbaum could have been in Germany at the time.

• 4 December 1890, Berne, Switzerland. I include this murder for several reasons, most obviously because it was looked on as a Ripper-type murder. The second reason is that it appears to have been undetected, like all the other murders discussed here dating from before Feigenbaum was apprehended. As for linking Feigenbaum to the murder, Lawton stated that he knew Feigenbaum had travelled around Europe in the past but gave no specific dates. Feigenbaum's whereabouts in December 1890 are not readily known. However, it is known that he was working on the *Eider* in November 1890 and could have left that ship after it returned to Bremen and gone off on his travels again. This is suggested as a possibility because there is no record of him, under any of the names we know he used, as having any working link to the merchant navy after November 1890.

• 13 February 1891, London. Frances Coles was found murdered near Whitechapel. Blood was flowing profusely from her throat, which had been cut, but there were no other wounds to her body. However, because the policeman who found the body stated that he heard footsteps running away, there is good reason to believe that the killer was disturbed before he had time to carry out any mutilations. Two merchant vessels from Bremen and Hamburg were docked close to Whitechapel. If Feigenbaum was still working as a merchant seaman then, he could have been here at this time and committed the crime. Certainly, this murder has all the hallmarks of the previous murders under consideration and fits in with the pattern and timescale of the other murders, so it should not be readily discounted as being the work of Jack the Ripper and Feigenbaum being the killer.

• 25 October 1891, Berlin. This murder again had all the Ripper's hallmarks. The victim was a prostitute who took her killer to a known location for the purposes of sex, as in the Whitechapel murders. The date and location and the timescale suggest that Feigenbaum could have been back in Germany at that time and committed this murder before returning to the USA. It is unclear whether it took place on the date it was reported or on 24 October. Feigenbaum may have been working at this time as a merchant seaman on the transatlantic route and may have been responsible, but what is known is that the *Eider* sailed from Bremen to New York on 24 October.

On the negative side, the description that was given of the suspected murderer does not match Feigenbaum, most importantly in terms of age. But, as we know, the Ripper mystery is full of inaccurate and misleading descriptions which have continued to lead researchers down the wrong path.

Then there is the second murder in Berlin, which occurred on 3 April 1892, but here details are very sparse. It was suggested that this was also the work of Jack the Ripper. It is linked to the Berlin murder in October of the previous year in that the victim was a prostitute and was strangled. In the Whitechapel murders, all of the victims were prostitutes and some were strangled before being mutilated, while one, Martha Tabram, was stabbed to death. In the US murders, Carrie Brown was strangled before being mutilated. The exact whereabouts of Feigenbaum at this time are unknown. So, having regard to all the known facts surrounding Feigenbaum, he could have been back in Germany and could have been the killer.

The murders in the USA in 1891, 1892 and 1894 that I have previously highlighted occurred when Feigenbaum was there – this is fact – and culminated in his subsequent arrest for the murder of Juliana Hoffman, for which he was executed. It is also a fact that there were no Ripper-like murders in the USA before February 1890, when, according to his own statement, Feigenbaum arrived in the country, and there were no others after his arrest for the Hoffman murder.

The evidence of his lawyer, William Lawton, is also crucial to my investigation, although the whole case against Feigenbaum does not stand or fall on this, as this evidence is only hearsay. However, we should recall that Lawton explained why he broke his confidentiality. He did not seek media coverage for his disclosure and, indeed, it appears that his statement was not highly publicised. It might have been helpful if he had volunteered more information about the enquiries he carried out which resulted in his establishing that Feigenbaum was in London at the time of the Whitechapel murders. However, Feigenbaum himself did admit to being in London. I have no hesitation in accepting Lawton's statement as honest and genuine, given that the results of my investigations tended to corroborate it.

As hearsay, Lawton's evidence would not have been admissible in a court of law up until now. However, in England, the laws of evidence with regard not only to hearsay evidence but also evidence of bad character and evidence of similar fact have recently been changed, so that, subject to certain provisos, all of these may be used in modern-day murder trials. The evidence of bad character and similar fact as far as this case is concerned would revolve around the murder of Juliana Hoffman.

On the subject of modern-day murder trials, it is a fact that there have been persons convicted where the prosecution has had to rely solely on circumstantial evidence, yet a conviction has still been reached. Equally, there are cases where the body of a victim has never been found and a conviction has been obtained. These changes have had a major impact on my investigation, strengthening my belief that it can be proved that Feigenbaum was Jack the Ripper.

Another major issue with Lawton's evidence is that when he made his statement he invited the police to investigate Feigenbaum and his movements in relation to the Whitechapel murders. Neither the New York Police nor the Metropolitan Police in London seems to have pursued this line of enquiry. Why not? Surely if they had spoken to Lawton he could have given them details of the enquiries he conducted, and this is where his credibility as a witness is confirmed, for he would not have made that statement if the facts contained in it were false or untrue. As a lawyer he would have been fully aware that anything he stated as fact in connection with this case would be closely scrutinised and tested.

A related question is that, if Lawton was fabricating his statement, as I am sure some will suggest he was, why did he not simply come out and say that Feigenbaum had confessed to being Jack the Ripper? After all, who could have refuted this? Certainly not Feigenbaum.

Earlier, I stated my belief that the police officers of the Metropolitan and City of London forces were blinkered in their investigation of the Whitechapel murders, as have been all the Ripperologists, in assuming that the killer came from Whitechapel. My findings lead me to further conclude that the police were negligent in not investigating Feigenbaum. They would surely have been made aware of his arrest in the USA and the circumstances surrounding the murder, and of what Lawton was suggesting. Despite all this, Feigenbaum was never even considered as a Jack the Ripper suspect. He languished in Sing Sing Prison for almost two years before his execution. The police in London missed a golden opportunity to positively identify the Ripper and solve the mystery of his horrendous crimes. In their defence, I can only say that, owing to the passage of time, namely six years after the Whitechapel murders ceased, officers had retired or moved on and the Ripper case files had been filed away as 'case closed'.

Before finally closing the door on the Whitechapel murders, I must turn again to the Goulston Street graffiti and the previously mentioned letters allegedly written by Jack the Ripper. Earlier, I said I do not believe that the Ripper wrote either the graffiti or any of the letters. This assertion is now borne out by the evidence against Carl Feigenbaum. At the time of the Whitechapel murders, he would have had little mastery of spoken English and certainly would not have been able to write in the language. This reason alone is enough to convince me that the graffiti had no connection with the murders and that all the 'Ripper' letters are hoaxes.

I also stand by my earlier assertion that the killer did not remove the organs of some of the victims. Here there is one issue relating to two of the Whitechapel murders which I failed to expand upon, so I will do so now. This concerns the murders of Annie Chapman and Catherine Eddowes. It has been documented and suggested in the post-mortem reports that the killer took out the intestines of both women and placed them over their shoulders. I completely disagree with this and suggest that the explanation is much less dramatic. The intestines are contained in the abdomen. The small intestine measures approximately 15–20 feet and is coiled tightly in the stomach. The large intestine measures approximately five feet and is also coiled tightly in the stomach. I believe that when the bellies of these victims were ripped open the intestines were exposed and simply recoiled outwards and upwards, giving the impression to anyone looking at the body that they had been strategically placed in those positions.

The final question is, how many murders did Feigenbaum commit? This cannot be answered with any certainty. I have discussed a number of murders in different parts of the world, and of these I firmly believe that he was responsible for the majority, including the Whitechapel murders. There may have been others which, because they were not fully reported in the press and many years have passed, researchers like me have been unable to uncover.

In the case of Carl Feigenbaum, it is a fact that very little is known of him and his movements in the early years. By the time he was arrested, he was 54. Feigenbaum may have been unique in being a serial killer who killed in different parts of the world. Most serial killers since kill their victims within specific local areas (those where they live and those that they frequent).

At 11am on 27 April 1896, the final chapter of Jack the Ripper's story was about to be written. Feigenbaum was transferred from the condemned cell on Sing Sing's death row to the execution chamber. Warden Sage, two keepers and the prison's Father Creeden attended him. During his death march, Feigenbaum repeated the prayers of the Roman Catholic Church and kissed the crucifix which he carried before him.

He was self-possessed and took his seat in the electric chair without any urging. As the straps were being fastened, he took Sage's hand and warmly kissed it, then with a smile bade the warden and the priests goodbye. He took off his spectacles and handed them to Father Bruder, with the request that they be buried with his body.

The death mask was then adjusted and at 11.16am an electric current of 1820 volts and 7.5 amps was turned on for 20 seconds, after which it was reduced to 300 volts for 40 seconds and then turned off. A few seconds later, a second 1820-volt shock was given, and after the current was turned off doctors pronounced Feigenbaum dead.

The body was then removed to the operating room for the post-mortem. This showed that death had been instantaneous, which is more than can be said for many of the killer's victims. Feigenbaum had made his will that same morning, apparently leaving money in a German bank in New York to his sister and reserving $90 to pay his funeral expenses.

The warden and the clergymen said that he protested his innocence of the crime for which he was convicted right up to the moment that he went to the electric chair.

Prison records show that after the execution Feigenbaum's body was taken to a Roman Catholic cemetery in Poughkeepsie, New York State, and buried. This was probably St Peter's Cemetery, at that time the only Catholic cemetery in the area. Burial records from the cemetery were destroyed in a fire in the 1900s, so the whereabouts of the grave are unknown.

The closing chapter on the long-hidden identity of Jack the Ripper, on what made him commit these horrendous crimes, and what became of him, is now written. After years of painstaking research, my investigation has ended and the mystery has been solved. It is one that Ripper enthusiasts and other experts all around the world have been struggling with for over a century. I firmly believe that Carl Feigenbaum was Jack the Ripper and that this name will now enter history as that of the world's most notorious serial killer. For this man was responsible for a series of horrific murders of poor, unfortunate, helpless women on three continents over a period of six years and, even after going to the grave, evaded detection for over a century. However, there will be Ripper enthusiasts around the world who still will not be convinced that the mystery is now solved, and never will be. To this small minority, the Jack the Ripper case has become a part of their lives to the point where they are now obsessed by the mystery. I have conducted a long and protracted impartial investigation and presented a case based on proven facts, which I feel has been lacking in some of the efforts of others. Most of these investigations are based on nothing more than wild, uncorroborated and speculative theories which have failed to provide any direct evidence. The real facts surrounding the mystery, little as they are, have been distorted over the years to the point that the public now accepts the fiction more readily than the reality. I hope that may now change.

By way of conclusion I would add that, despite the wealth of sophisticated technology now available to law-enforcement agencies throughout the world, my work has proved that there is still a place in crime investigation for good old-fashioned investigative techniques. I just wish that today's police detectives would spend more time physically investigating crimes instead of relying so much on current technology to solve crimes for them.

JACK THE RIPPER 1840–1896
REST IN HELL!

ACKNOWLEDGEMENTS

Her Majesty Queen Elizabeth II
Lord Salisbury
The Rt. Hon. Tony Blair
The Rt. Hon. David Blunkett
Pamela Clark, Royal Archives, Windsor Castle
Robin Harcourt Williams, Chief Archivist, Hatfield House
Jill Brassington, National Public Record Office
Stephen P. Ryder, author *Casebook — Jack the Ripper*
Casebook Productions
Larry S. Barbee
Michael Barrett
D.P. Hardy & Co
Patricia Cornwell
Daily Telegraph
The Times
Heather Wareham, The Marine Institute, St John's,
Newfoundland, Canada
The Memorial University, St John's, Newfoundland, Canada
Dr Adolf Hofmeister, Bremen State Archives, Germany
Ulf Bollman, Hamburg State Archives, Germany

Peter Kiedel, German Maritime Museum (Deutsches Schiffahrtsmuseum), Bremerhaven, Germany

Richard Tuske, New York City Bar Library, New York, NY, USA

William Mantz and Nuchine Nobari, New York County Lawyers' Association, New York, NY, USA

New York Municipal Archives, New York, NY, USA

New York State Archives, Albany, NY, USA

Roberta Arminio, Sing Sing Prison Museum, Ossining, NY, USA

Westchester County Surrogate Court, White Plains, NY, USA

New York County Surrogate Court, New York, NY, USA

Vick Green, Southampton Reference Library, Southampton, Hampshire, UK

Joanne Smith, Southampton City Council Archives, Southampton, Hampshire, UK

Rachel Wragg, Southampton Maritime Museum, Southampton, Hampshire, UK

Aspley Identifying Solutions, Hatfield, Hertfordshire, UK

Arquimedes Gonzales, Managua, Nicaragua

CONTACT AUTHOR

To arrange speaking and other personal appearances by Trevor Marriott, please contact: t.marriott_info@btinternet.com. Web page: www.trevormarriott.co.uk